The Rudiments of Poetry

New Poems 2017–2018

Iván Argüelles

Some of these poems first appeared in *Caliban*.

© 2019 by Iván Argüelles

All Rights Reserved.

Set in Williams Caslon Text with LaTeX.

ISBN: 978-1-944697-98-3 (paperback)
Library of Congress Control Number: 2019954899

Sagging Meniscus Press
Montclair, New Jersey
saggingmeniscus.com

For the Angels and Demons who have ridden me all these years, and the Muse and her Nymphs who from Antiquity have continued to inspire me.

Contents

CROUCHING LOW OUR CAMERAS CAUGHT THE SHADOW OF ONE FLEEING PARADISE!	1
GERUSALEMME LIBERATA	2
STANZAS ON THE NOVITIATE IN HADES	4
AQUA PLUVIA	5
PIETRADOLOROSA	6
PALINURUS : AN EPITAPH	7
INSOMNIA	7
DEATH-WATCH	9
ULYSSES AMONG THE LOTUS-EATERS	10
"MORTAL COSA SON IO"	11
THE POETRY READING	12
POETA	14
AN ACCOUNT OF THE DAY OUTSIDE OF TIME	15
"THE GLORIOUS TRIBES OF THE DEAD"	17
SAYING GOODBYE TO MARY LOU	18
GEMINI (i)	19
LOS GEMELOS (GEMINI (ii))	20
A CAREER IN POETRY	21
WHAT EYE CAN SEE THE PASSING OF THE YEARS?	22
GRAFFITI	23
THE *MUSE* ADDRESSES HOMER	25
ΑΓΑΜΕΜΝΩΝ	26
ACHILLES, MY BROTHER	27
LINEAR-B	28
ELEGIAC FRAGMENT	30
PUELLA	30
IMITATION OF SEXTUS PROPERTIUS	31
SONG OF SAN FRANCISCO	32
THE UNFINISHED HYMN TO *PERSEPHONE*	33
ENIGMA ME THIS	34
ABANDONING THE MIND	36
TESTING THE SPIRIT	37
MAYOWOOD 1956	38
JUNE-SONG BY THE RIVER STYX	38
AN ACCOUNT OF THE TWINS, SUMMER 1957	40
VENUS DECONSTRUCTED	41

A WAY TO WEAVE GOODBYE	43
IN EXILE WITH OVID	44
ULYSSES SETS FOOT ON ITHACA AIR LIGHT AND THE GODDESS CLOTHE HIM IN A DIVINE MIST	46
FRAGMENT TEMPLE RUINS	47
WHIRLWIND	49
DOWN TO THE HOUSE BEHIND THE SUN	50
DOLCE STIL NOVO	51
ESCHATOLOGY	52
HYMN TO OSIRIS	53
A SMALL ELEGY : JUNE'S END	54
FRIEZE : SUMMER NIGHT 1953	55
puella dixit se Venerem esse	56
AN ELEGY : THYSELF	56
WEST WIND	57
VARIATIONS ON A LINE BY OVID	58
ATHENA APPEARS AND DISAPPEARS	59
EPYLLION	60
POET , THE	63
FOUR SONNETS	64
CANZONE D'AMORE	66
TRIONFO DELLA MORTE	67
OMBRE D'INFERNO	68
THE FORGOTTEN MOMENT	69
LAMENTO D'ARIANNA	70
AN ACCOUNT OF THE DAY SUMMER ENDED	71
LUNA PLENA	72
ELEGY SUMMER	73
LOVE IS—	74
MEDITATING ON VENUS	76
SIRENS' SONG	77
INTO THE LETHE	78
KISSING THE STATUE OF DISTANCE	79
MY SPHINX	80
NEOPLATONIC	81
Ἀχιλλεύς	82
MY SO-CALLED LIFE REVISED	82
A VISION	84
A PERFECT LOVE POEM	84
ELEGY FOR JOHN ASHBERY	85
DAY-DREAM LOVER	86
CLOUD-SAMPLER	88
FOOTNOTE TO LUCRETIUS	89
SECRETO DE AMOR	90
INSCRIPTION FOUND NEAR HELIOPOLIS	91
ATHENA STEPS INTO THE FRAY	93
DIDO	94

LETTER TO A GHOST	95
CREUSA	96
THE ORACLE AT DELPHI	97
STANZAS : ULIXES	98
"no more war!"	100
AN EPIPHANY	100
IN THE ANCIENT	101
A NIGHT IN ITHACA	102
IMMORTALITY	104
THE FIRE THIS TIME	105
STOLEN KISSES	106
EROS & THANATOS	107
JOE READING THE TIBETAN BOOK OF THE DEAD	108
THE DATE WAS THIRTEEN DEATH	109
THE SHE-DEMON ANNIE	110
THE HYMN TO KIPKH	111
THE FATE OF THE SUITORS	113
PROMETHEUS	114
DAY OF THE DEAD (vii)	115
DIA DE LOS MUERTOS (vii)	116
PRE-SOCRATIC	117
ON THE WAY TO MENDOCINO ONE FATEFUL WINTER DAY	118
LOVE POEM IN AN ANCIENT KEY	120
YOUR HAIR	121
TWO UNRELATED LOVE POEMS	122
INEXPLICABLE HEART	124
RETURN FROM PARADISE	125
"UNFORGETTABLE , THAT'S WHAT YOU ARE . . ."	127
BEING WITH YOU CONFUSION	128
SALVATION	129
MAYOWOOD FOREVER YOUNG	130
THE NEXT TIME I SEE YOU	133
SONG : I AIN'T MISSING YOU AT ALL	134
THE VOICE WITHIN	135
APHRODITE REDEFINED	136
MYSTERY WHO SHE IS	138
NARCISSUS & ECHO	139
MYSTICAL YOU	140
TWO SPIRITUAL POEMS	142
CHARLES MANSON DIES AT 83	144
BECOMING MYTH	145
"YOU CAN'T HURRY LOVE . . ."	147
THE HEART IS A TORNADO	148
BITTERSWEET	149
THE LAKE OF THE HEART	150
THE IDEALIZED *ANNIE*	152
SMALL HANDS SMALLER RAIN	153

ADIOS, AMIGA	154
THE FOUNT OF ARETHUSA	155
KISSING DARK	156
THE LANGUAGE OF MADNESS	157
A SMALL COSMOLOGY	158
C*R*A*Z*Y	159
NIGHTINGALE FLED	160
A PHONE CALL	161
TWO CRAZY POEMS WRITTEN UNDER THE INFLUENCE OF THE FULL MOON	162
FOREVER IS *"YOU"*	165
HOW THINGS STAND TODAY	166
THE LAST TROJAN WAR	167
FORGET YOU ?	168
'EKTOP	169
STATE OF EMERGENCY	170
ASLEEP AT THE WHEEL	171
MORTALITY	172
UNBEARABLE	173
YOUR VOICE IN THE LEAF	174
BRIEF HISTORY OF THE ORIENT	175
THE HIGH HOLY DAYS	176
RAY OF LIGHT	178
RENUNCIATION	179
THE POEM IN YOUR EYE IS THE POEM I CANNOT READ	180
THE SOUL ITS SHADOW & ITS OTHER	182
YOUR VOICE	183
CONNECTED	184
SILVER BULLET	185
"Io sono Aglauro che divenni sasso"	186
CIRCE TODAY	187
VERTIGO	188
annieannieannieannieetcetera	189
THE NEXT TO LAST LOVE POEM	190
THE LANGUAGE OF DISTANCE	191
THE LAST MUSE	192
THE POEM	193
O*B*S*E*S*S*I*O*N	194
BODIES OF LIGHT	196
WEIHNACHTEN	197
PHOTO-CELEBRATION	198
BLACK MAGIC WOMAN	199
THE ENIGMATIC	201
THE INNER YOU	202
THE DREAM OF LANGUAGE	204
THE MUSE MNEMOSYNE	205
THE DEATH OF THE END	206

THE HEAVENLY STAIR	208
DANTE SHIPWRECKED	209
THE ELEVENTH HOUR	210
A HELLESPONT BAEDEKER	212
LACHRYMAE RERUM	213
THE VOYAGE TO PLUTO	214
CHASING SMOKE RINGS	216
MY LITTLE QUEENIE	217
THE NATURAL HISTORY OF ECSTASY	219
SAINT NOTHING DAY	220
HYMN TO THE GODDESS OF THE UNKNOWN	221
SITA—BELOVED OF RAM	222
HIATUS	224
ADONIS	225
SWEETS OF SIN	226
MYTH OF ETERNAL RETURN	227
THE SOUL CUT FROM ITS MOORINGS CIRCLES WITHOUT NORTH THE SEAS	229
NUMEROLOGY	230
ΦΙΛΟΣΟΦΙΑ	232
ADDICTED	233
ON THE DEATH OF JOHN OLIVER SIMON	234
TO THE UNNAMED GODDESS	235
BIG BANG	236
PERSEPHONE THE NEXT TIME	237
PARIS & HELEN	239
THE MYSTERIES	240
TRINACRIA	242
CONSULTING THE DELPHIC ORACLE	243
RITUAL MADNESS	244
BACON FAT	246
LOVE : A DEFINITION	247
ON OUR 79TH	248
THE DEPTHS	249
ULTIMA !	251
THE SPACE WHERE DARK IS BORN	252
AFTERLIFE	253
NEFERTITI	255
MYRMIDONS	256
THE DEATH OF HERODOTUS	257
SHAKTI	259
PHANTOM HELEN	260
THE RUDIMENTS OF POETRY	262
CORPUS	263
NOCTURN	264
THE ENVELOPE WITH YOU INSIDE IT	266
THRENODY	267

THE END OF THE WORLD	269
EROTIC	270
BROWARD COUNTY	272
INEFFABLE	273
ELEGY : HENRY THOMAS r.i.p.	274
THE GIRL I LEFT BEHIND	275
IUDICIUM PARIDIS	276
PERSEPHONE : THE DIFFICULTIES	278
FOOTNOTE TO HISTORY	279
THE ARCHAIC	280
ISIS MY ISIS !	282
A SMALL LOVE POEM	283
JOE ! INTIMATIONS OF ETERNITY	284
HIATUS ii	285
ENIGMA	286
WHAT ARE THE GODS UP TO ?	287

The Rudiments of Poetry

CROUCHING LOW OUR CAMERAS CAUGHT THE SHADOW OF ONE FLEEING PARADISE !

"Canzon, tu cercarai Cariddi e Silla"
Simone Serdini

I am a window
I am the thread of light passing through glass
and I am the Leopard's eye filled with flame !

lordly Alcinous seated next to Ulysses
could not help but notice tears brimming
from the god-like hero's eyes
so are we all strangers passing from darkness
to darkness ever grieving a lost home
islands cast in a truculent sea
ignorant of the address of the one
who receives us in the midst of sleep
unconsciously touched by a goddess
standing as a wraith beside our dreaming
what will we ever know but the sure passage
straight to the end of things and dust

a reflection a negative image
captured upside down in the retina
a fugitive fleeing the jail-house of knowledge
witless beams swirling endlessly
chaos of information loading the brain
flame and frost tree and stone
what happens the instant light
retrieves its own *image* and surrenders it
to menacing night
is the flash of consciousness
ignited between ear and ear
a thunderclap a summer of dazzle
image of bees swarming a single thought

photons
     absence of form

with a crew of select oarsmen
the finest of the Phaeacians set forth
into the wine-dark sea ere sunrise
looming clouds the dark of forethought
booming and drizzle
       torn sails
ropes snapped by the invisible
cries of lightning zigzagging momento

to places where men have never been
where electric fish with eyes of the Fathers
and where the infinite is stored
in the impossible smile of the Nymph
hidden worlds
         to partake of the *moly*

through the window of time
sleepers in dusky hulls
hills where speech is modified
and the agony of waking

thread of light piercing matter
and the animals of the other side
peering with lantern-eyes
at the shipwrecks
Scylla and Charybdis

AOI

I am Nausikaa
you will remember me
for giving you life again

04-11-17

GERUSALEMME LIBERATA

I have nothing left to say
I have seen the ancient city of Nimrud
destroyed piecemeal by jackhammers
I have nothing left to say
and the president of the United States
shed crocodile tears over images
of babies gassed by the Infidel
while denying access to 500,00 refugees
what is left to say
the Russia is angry because it lost the Cold War
the Zion is stealing land from the Palestine
it's all in the Bible
nothing left to be said
Hermione daughter of phantom Helen
aghast at the news from Kandahar
Cassandra raving on rubble steps of Troy
sets sail tomorrow hostage to wild Mycenae
Taliban S.O.S. to the moon !
day will come when all of us spears
missiles and bow-shafts sturdy in our hands
will fend off the foe in their armored beasts

earth will lose its ionosphere
coral reefs turned to blanched cabbage
who has anything left to say
conspiracy theory fake news alternative facts
lessons of democracy lost in South Sudan
magnetic needles sent spinning in arctic floes
amphetamine induced politicos declare Void !
with nothing left to say
who will write the following lyric
who will attest to the once and former Homer
who will say the Muses were not bankrupt
courtesans or mule-skinners' brides
it is the world that is illusion
it is planet Nothing on a death trip
lunching on Gorgon and Medusa
it is too late to have anything left to say !
it is the religious right to blame
it is neo-con liberal isolationists
it is drum-thumping head-band hippies
grown senile in their lost caravanserais
it is Gaia strapped to her final tom-tom
doing Ojibway fox-trot in the sump
recycling all her plundered minerals
into the once deathless sea
I have nothing left to say
I have Uranium dust in my veins
I have plutonium cyanide cocktail
I have talking-death blues wanderlust
to leave the planet forever !
and the vice-president of the United States
is a flag wrapped around a fetus
dumped into the Gowanus canal
it can be the year 1972 AD
or the year when everyone dies
but I have nothing left to say
erasing line by line the last epic poem
the one about the re-taking of Mosul !
and the countless nameless warriors
each who pledged to his god
to capture once and for always
Jerusalem

04-13-17

STANZAS ON THE NOVITIATE IN HADES

the heat the innovative oils the circularity
the force of destiny the talking air the dreams
within and without the sleeping mind invoke
Muse O ! clarity and tenebrous the fierce
paradigm how much we use and how little
comes out of the clouds looming a message
statecraft of threads and who has and has not
right to cut life to the quick marrow transfer
idiomatic recurring of summer the intense
grasses praying for night to descend dense
the darkness of the longing when just a
minute ago we lay *here* in the soft listening
for the secret aircraft the deathless ones
who govern the dustless immortal realms

or to put it another way in the landscape
of the Upanishads where distance is zero
supreme integer of meditation out of the body
total as the nothing that comes after attainment
Mind O ! everything in the pale languishing
on porches of rotting timber revolving palm
fans tropical birds of electricity flashing bright
and the song the radio held to the glass for
reflection the endings of words unheard zzzing
forever a glisten the intricacies of silence

a third of the way through the BIG BANG
evolves the mystic union the string that unties
the midden heap of history smoldering rank
edges of time slowly erased by
body corrupt betrayal of
long winter train ride to nowhere
dimly remembered underscored by soughing
of invisible pine tree branches bent to earth

light years fade
no greater grief than absence unexplained
planets shaking their hair lose their asterisks
Mater Dolorosa O ! the great flight out of time
You the once and always charades
switching chairs in the middle of the night
how many stops did you make before
you got to the snowbound trestle in Mankato ?
what a resemblance to mighty Pluto !

down there where shade counters shade

for an inch of dwindling light
ashes sown in the fierce atmospheres of Uranus
vertigo and consequence of traveling
in the fourth dimension

zing thrip tump !
ear to the sand
nose-bleed !
lost finger
grass

04-15-17

AQUA PLUVIA

too weary the rain
it doth to make me moan
can dying be a lesser thing
these days without end
nor light nor grief nor
any how distills the brain
its adders and poisons gale
to look yes upon earth's
sodden circle and eye
a firmament gone mad
with night's constant being
a sorrowing a wither a
mind in its own sleep
to dream a summer's coil
green heat and spikes
verdant and wild of grass
how came we to be here
after so many years
suddenly infirm and down
brown weathers that
flood memories of who
that was we were at play
things shouting aloud
the one to the other
kids on a gambol drunk
just once before clouds
the shape of errant death
glass stained all lamps
blotted out by rain
the weary to grieve
and to bed at last
all hope

04-16-17

PIETRADOLOROSA

this gash of prose mud and rains
Florentines with 2000 infantry
and 800 horse on route to Pisa
details of the day the battle
Pietradolorosa walls knocked down
fugitive compartments of memory
who will remember the year
the month the day the hour and
where was the goddess of Love
and the Cupids with venomous eyes ?
Paolo Vitelli on the ridges above
the Arno surveying where best
to thrust against the besieged
though Ovid says the best place
to pick up a girl is the Circus Maximus
watching a mock sea battle
let the powders fall where they may
pretend to brush off the dust
from her innocent lap !
red skies looming over the centuries
bruiting Mars his metal flak
hills they roam and darkened dells
lemon puce maroon and rouge
warring demons beset the underbrush
orators disguised as trees
announce the advent of the sea
or at the horse-races too
ideal for plucking a puella
roar of antiquity face paint steams
centuries of heat the blazing air
and as for the Cyclops a man larger
than any other in girth and height
his single eye the sun's emblem
insolent and lawless a cannibal
but blinded a bawling pity
hurtling boulders into the surf
turmoil of historiography thunders
flint and scintillations on Olympus
who of the countless deities
will preside over the rash Pisans
by the glassy Tyrhennian surface
by midday in the relentless heat
drawing circles in the roiling waves
star-count bottomless night
none to number the dead but

forsaken of chronology
writing these chaotic verses
in the year 1498 . . .

04-18-17

PALINURUS : AN EPITAPH

two lamps burning the night through
the last for loss and the first for grief
simple ropes pull the dark in
sound of lapping water against the hull
of dreams rent the sailor drowns
how many times above the surface
how many hands did reach for sky
lesser the surfeit of breath and light
lighter the lasting moment of death

04-20-17

INSOMNIA

wherever I go
    by day the sun follows me
by night I wander among the stars
looking for you
      wherever I go
which is not far
no farther than the nearest
    earth nor more distant
than the afternoon's lawn
    looking for you there
and there too in Culver City
or in the more remote Cannon Falls
where strangers linger
    on crudely carved picnic benches
a greyhound bus could whiz by
an unseen train blow its whistle
    how many place names there are !
common ground on folded maps
where is everybody going ?
stepping down stairs slowly
toward the imagined pool deep
    in an enchanted wood
skin shivers in the cool glade
hair stands on end hearing
a voice calling from a leaf
    a voice torn from its soul

wandering among the stars
    looking for you
a single drop of blood stains the air
a something cannot be named
a root pulled up in a field
    ghosts running
through rows of dried corn shocks
the sadness it makes me
to think there are no more days
when perched on invisible bluffs
    we watched spirit-buffalo roam
on the plains as far as the Oglala
stirring in their ancestral hides
    what is to imagine
if not the death of things
    all things in their time
the sun in its ethereal heights
the stars in their vitreous passage
the greyhound bus whizzing by
the picnic benches in Cannon Falls
Mom too in her distant house dress
weaving a shadow between the hours
    listening for us to come home
        for us to come home
yet to this day I go looking for you
a sound a voice a leaf falling
when sleep does not come
    and all the great sands
that populate the listing mind
all the great sands come pouring
through the darkened ear

    turn the lamp on
no more

04-21-17

DEATH-WATCH

all these guys lined up waiting
some waiting so long they've
forgotten their own names
waiting for the sea to reclaim
waiting for the sky to cancel out
waiting for the winds to lift
waiting for the north in *her* eyes
to change direction becoming blue
waiting for something else to happen
it's Saturday springtime tulips up
crocus chrysanthemums daffodils
narcissus hyacinth jasmine
Joe ! let's go down by the water
where they say the Greek heroes
have landed looking for a restaurant
lamb kebab ouzo olives and squid
photographs of Troy after the fall
seas in upheaval waiting for more
forgotten their own names waiting
the death-watch they call it
can we only see it from the outside ?
have they all lost their shadows ?
waiting for the stygian summons
waiting for a goddess in gossamer
to deceive them once and for all
heaven's priceless nickel cloud
Neptune's furious salty spume
waiting for *never* to come again
Joe ! you're waiting there too
Saturday's in the bright effusion
Primavera in her see-through breeze
skinless the sheen of infinity
and you puffing a marijuana "joint"
hitchhiking without moving an inch
cars of enormous immobility
come and go chauffeured by demons
they won't stop for you *ever*
big High on the way to eternity
the thousands of guys sailors
dead-end high school drop-outs
earth worms galley dogs freaks
waiting just waiting for BIG BANG
and you cool elite button-down
staring that cigarette in the face
burning just burning with desire

for the perplexing complete Unknown
it wasn't the rain it wasn't the hospital
it wasn't the lawnmower on the
      precipice of time !
it was all inside out outside in
up the interminable hill of tricks
down the slope to the bottom of space
legend and myth history and lie
you tied yourself in knots
trying to explain the very *why*
traffic of half-finished deities
revolving doors and the Morgue
right next to the county Jail
where they left you to dry out
tomorrow will never come , Joe !
Dante wrote it all on the back
of a grain of sand !
guys waiting just waiting
for . . .

04-23-17

ULYSSES AMONG THE LOTUS-EATERS

planted oranges next to the house of *Idols*
from which issued darkness and reek of human blood
to name distant sierras for their snow
or listen to the vengeful pounding of the seas
sorrowing for the plunder of earth's veins
and they talk of magnificent fountainheads
where the spheres show their faces crystalline
and of cities of pure gold and alabaster
capitals of the heavens situated on ochre dust !
some came back arms full of precious stuff
others returned in rags raving to have seen
at the bottom of a well the hell of androgynes
sulfur and iodine flowers
      bees of oracular transparency !
what seemed to be an island a floating trunk
our ships anchored like ghosts to saliva
listing in waters of a tropical antimatter
waiting for a dawn to come if ever again
consumed by mosquitoes and jellied larvae
the hulls of our corporeal selves flung down
thirsting for the oranges planted a year ago
knowing full well the underbrush is alert
with tattooed spirits of the mountain race
lurking in anticipation of our one false step

to eat of the lotus just once more and forget !
the many we have already lost to head-hunters
to cannibals to the gossamer witch *Κίρκη*
for them we weep night after unending night
the fitful make-up of the stars rains down
washing away time's febrile shoreline
do we move are we animated by a soul
or are we merely retracing lost circles
in some enormous remove from the planet ?
what does it mean to wake next to the house of *Idols*
to be *other* than before a somnambulant
in the unwritten text of dreams ?

04-24-17

"MORTAL COSA SON IO"

(for Nikki again)

in May the fronds the moon eclipse
no longer sky in sight the azure pales
small meadows down slope phrase
yet I undecided the stammering O
sections of air aces pinwheels miles
how far to go and lend to distance
a greensward from the leaning eye
suddenly to wake this was a sight
a dream a thing undone unutterable
someone's face lingering still alive
though these many decades ashes
alone claim her vivid shadow-form
take me away from this moment
erasing all future hours senselessly
can it all ever have happened
the train rides rocking to and fro
from job to job and put through
days of malaise unwanted portfolios
lies deceit harbinger of promotion
to what higher rank and hold her
noontimes furtive on the riverbank
would that a birth a name a title
none of that placing identity on hold
jammed the lever thrown the dice
suddenly a sordid hospital bed
lice decorating memory of Eros
an inscription erasing itself a Spain
sequestered in the fade of water
as she too brown beneath the nails

pales into walls of oriental cryptology
a murmur a thought like a park
fast and dark beyond the Avenue
searching there for the darker leaf
the underside of eternity pulsing
slower and slower with each step
hand hold Thyself !
all else a little sand a sliding into
the dense and unmeaning netherworld
with its red calligraphy
improbable as the night
beneath her eyes

04-25-17

THE POETRY READING

"turba docenda venit, pulchrae turpesque puellae"//
"Cura deum fuerunt olim regumque poetae"
Ovid, Ars Amatoria, III: 255; 405

hello, my name is *Iván*
tonight I am going to read a *lifetime*
mostly botched translations
mismatched dreams rejections
two and three times over then tossed
obscure references to the many dead
cancer victims aviators lost in the jungles
suppositions about what is and what is not
ego transfer soul emission depth charge
luscious undergrowth of hell-plants
heavenswards leanings toward eternity
infinity in a nail-file fits and starts
toward a proemium consisting largely
of the endings of planets and angels
how I came to be aware of and ignorant
of almost anything moving beyond my ken
loves saturated with ammonia and wine
perfumes spilled musk oriental mirages
silk patterns woven into cuneiform thoughts
what I learned in the book of Omens
what I forget the day following the big Bust
but mostly lacunae and silences
the omitted jazz of the circling moons
high above my adolescent and concupiscent head
brain fodder of lyrical madness stalking
magazine models of fabricated pulchritude
in order to bring the cosmos into line

pitching sand into the sleeping grass
where a single finger signified
the immensity of the unknown universe
houses and more houses of mystery
paintings enigmatic yet shifting across walls
into a doomsday series of footnotes
more important than the text they refer to
readings of the midnight looking-glass
speculations of dust as the origin of things
lacking matter or any other substance
falling as ever from error to error
amorous longings for the Unremembered
who in her white sheer through stockings
waited beside the entries to Japan
in a music of red hair and asterisks
will I ever make this understood ?
what little breath remains of this passage
what small lights still flickering in my eyes
what sort of crazy mixed up dream is this
in which an assortment of poetries vies
for depth and meaning even though
even though *what* ?
I am obsessed I am overwhelmed
I am not the thing I thought I was
I am in fact not here tonight
I have forgotten all the lines I meant to read
and look out over the audience
recognizing no one and nothing
empty papers in my hand a
glass of water knocked over the words
smearing and erasing the syntax
a jibber jabber of nonsense a manic rumor
a vision of zodiacal mansions whirling
taking me away for my very *self*
this is not skin the song
this is not a body of bones
but a sack of language with its broken lamp
there must be a doorway somewhere
there must be more to space than time
yet where oh where dear Listener
is your ear ?

04-27-17

POETA

"Est deus in nobis et sunt commercia caeli:
sedibus aetheriis spiritus ille venit"
Ovid, Ars Amatoria, III, 549-550

what is the light that shines within
from the ethereal heights from sand
that sleeps in the profound mystery
and the darker the leaf the diminished
burning an ardor from the depths a
finished writing one of the pages a
to the left a voice or voices hidden
inside the wall wailing moans sighing
confusion of sounds grating against
to look up and see through the window
a shape a hand of clouds a dense
like singing through stone the clear
and bright that shines a god immense
yet invisible emanates a breathing
instills some luminescent enigma
that sheds and spreads across night
unfolded plains of stars lost planets
traversing and yet music and sound
striking grandly on the map of skin
a gathering of nymphs and death
waters rushing through the Word
can translate and become different
other than whatever went before
in myth the famous fountains whence
spring those clear-eyed Muses
or longing and yes distance dusky
memories laden with greenery
never to return unless the symphony
clarion of flashing metals and sky
heavens one after another raveling
just outside the Sleeper's eye a
page unfinished this one a blank
suffusion of unspoken paragraphs
archaic symbols and aloft Lo !
what forgotten land the Mind is
put to rest and listen to the Inner
a deity a flashing radiance between
the ears the attempt to articulate
but only dust without memory
ruins of the Ineffable meter

uttered in trance then vanished
the poet his brother the half
. . .

04-29-17

AN ACCOUNT OF THE DAY
OUTSIDE OF TIME

wasn't that a day shadow boxing
listening with intent ear the green
increasing its fold in the inner light
out we jumped from the vagaries
of space travel on to solid earth
each the other or no one at all
playing with maps on evanescent
lawns *this* would be your place
and *that* one mine where a drawing
of water and the many plurals
the mythic mines and hills the very
and gods too innumerable to count
doorways and ceilings and lamps
redundant with divinity shadings
or were there windows for the sun
and by nightfall cool the moon
circling a mystery to regard sleep
would we wake again the voices
became us and like wall paintings
come to life we consorted with beings
much like us in skin and intent
alive ! statues of the mind we assumed
immobile or chasing flying things
an air alert to the possibilities
of breath the way clouds have being
transformed into distances of dust
longing the immeasurable white
by day's end where the road lost
in darkness turns into a dream
of trees and streams and stones
talking the strange dialect of ideas
what is a past if not the whole
that has become sundered from
and the stars too invisible high
to catch a beam and to drink until
altered the very substance of thought
visions of a city on top of the sky
with its illusory pedestals and cars

routes in and out of memory
alas ! to fall from such splendors
and from there made our way
to Circe's house in the woods
touched the grunting swine
with her wand and transformed
our comrades wailing lamenting
would we never find our way back
spread a lavish banquet before us
for upwards to a year we dined
in abundance with priceless wine
careless of the passing hour
of the day outside of time
. . . winged words spoke saying
a different voyage must take
many . . . is the sunlight you
won't see again . . . to Persephone
the dread where only flitting
shadows as are men the remains
upon a . . . will not each other
recognize but for a scar . . . or
the dog you shared and the cart
bright red and four-wheeled . . .
sat as princes upon it . . .
moving as characters in a spell
through and beyond rock crystal
to come out . . . where no black
ship sails and the entrance
not far from the corner store
enticed by . . . a red-head waving
as to ghosts in the bright air . . .
nevermore and the music . . .
to bring seas from their bed
and rushing through one ear
the sound of light !

05-01-17

"THE GLORIOUS TRIBES OF THE DEAD"

I felt their skin as if it were mine
where was I ?
names from another world
from a past that was not my own
from occlusions and submersions and
their skin cold and wet and their eyes
lightless and opaque searching through me
to the world that was once theirs
was I or was I not one of them ?
a song mysteriously elided in the air
a darkening of contrasts without shadow
smatterings of a speech in a public forum
a defense of virtues and afterthoughts
about a decision which was not mine to make
coming along slowly against smooth rock
syllables truncated and put in a bottle
yet I moved not among but through them
as through a dream of non-existent figures
mysteriously endowed with voice and accent
a tone above the muffled roar that ascended
from some precipice below my feet
a circular gesture of heat and suffocation
hands emerged like clouds from stone
holding bits of leaf or grass
invoking a summer of distant waters
half-pronounced names or asterisks
pronouns meant to include the shapes of dust
forms of the enigma hovering like absences
in the magma of the near distance
miasma and shattering of tragic intensity
violation of metal and sand crashing in the ear
their remonstrances pitiable and frail
imploding against the senses
was I to fall into the immediacy of their night ?
clinging to a mere rush-plant
and hearing the awesome echo of an underground stream
taking in its torrent the myriad daylight of memory
I persisted in the sleep of unreason
demons like the spectra of serpents
gliding between the vowels of a chant
wrapped their parallel selves around my mind !
this was the idea of death the skin
which was not mine but which I embraced
locked in a glass of dusky of oblivion
walking me through the paces of a remembrance

going back and forth in and out
of some porous substance some planet
gyrating forever around the semblance of light
a thin flare on the brow
and the faces of leopard or fox peering
through a crystal substratum
of language trying just trying to articulate
something about the world
I was about to enter

05-02-17

SAYING GOODBYE TO MARY LOU

don't let the ghosts too near the pit
their thirst is not as ours
the life was not ours those years ago
when I set a sprig of lilac in your hair
or held you fast against the frozen metal
kissing you for all eternity
each was already to the other
what a lost star is to an absent paradise
a wheeling disorientation of the mind
love was young then a poetry of breezes
green auras hill slopes a sun in decline
dipping into a mythic western pool
the darksome evening when fresh
budding plants yearned to be white
like the moon in its first dance
high above the Egyptian sky
before it started it was over
the death in the back of the eye
unable to say *goodbye* or to even wave
the furtive blank hand
emerging from a cloud in the drugstore
itself glass vanishing
into the dense and infinite night

05-03-17

GEMINI (i)

where it is deepest and darkest
on soundless rock
we left our sainted mother
bewildered as to where and how
her two boys went astray
far off into a distance bereft of leaf
or winnowing grass that no flames scorch
toward ultimate heaven or furthest hell
rounding abysses of space and time
each a voice broken from its branch
each an echo of senseless stone
which of you smote with your sturdy oar
the nameless passenger sending him
surely into the shadowy mansion ?
which of you dallied ever so long
in the chambers of the goddess of animals
pleasures and wines and sleep ?
why did you not write of your travails
of how the black and hollow ships carried you
into ports of opium and jazz ?
nights I spent by the small lamp
searching the window for your shapes
to come ambling home as children
hours near dawn to hear staggering
your footsteps on the broken stair
yet morning found the sheets unslept
the gate still locked with rust and dew
abandoned her there in time's small cell
fused to the Braille of the rolling stars
plying the loom of chance and death
which of the constellations was ours
which was Castor and which Pollux
drunken sailors on a rout or gods to be ?
Mom , we never really left you
we just went out to play in Elysium
gardening and mocking the empty dead
holding to the mirror breathless mouths
promising to return before next daybreak
fondled in Aurora's dewy embrace
each more the less of the other
years have passed and not a day
planets have changed their course
the moon turned red and lost its gyre
heavens have been renamed and seasons
come round to the infertile tract

nowhere do your graceful shadows flit
playsome figures of a nocturnal dance
what have you been drinking
where have you gone to hide from the law
why does the phone never ring
telling me your bodies have been found ?
by the margins of an eddying stream
we left our hallowed mummy
by the tree of archaic memory
bough and bud sprinkled with ambrosia
the gods invisible watching over her
even as the constellation that bears our name
switches gear and dives into some black hole
knaves and fools and sages all
some reminiscence of a life gone by
of star-traces bright and pools
where our faces die

LOS GEMELOS (GEMINI (ii))

the world waning what it was
we thought we were representing
in a photo now faded beyond and
darkening shadows would loosen
boats from their moorings setting
sail south by southwest night dust
could scarcely see figures clouds
hands undocked fleece lace waves
bearing mystery to other shores
us them bent over drawing maps
equations of mountains and ford
through liana grass dense cutting
arrived one heat-choked afternoon
at the motel in Tamazunchale
off the mythic carretera Panam
distances unbearable to the eye
holding weights of air and voice
looms shuttling behind drowsy
lids Bang ! of suction pumps
drawing fluids vital and dark
walls of sleep heaving a breath
where hearts flung maze tongue
cannot recall precisely why or
the smell of automobile grease
staining ether pages of codex
here and here the great moves
stone and grass and heights
untranslatable the pyramids hewn

roughly out of legend aerial flight
coming back recurring the novel
unpaginated heroes in chain mail
praying devoutly to serpent goddess
breast feeding cloaks the carmine
adhesive strips wrapped around
mind's subtle flues will remember
often the how cactus and flies
green gauze the size of cities
where we will together partake
of the swiftly devouring whole
looking up to greet lost relatives
bleached soaking wrappers flap
immediate the grammar of maze
and lattice a siesta beside motors
droning whole afternoons sweating
will it ever wake the eagle the
hiatus of norms slept restaurants
courts where Spaniards fork death
heads falling to the side lanced
by feathers and fierce grains maize
burning at the root fields running
fast circles sun-orbs fantastic why !
the two the them the myth twins
makeshift polar stars concourses
in the preterit sky that never was

05-05-17 (cinco de mayo!)

A CAREER IN POETRY

statues of snow irregular verbs
sidestepping from the moon
nights shifting vowels archaic
sudden the once of always and
watching graze slowly the deer
the feldspar the underbrush
planets unnamed becoming red
bright larger than a man's thought
about the afterlife a goddess
shaped from an air of marble
lessons in an afternoon tongue
how to and wherefore and why
girls behind plate glass playing
at wistful their hair full blown
sicilian carmine saturated with
light or the verdigris reciting
platelets unfounded pronouns

hasp of the back wavering dark
inching the frame of a form
shadowing of memory verse
told to re-enact the blind sea
vertigo wine-deep swooning
in the absence of mirrors ink
billowing cloud-like over
image of what is to achieve
if not the final vowel :
musk ivory drum and tin
did not ever the crescent
and waning stars the distance
what is to sing what is to die
longing dawn over hills rising
dappled rose the fingered cloud
evanescent as ever until fade
the pale a life margins white
burning quietly in stone years
ancient coming full circle from
what started in a blade of grass
winding through a wish of light
into the vast and enigmatic
Unknown the

05-07-17

WHAT EYE CAN SEE THE PASSING OF THE YEARS ?

the tributaries of the streams of heaven
gorgeous pink anonymous nowhere
like the imagined Nymphs of the Lethe
perceived for what they are *not*
skin tissue perforated bone ear-rings
swinging in a classical poetry of Beauty
nonetheless all falls fails to register
springs come and go greens turn to rot
lonesome skies gathering knots
over the fading of all photographs
hills and commons and echoes of echoes
distances hove into view astral projections
metals that ring hollow sleeping in the dense
seeing in the night stars a passage to otherness
what is not seen what fixes in the lens
as a migration of black energy invisible
ineffable as the tormented histories of art
that describe the ages of man decaying
on murals in a renaissance portfolio
opened up for exhibition in the Mayo Clinic

x-rays fantasies UFOs optical illusions
the brain cannot transfer back to the Mind !

forever the what was once no more
dying to seethe in the mortal seas
rupture of the senses the complete *End*
cities that are no more as such
mere smoke traces in the empyrean
quays where lovers once lay in the fog
stanzas of broken stone and bilge
or greek letters iota and sigma
stained and floating in the ether
when is the body not the body's ?
when is the soul not the soul's ?
a year ago today
how many times in passing do we
and under the bridge in the mirror
reflected in the flashlight glare
beneath rubble and mulch
gone even the aspiration to breathe
words come and eventually go
wrapped in the maelstrom of thought
childhoods in a trice and leaves
torn from their own voices !
soon it is when it is over once
never the return coming back
on screens blanker than
a year ago today
was it only shadows
we were playing with ?

05-12-17

GRAFFITI

. . .and a great wave dark
as cyanide stood up over them
while they coupled ignorant
of the god joined to her and
awash in the pleasures . . .
bright flecks in clear air
. . . Zeus or Poseidon ?
thighs pure as marble hewn
. . . a . . . islands adrift and
swooping birds of prey . . .
meat off the plate . . . her hair
in the sun's late glint auburn
. . .or the spear that strikes

the animal sacred to Diana
confusion . . . Mother , I am
wounded and in turbulence
the small skiff listing in spray
. . . to drown in the Sirens' song
hands a poetry of . . . lifting
toward the ether a presence
more like a statue of . . . and
her smile enigmatic and of
stone and the . . . what surrounds
the earth an azure depth a song
of fathoms sinking a legend Nymphs
cherished of the dead . . . furious
tempest . . . a slave girl brought
night-time to the beach where sleep
the wasted heroes a dream a . . .
wrapped in saliva a vague skin
shimmering if would but call out
to the stars a warning . . . touch . . .
who it was they were praying
syllable by syllable to the deity
who governs the distance between
. . . and . . . lips chapped cracked
salt pained the bite . . .loose
teeth some . . . appeared fulminant
a regard to the whatever it . . .
I was whelmed by the sound !
waking in sheets of . . . tipped
the mind in its sand . . . spine
buckled nerves jacked a verve
to have at the phantom and
have discourse . . . come the
many daughters to drink of
the blood poured into the . . .
cannot return by the same route
but over a different sea a . . .
howling with rage the . . .
and by the fire told stories of
tales of languorous lying there
after the tumult of sex unknown
unbidden a . . . watched as
in a trance the steep wave lift
and the haunting noise of
horses racing over the watery
surface . . . who were bound
never to get home . . . again
. . . in an immortal embrace

and the sobbing and hair
falling damp and darkened
over her face . . . the remains
of light . . .

05-13-17

THE *MUSE* ADDRESSES HOMER

to continue is to not be home
neither at sea nor when at moonrise
finds the hollow ships beached
waiting and the monotony of time
was one ever born to simply waste ?
foster illusions of the island
and its labyrinth to consume hours
bewitched by the dream of a red head
and the rain and the vehicle
pursuing an errant course
to the banks of the Acheron where
from afar see the flames and brooding
Pluto's queen in her grassy filaments
lamenting the verses describing
her abduction and sleeping hard
in rock the remote drill of memory
is to recall one by one the failures
mounting the steps of age
planets also succumb to the Wheel
darkness plunges slender daylight
into the lake of despond a warning
of the futility of pronouns
as one wanders the magnificent
but empty halls of the afterlife
questions doesn't one the reason
and air seems to weigh and waters
burst their walls drowning cities
of mud and reed and the heroes too
deceived by promises of the goddess
this spear shall miss its mark !
all of this I offer you , Poet
are there things and concepts
for which there are no words ?
I am vast and insignificant
there is no future
only Mystery

05-15-17

ΑΓΑΜΕΜΝΩΝ

"Venit et ingenti violenta Tragoedia passu"
Ovid, Amores, III, i, 11

in comes Tragedy slow of gait
and wearing that violent look
how waving the afternoon is
and not an ink in the sea breeze
though suspicion sets its red curtain
flapping in the women's quarters
where is the switch that turns
everything off ? where's the dime
Cassandra swears by the truth
the space of air that suffocates ?
how is it children come running
deaf to the cries of gulls and kites ?
does it ruminate in the chance
that life is a mistaken dream
that stone and hewn marble
quicken and start talking wildly ?
I am but an hour away from either side
an asterisk a comma a derelict
punctuation in a sordid drama
food tastes bad plates unclean
menacing looks from kitchen help
a dagger scintillating in mid afternoon
when drowsy the fleece keepers
paste their sleep to oaten reeds
swinging back and forth on melody
muses prink on faithless lawn
digital references to a stuttering god
that makes woman a homicide
is it Greek to speak so endlessly
and pair the sounds of longing
to the leaf's perpetual grief ?
echo is in the winds high mountains
etched in waters that don't exist !
poppy trance ether overdose siesta
dandelion wine small senseless words
going to sleep not once but forever
forget the meadows in their myth
the caves grottos and dwelling holes
of deathless beguiling nymphs
I am arrested in my breath a pawn
a symbol evermore of love's antonym
a bath in sand a statue at high noon
why did we ever move our ships

across intransigence of thought ?
horses come to bay in grasses
that harbor idylls undying green
storms in flickering lips of rock
poetry lacking eyes or blood
the nature of the universe in *what* ?
chariots careen off violent cliffs
surging seas take away my knees
redolent of lyric embolism
my brain waves its fast goodbye
to myriad gods of toxic brow
slips of the tongue and gold
unerring price of the *mask* !
me buried in the somehow
beneath the shaking walls
and howls into midnight
the dozen bloodied moons
each what mice the king
declare !

05-17-17

ACHILLES , MY BROTHER

and earth hugged the shadow
of the one just gone a spirit-whisper
fled through blind stone and air
smothering heat in swaths came down
into the fray in the low hillocks
what was the name of the fish
that swam in the eye ?
who were the kids tossing pebbles
across the stream of oblivion ?
what were the small white things
swimming back and forth on the surface ?
was it because the ants got into the larder
making war with the ghosts of ink ?
whatever that was and whenever
it meant to scale a blade of grass
before evening with its *Mystery*
shouting distances inside the ear
as traffic of fireflies loomed on the leaf
darksome brother lordly in shape
your ever remote claim to skin
to sing that verdant but somber tune
how did it happen the spear ?
which the masked phantom across
the way with such sure aim ?

they say that death is nothing but dust
a storm of instantaneous motes
that disintegrate memory
nothing of substance ever comes back
was ever aloft a finger so great
carving an arc from sky
yet in a trice went deeply lost
in that recondite lawn of darkening
hues sizes losses echoes
something more it must have been
that earth hugged so sore
a shadow a

05-17-17

LINEAR-B

what is the etymology of *Apollo* ?
  or the bright spheres that signal
in our sleep
      belt of memory unwinding
with pictures of battles murders
    slaying of men
would that *august* Persephone
        lead us forth out
away from the throngs of the myriad
    dead their eerie cries
back to our hollow ship
    tarry forth both rowing
and aided by a good wind
        to reach in the next canto
island which is of Dawn the dwelling
    the dancing places the risings
of the Sun and there we fell
    into a deep torpor
not understanding
    invisible words winged things
that leave signatures in the eye
      a rotation a delving
a depth from which never
    and the haunting of those cries
the myriad throngs and held
    leaves over our ears
and smoked a hempen substance
    before our very eyes the *Lyre*
from a tortoise shell carved
    nproduced such harmonies
would Dawn ever rise again ?

      there is a limit to mind
water is only so finite
          wake to find the companions
scattered gone to the other *Side*
      metal ringing in sea-air
brine-taste sours the mouth a
          dead-end to time in the grotto
God-of-Plague ! send your mice
          devour the earth with echoes
to wander evermore on islands
          without boundaries wary
of the bear the wild boar the lion
        flashing eyes in the text
where nothing can be deciphered
        a woman was here a veil
a departed soul a sandal astray
        losses mount by forenoon
edges of air sapping breath
        like the color red
meant to blind and the wound
     somewhere in the left flank
and the ineffable clouds racing
        to discover a double moon
++++++++++++++++++++++++
what more can there be ?
     incisions in wax a prayer
invocation to the goddess
     twin of Apollo her unwritten
hair flaring in late afternoon
     chasing a human ghost
ululating in blond triumph
     cavernous syllables
the chill of a death warrant
     come to a stop by the pool
where the Nymph unclad
    awaits

05-20-17

ELEGIAC FRAGMENT

it is the late time
the small white flowers
have seen their god
sun sets behind their eyes
sea shades deep violet
washing against rock
that night embraces
then silence comes
out of the dizzy sand
to fill the ear with song
starspent dust fade
remember nothing
of daylight on earth
nor the crocus on the hill
nor the darkening fen
where hide the souls
of the before gone

05-20-17

PUELLA

poet ! a ton of Beauty walks by
and you sit there stupefied
enmeshed in your platonic saliva
a seashore of illusions and losses
and there she sits hair a mess
lachrymose despising the perfidious waves
that have born some errant sailor away
you signing letters of eternal promise
and regret a stoned devotee of the god
who musters storms and catastrophes
you don't see her you don't get it
Puella in front of your damned bedimmed eyes
the stars go through their myriad exits
planets angry with the constitution
go plunging their destinies into an inferno
suns a million of them become an atom bomb
mesas and deserts and plateaus of sand
the very junction where Venus and Adonis
combine to suffer witless ecstasy
and *Puella* in the midst of this maelstrom
largely a figment of your imagination
sits there a disturbance of Mind
watching the various seas of Homer disintegrate
in the holocaust of a single ray of light

matter and anti-matter photons and beta particles
frustrations of the memory of time
rounding the single bend of a lost river
poet ! a ton of Beauty has just passed
lingering fictions of sputum and vomit
tossed in the mirror of no-reflections !
why can't you see her for what she is
Puella the one and only in her massive disarray
did Love ever split the comb of chaos
just to fit your reveries of Never-again ?
universes come and go in a tiny afternoon
pools where Nereids abandoned wipe the air
with their misapplied cosmetics
grottos and caverns mountaintops and hells
other worlds dreams sleeping potentialities
poet ! stupefied in the luster of a spent moon
unable to look away from the Hallucination
that binds you to the apotheosis of Idea
it is only death *Puella* wants of you
and you just sit there myopic and grieving
for something you never understood !
what poetry is about : the noose the snake
the stone the weeds the smoke the blind
in the sad labyrinth of her skin *Puella* cries
Don't come back !
I am the unkenned mystery

05-22-17

IMITATION OF SEXTUS PROPERTIUS

"quare, dum licet, inter nos laetemur amantes:
non satis est ullo tempore longus amor"

rocks , solitary , abandon , resound , woods ,
and , echoes , dolorous , heart , my , grieve ,
you , Cynthia , bones , lasting , ? , will , if ,
ever , longing , suffer , like , Hylas , lost ,
among , and , lovers , pool , bland , images ,
hurry , avoid , chance , remember , ? , whom ,
call , Dryads , ensnared , mind , error , whim ,
aging , not , nothing , lasts , Cynthia , why ,
doors , listen , night , lamps , beds , grief ,
other , who , ? , vestiges , smoke , trails , sky ,
obdurate , heart , yes , yours , again , dawn ,
the , unwilling , sandals , back , forth , and ,
red , illumines , streak , heavens , clouds , moon ,
white , pale , fading , me , weeping , turgid , eyes ,

turn , walls , silence , mine , whenever , light ,

, tears , cheeks , hair , mess , robe , torn ,
lies , deceit , lips , tongue , and , stars , loss ,
forget , ? , how , ever , yours , mine , break ,
naked , skin , pearly , moist , again , once ,
now , more , sweat , whispers , shadows , me ,
you , believe , ? , tomorrow

05-23-17

SONG OF SAN FRANCISCO

half of all men are dead
half as many more women
might be dead also moon-struck
delirious watching the envy-sea roil
deepening red and poisonous
through fathoms of lost poetry
ichor and iodine and ambrosia
whatever pours through the veins
heroin and meth and bad dago red
sitting on the rotted pier as fogs
roar in silent as the planet Morpheus
and cities of sand and cities of thick tar
rear their ancient skyscrapers
behind us and a noise of ivy
or bacchants ululating in cafes
sipping week-old espresso
thrills our algae-filled ear-holes
it's already the first Saturday
of the rest of the Holy Week
lunatic italo-americans want to eat Jupiter
their hyphenated greek relatives
are on a binge for asterisk and ouzo
large domains of Homeric verse
made bright by peyote hallucination
it's all out war on the telegraph and
the ever more omnipresent iphone
the ones who don't get it are on a slab
the ones who do cannot get out of bed
the walls are sticking to thin air
gypsies with faces of luminous dogs
enormous cetacea behind plate glass
make mustache-eyes at the girls
who glide by in their Chinese skin
what else is there but enormous memory
of when Kerouac dived headfirst

into a bucket of 100 proof ice at Vesuvio's
and the then poets and hipsters
trotted out in caparisons of Blakean meter
recited for all the world to end
directories of unedited stream-of-consciousness
wailing like unfettered saxophones
at the budding new-star of the last night
of the already cancelled Passion Week
holy ! holy ! holy !
more than half of everybody is dead
the remainder are waiting on the corner
of Columbus and Grant
for a god to undress the heavens
before their very eyes
symbolism of the color blank !
it is already the tomorrow of electricity
sacred the Mind
that does not Understand !

05-23-17

THE UNFINISHED HYMN TO *PERSEPHONE*

daffodils
    reunion with light and air
wisps of auburn hair caught
    in the infernal comb a
gasp a sigh some tears a
    whatever was lost that fatal
month when
    nand the lights went out
and stems of great greenery
    climbing some invisible trellis
and exactly how many skies
    rushed through the vowel
held like a song in her mouth
    the leaf hidden in stone
small insect chirping in glass
    evening's softening din
hills where echo remains wounded
    unable to return the consonant
to its vatic tongue
    surges of water in the dark
multiples of the letter Pi
    to stand there dazed
holding a simulacrum of metal
    daybright scansion of memory
where it was before a ruin

    piles of unhewn marble
which should have been a god
    come running to meet
the shadow the Nymphs
    wet with night
and to embrace the form
    but not the substance of
a sobbing in salty tamarisk
    what other words are there
but the unspeakable ones
    purplish haze veils the eyes
dust of longing in the ears
    which are the seas to approach
undying waves restless white
    to set foot on the unseen shore
to embrace the incoming fog
    to relinquish the pronoun
senseless brain meal
    open arms to the Opaque
nothing of stone and mineral
    to lose foot in the deafening
marine roar drowning
    syllable by syllable
in the gradual labyrinth
    of cloud and
to be returned unexpectedly
    to the House of Mystery
to go lost again
    a grain a seed a
tossed in the summer wind
    Mother ,

05-26-17

ENIGMA ME THIS

"I will go down to Hades and shine among the dead"
Odyssey, XII, 383

the frail a rose is a cloud the sky
stemming from such a which it was
never on earth what a chariot is a name
by wheels run the course a fane a ruin
some dumped into the water a running
rain is a faint the night through a pane
same as dark as metal her mind a memory
of days without end on floors rugs animals
peering from walls a scene without back

she stayed and legs and frame a picture
some shades a shadow a thing falling
through here and here shaded halls
among and transient as a voice is a sound
naming what a number is are you too
a body years to relate and counting
stopped to fix the stocking a run in
the seam and words other than a vision a
section at a time the air halved by azure
temples of the once gods they were adorn
necklaces of pure jade the pearl afterwards
in her mouth a single jewel an entity on
the brow please as to enter this way ,
winding and unwinding discourse between
whomever is guiding and the path obscure
they are like spirits breaths rising fogs
change of flowers pattern days in chain
if she could and then heads turn watching
as pass by her outline a form without matter
shaping wit and signs beckon hands whiten
making of myth a single most what if
sinking too and alabaster and statues
commerce with speech to bring back
if could and the eerie flute song the ring
in the ear the signal to alert rock a !
writhing a piece of small almost pink
the buds in the hair and a wind raising
waves to sail like that forever blanched a
planet of grass something darker still what
can never know waking or asleep the mast
totters storms without vowels that whipping
a siren blast a fiction the poet in his blind
cupping between palms of time a recall
softness when it was there an afternoon
with music and her breasts opaque a fade
slowly the motions of going and coming
through what seems like lawns of eternity
come now won't , you ?

05-28-17

ABANDONING THE MIND

> "... *found four abandoned temples, called cues, with many likenesses inside, mostly women, tall women* ..."
> Bernal Diaz del Castillo
> Historia verdadera de la conquista de la Nueva España

am I my breath ?
am I my name ?
am I the thinking in my head ?
how many are there of *me* ?
when I was three years old
was I someone else ?
why am I not the cow grazing
by the side of the moving road ?
when I was twenty one years old
getting inebriated was that somebody else ?
time and again I wake from a deathless sleep
struggling to remember the day before
was that the day of the accident
when the world dissolved in a glass of milk ?
how was it I embarked on that frail craft
and crossed so many raging seas ?
how did I reach the other side
still remaining breath and name *me* ?
and as for the suture in the page
that tells about the history of things
or the rust on the tip of the metal
stuck in the air of the many wars
they are nothing they are illusory
abstractions in the library of memory
as many as accompanied me
on that errant voyage across the dark stream
they have all fallen by the way *shadows*
am I the voice that proceeds from my lips ?
am I the face in the mirror ?
restless sand rushing water
moons that enlarge and diminish
stars identified as fixed in the firmament
suns that rise and set monotonously
am I the sentient being that experiences these ?
are there exactly one thousand demons
arising from the pentacle drawn in the Colosseum ?
when it is midnight and my head has fallen
from the tree branches into inferno
and all the noise and chaos seething
around me am I dead ?
if I look out the window and thirty years

have passed in that minute staring am I dead ?
I am not Nagasena
I am not Milarepa
I am not Hernán Cortés
is it the year 1519 or is it not known
what month on the Via Sacra ?
and the sound of the drums is powerful
and the tramp of so many feet
crossing the inlet splashing
and by mid afternoon reached
a desolate place where stood abandoned four temples,
called *cues*, with many likenesses inside,
mostly women, *tall* women . . .
lying there in the stifling summer heat
to make out on the walls designs
cloud efforts fading simulacra gods
most likely come to drink our sweat
and the gong at dinner time
and the Captain in his great armor
standing there trembling
poised to enter eternity
dust !

05-30-17

TESTING THE SPIRIT

season of funerals burning hands
invisible gods raining in sleep
room after empty room bewildered
wandering bodies go searching
for leaves that read for the wind
that circling takes away thought
no longer a difference between selves
talking through a paper of signs
nothing is understood for what it is
or is not breath and light and
passing through doorways and
coming forth into unending hours
sorrowing for the other who went
lost in fogs and smoke behind the hills
why couldn't the answer be heard ?
who translated the footnotes ?
where have the long houses gone ?
to be absent communing with silence
listening for the single raindrop
to finally fall from the eaves
into darkness

05-31-17

MAYOWOOD 1956

the spot where the small deer
come to nibble grass and drink
deep from the dark pool
where is that spot ?
will brother ever come back ?
road taken dust fade of time
turning round the bend
waters vaster still shadowy
where does everything go ?
cloud spackled western sky
trees overgrown ancient path
echo and echo verdant hue
set the mind down on stone
lay out the shape in its suit
nacre buttons and silk sleeves
how little the wind knows !
abide with me it says on the knoll
where a circle of grass seems
to linger praying for evening
from afar the once-city pales
its carillon tower now dust
when were we ever there ?
to go down where the silent ones
throng thirsty for memory
and mingle there asleep yes
becoming one with the small deer
bending in darkness to drink
from the deep deep pool

06-02-17

JUNE-SONG BY THE RIVER STYX

what a lovely day to step aboard
      the Stygian bark !
lark robin sparrow and crow
are there to sing their latin verse
and Tom and Ann and Nancy too
their flailing pallid spirits play
one last time shadows in the wind
how is it on this cloudless day
that sky seems so menacingly blue
and hover over grass flitting
insects with human eye and voice
lament that makes leaves bleed
words that none can hear

who walking still on earth's curve
tremble in their inner *me* knowing
that round the bend the final hill
rears mysterious turf into the void
and crowding round a small spectacle
of broken glass and blood
onlookers mere reflections peer
wondering whether to pray or fear
what's next for them by the Stygian bank
will hands descend from eerie heavens
suddenly to transport them to gods
who judge by the sand they've wasted
how long the endless trail will be ?
what hapless soul will be Prosperina's
choice to dance the stately sarabande ?
month of May has passed merry
beyond all recall green of Troubadours
full song and joysome for the quick
no less for those departed from the light
how we recall the dance the circle
bright fane in the center of revolving time
new stream running silver rivulet
flowers in polychrome clusters shining
in the melt of the hundredth sun
was there a shiver in unfolding air ?
was there some bane on the blushing petal ?
it's June now month when Persephone
returns down under to dark mold
her arms full of plundered flora
gaze not back Queen of Hell !
stepping out from forenoon's knell
to the muddied quay the ferry to await
the grizzled boatman with flaming eye
weightless stone of the unrelenting barge
rush and eddy of the dark flow
come Jane and Alice Harry too
shuddering wights in blinding glare
with thin wavering hands set down
the remainder of their human form
torn shirts muddied cuff a missing finger
what's oblivion but a penny lost ?
what's tomorrow but an unknown window
a tortoise shell a fraction of a vowel ?
it's a June day a fragile brightness
on the fade a pale and wan of distance
longing a fierce desire to overcome
the once and only end of time

with something more the Muses give
dancing luster of the gone world
fringe and dun the wasting hour
and poetry fragmented misunderstood
immensely fired the burning woe
altar root and stem a goddess
white-armed the moon a ruddy crown
a something glimpsed an error
heat and then a lapse of sleep
wave after purple wave lapping
the dreaming ear into lull a sing
a song an unremembered sound
goodbye to one and all
goodbye

06-03-17

AN ACCOUNT OF THE TWINS, SUMMER 1957

lying there in a glaze of blinding light
was it Apollo's voice of marmoreal distance
that shattered something deep within
summoning from every fiber a music
a sweetness of melodies beyond compare
a mass of chords that sculpted the air
into infinite choirs of ascending luminosity
and yet and yet we lay there stunned
as if poured into a sleep of heated glass
transpiration in rivers drenched the bed
someone was calling us from a stairway
that did not go all the way to paradise
a cigarette as if by magic lit itself smoking
in the imagined lips of still a third body
invisible inserting itself between us
I am the planet Gabriel it seemed to say
it was a warning from the next life
a warrant for our arrest a denunciation
for we had more than once passed
the limits of intoxication and inspiration
in the following instant the world
became a desert a vast eeriness of sand
of monolithic structures and a sky low
and yellow so small it fit under an eyelid
orange spectra dizzying violet pinwheels
moons of radiant noon throbbing bleached
asterisks and great rounded exclamations
that seemed to finalize a typescript
existing only in the mind's pale flux

a dream a scandal of various orients
a version of heaven pasted to the heat
that revolved around us in hourly cycles
were we to arise and get up and walk
would we simply return to the hospital
where we were employed as dishwashers ?
what about the burning bed and its disciples
and the tale of Horus and the muddied flats
who would be first to lift the carapace ?
what was the awesome illegible message
slipped under the door of our tombstone ?
an afternoon like no other with metals
of pythagorean mystery and the Rhombus !
enigmas windows abandoned movie theaters
the hundred years of delphic silence
endured in the very instant we reached
the hilltop with its enigmatic water tower
where we entered a second phase of time
an evening of flagstones and exhaustion
thought was no longer thought !
insect transformations of consciousness
black matter sunspots space travel
whoever we had been at birth was no longer
meaningful a puzzle in a ruined temple
stone set upon stone impenetrable rock
leaf imprints in the ceaseless breeze
 a wave !   a fading
falling away from the once imposing light
weightless zygote passing
through an ineffable
              maze

06-04-17

VENUS DECONSTRUCTED

Queen Venus ! take this dove
and wring its neck burn it
on your fragrant altars
enough of love and grace !
let those who are incinerated
by your frequent gaze testify
that yours is a heartless blaze
there is neither heaven or earth
there are no days of the week
there are no months of the year
there is only treacherous hair
anklets that sound like rust

eye make-up and lip gloss
ash and mercury on the tongue
as for memory ! stupendous
ingots of chloroform and lye
one-way ticket to Krete
seas incarnadine & upside down
a Sicily fuming with regrets
Bacchants that rage like bees
consuming entire wooded hills
in their passion for Thought !
Queen Venus ! when was love
anything but anachronism of rock
like sleep in an obsidian heat wave ?
are there cigarettes of virtue
cauldrons seething with vowels
grammars of ineffable silence ?
puellae naiads nymphs hamadryads
goat-footed boys lost in libraries
summer afternoons without beginning
folded inside a butcher store wrapper
what is the function of dream ?
what is blood what is nonsense
what is the hand writing ?
what is the hand writing ?
if everything were as beautiful
as the inverted snow of time !
hummingbirds pasted to photons
wings gestating monuments
elaborate with speech acts
statues and more statues
gripped in the ennui of eternity
the whole classical world caught
in a single glyph of sand *KLEOPATRA* !
incest of the embroidered eyelid
shadow and effigy of hemlock
scarabs mutilated by the sound
of mountains crystallizing in honey
Queen Venus ! you are ancient
a museum ruined at the crossroads
filled with languages of fading light
clouds glaze in the cataracts that
tumble senselessly from your eyes
a thimble a spent thread a needle
skin that has lost its music
tattered piece of cloth
once the city of *Adonis* !
step by pitiful step you totter

dumbfounded an element
blackening on the island of Cos
musk fermented in vats
a pitcher without ears
rattling in dust
a snake hissing
a snake hissing
is it a wonder today
is no day at all !

06-06-17

A WAY TO WEAVE GOODBYE

ACHILLES & PATROCLUS

long the last road lost so far
have we come deep now into mist
neither shoreline nor wind-spear
sung a various and roaring
mingled the angry white-caps and
flung from the boundaries of sleep
where winter on night's other
side hides in dry tamarisk
near the snowy ravine
where Selene separates her dreams
or the two gods so alike in beauty
a strapping lad the one the other
most like a maid fresh from dew
milking kine
           so dense the airs
wrapped us like robes and speaking
each to his own divinity suppliant
no longer a surety homeward bound
ships a mangled mass of timbers
at the bottom of the rock-grey depths
turmoil in the heart the head stoned
of memories incoherent with light
what was it to search we were sent
by the mouth of the issuing water
lay the ear to cold earth listen !
shapes of voices infernal and dark
telling us such was loss the fervent
lesion of flesh desire streaked numb
at dawn frozen grass like icicles
unaware of what we had slain sleeping
hands raw with itching madness
how did we turn from infancy

to a perilous drive off cliffs
crazed steeds frothing sweat
chariot wheels sent flying in the void
here come by me your body wracked
our souls together read the stars
what fate it was we met
and so much to grieve
        unknown statues
shadow of music lying slantwise
across the late afternoon ruin
from afar an echo
slings shafts and clouds
man's fragile bone
brassy greaves shattered
by the noise of the sun
rains mysterious as glyphs
obliterating spoken memory
two by two the worlds lie down
head first in the furrow
dusky and melancholy
as unwritten and
enigmatic
verse

06-11-17

IN EXILE WITH OVID

if a canal could cut through the isthmus
of the mind connecting the two Seas
of Ignorance and Fatality would the mind
be any more at peace with the darkness
that consumes it ?
here on the Barbary coast with zero
for a horizon and arrows from nowhere
what one pines for what one misses
gardens of intellect loves at war with Love
fallen from grace the body of Poetry
dense smithy of image and cloud-work
the entire antiquity of memory !
marble bits of shattered planets litter
the blackening shore where shadowless
the exile paces in the maze of longing
what was it about life among the spirits
among the spirits of Alexandria
hexagonal seas issuing from parian marble
voices infernal and sublime rising up
from the mysteries of stone and time

was it one word too many or a misplaced
accent on the Homeric sun-slant ?
the tears of the Pleiades freeze
the Wain staggers under an icy weight
Selene displaced among motionless fogs
weeps for her namesake Helen wafting
amidst tortured pharaonic sands
was there ever such a thing as heat
the buzz of maddened bees nostalgic
for the endless noon of Mount Olympus ?
the gods are no more ! effigies of ether
napalm carbon dioxide or benzedrine
hallucinations metamorphoses trance !
animal becomes leaf leaf becomes goddess
rains of night-shade and decomposition
man devouring man in power cycles
neon atavism of the original Thought
one single image the sad and lasting
tossed into an oriental ditch Beauty
left to drift in the pale myth of light
does the *other* ever become the *self* ?
how many are the persons of Orion !
such distances in the unseen cosmos
that burns to the nerve of the Muse
who dictates nightly this discourse
of saliva and disorder
patterns of darkness both ethereal
and crazy devour the human remnant
clothes washed up on the beach
bearing the shape of Ulysses
and in the low brush a sobbing
nymphs who mourn the passing world
this was where I stepped this was where
wandering I lay the head down to sleep
rock becomes mind mind becomes nothing
fire faces all directions

06-14-17

ULYSSES SETS FOOT ON ITHACA AIR LIGHT AND THE GODDESS CLOTHE HIM IN A DIVINE MIST

hands aloft beseeching the Nymphs
by their sacred grotto
is heaven the nearer for so much suffering
distances accrue in small waters
where faces come and go in a trice
was one ever otherwise

a surfeit plaything of the gods
writing and rewriting the unsent letter
to Penelope the same who abides
if only in memory's capsized bark
how is it one has died
yet persists in the envelope of earth
in the vain hope of discovering
as if anew the abandoned home
the deserted altars still fragrant
with incense and oblations
ghosts of so many shipwrecked
or sent to Hades arrow-spent
glorious ones their names are lost
who waxed and wasted beside me
does Athena disguised as a lad
still accompany me in her white raiment
interceding for the Thunderer
even as the days of the week vanish
into a single monotonous hour ?
face down in inert humus I spin
one single thought after another
embracing not light but what light
represents in the panorama of sky
dizzy winter of the stars outracing
the mind's cunning and guile
what ruins what shards and fade
the homecoming wastrel greet
wine-stained the brain lingering
in love's webbed artifices
no longer sustains archaic hope
music of ivy-twined remembrances
a cup spilt ire rousing men from the hip
to shoot the gold-tagged deer
sacred to Artemis and dire
nemesis to spread dread night's
porphyry cloud over mortal sight

ennui of decades lost in error
ever the butt of the sea-god's wrath
what was it all about ?
deceit miasma and snouting lust
men turned to swine
enormous rocks cast into the sea
roiling surfs and indecencies
and always nostalgia for the shore
dawn in the ruddy sands waiting
for the girls to come and wash
divine garments in the dark eddies
a flash of recognition before
the fabled inky curtain falls
blinding the eye to the moving world
a screen with phantoms arguing
loud in their aggressive silence
and by noon finds me
where ivory and marble construct
a palace and a riot of the dissolute
contesting the kingdom of *Absence*
with their haughty and stupid verse
unknown I remain
and weightless
an integer
ablaze

06-16-17

FRAGMENT
TEMPLE RUINS

stone in conflict with sun
whose ruddy steeds   flowing
over skin of earth all radiant
as shines the deity nameless
who   embarked ago
to cross from bed to bank
atoms   the soul now lips
now arms raised   a murmur
correctly pronounced the
ascendant vowel   limbs
articulated seated on holy
grass   the light that pours
making wide the sky   a
bird the holy wings aloft a
  from the dark issuing I
praise   ancient the rock
rent in two a voice and

distant   as if hanging
in mid-air   sound of hooves
racing leave   a
presence ! hidden leaf
shadow   what it can be
if not a portal   behind
a quiet dying a   summer
in circles of heat   high
in golden chariots as if
dissolving   saffron clouds
the   once night in their
eyes   lie down
not light but the idea
   of light
houses come crashing
    and whatever
else was solid
other worlds a   when
the pedestal bereft of the
goddess   window opened
wide to reveal unkempt
the   Love with anger
flashing eyes   the world
done wrong a corner
where shriveled and de-
composing still another
deity   to ruins
all come to ruins in this
   full circle a year
some beauty revealed
as in a shimmering
   small streams
running backwards
into the moon

06-19-17

WHIRLWIND

for james balfour

the fox and the fuse entry and exit
life ! this unbearable moment
shepherds quarreling
what's ambiguous about the day
bright hour first you swam the length
came out shaking ready to smoke
and learned to speak in dialect
in the midst of sun and stone
the arbor where you slept
sand where waking fast you stepped
who was the girl on the right
wearing skin of freckled light
married her divorced her wept
the following day was a year long
riding the waves so loud and clear
snapping sails furled the wind
espied afar the rock girt isle
jumped ashore learned to while
the hours bewitched in love trance
why did the gong devastate time ?
did you circle pointlessly the well
where for sure the shadow drowned
your other half the faster swift ?
how soon the quick turned dumb
the myth of green and swart ivy
the drum and bell the furious file
trees and hills and lengthening grass
face down you fall !
listen to the sun as it drowns
the wildest seas have gone away
night descends with its soft hammer
does flesh fail you knees turned soft
is the end less a future than a mile ?
come call your muses from the stars
where turning to rain they evanesce
this is the last poem !
what you recall is the *bang* !
an ear filled with yawning ink of space
whispers from the many you forgot
a hand a voice a drop a leaf
the silence of the what
the why of the unending

06-20-17

DOWN TO THE HOUSE BEHIND THE SUN
MYSTERIES TO OUR OWN SELVES

"let them go down quick into hell"
Saint Jerome

histories of the end friction of air
less dense than before sounds
emanating from a house where
the profound red birth of echo
takes root and blossoms white
cycles of heat prodigious clouds
filling the movie theater where
together we languished waiting
for the red sea to part—a fiction !
heaven of lice and abandoned ore
vatic nerve ! rooms where dark
gathers fateful looms weird
absence of sand and libraries
descent to the other world
ebb and flux beyond water
archaeology of memory and spit
before angels could speak
before light engendered light
chaos immense and ineffable
what weaves in and out of time
the self the many selves in One
if for a moment we could have
been as spirits exchanging lives
mind at the aperture to space
we could have traveled rivers
like gods living on monotony !
yet leaving that theater entranced
with the city that inhabited us
we were immeasurably transformed
gold ingots seething in the brain
flashes of immutability like Egypt
in its innermost recesses blank
simultaneously teeming
with balances and spoons and eyes
paintings of sight and hearing !
turning the corner where traffic
seemed to fly on concrete wings
we knew we *Knew* for sure
that when the red sea parted
a voice of a million vowels emerging
would burst an immemorial Sun
imparting to us the secret

that can never be revealed
one is not the other without death
a rush of mystic grasses
small pools underneath
a handful of soil
leaf and vertigo
the wind

05-23-17

DOLCE STIL NOVO

what color is dark on the other side of time
if rivers run through gods like shafts of air
Madonna moves her mountains to the stars
needle of intellect no mercy her love shows
below a stygian veil my brain to stone turns
and stone in deepest waters burns to know
where is the house where dwells the body
celestial which is the room shadows inform
a lie this pleasant world this meadow fair
greenery that adorns the blowing winds
flower plucked by hands invisible and rare
in a swoon I lie for hours unnumbered
as if to die were reality sublime a waste
this otherness of breath and longing
to see beyond the pale skin of her song
to *know* is the thing denied by her sign
eyes inward cast and strange designs
moving through screens of fog and pearl
jettisoned dreams like rocks tossed
to furious waves vowels unmeasured
in the enigmatic poetry of lost minds
powders of thought distant and unrealized
energies that devastate long afternoons
when rain and massive clouds conspire
to make chaos of the nostalgic lair
where once I thought to tryst with *her*
intelligence foreboding moons and asterisks !
bright noons suffused with blind statuary
marble quarried from the grammar of despair
who goes in and out following the errant
path of no return and sighs to die again
day after endless day in the obscure wood
who went to school to learn of ideas
and gyres that enlighten remote heavens
weights measures and equipoise of light
books that opened turn math to flame !

I am that *he* wounded many times over
who struggled to read then write this verse
mirror of caves and winding labyrinths
Madonna this poem is sent to you by lethal
cupids whose aspersions and mockery
make a hotel of aggrieved windows
false luminescence that pours like ores
from the smithies of far off Saturn
rust and sands of nothingness ablaze
and to sleep in the great dissolving *Arm* !
forgetting the day to the hour when
I first met you descending from ether
a blossom absinth-white in your hair
a grief your mouth a daze of coral
spent
      would I ever ?

06-25-17

ESCHATOLOGY

the last of the gods
    truncated words
meaningless syllables
    vowels that pass over the mountain
or in the evenings
    when dogs become suddenly silent
in the copse by the drainage canal
    you can sense something a
few fireflies emerging from a leaf
    whisperings like echoes
of a name trying to be recalled
    a light that goes on in a window
in a house missing for years
    grass the abode of the invisible
sense their aching to be
    fear in the tree trunk
where an alphabet has died
    the hive where winter sleeps
ghosts of bees spinning glass
    what is it about rust ?
or in the stillness of midday heat
    when only statues move
immense prescience of the end
    thunder in the wheel of light
as it revolves in and through stone
    thoughts that are only darkness
sleep in the motionless water

    that floods a lost mirror
how do we become more than
    the other ?
is there a body of air that transcends
    or is infinity simply
breath issuing from an earthen crevice ?
    all things are haunted
by what they are called
    every creature is at once nothing
or the thing that proceeds from death
    ineffable the being of the gods
shrapnel of myth and rock
    dew-drop size of the sun
anti-matter that is nowhere
    Apollo Bacchus Mercury Minerva !
rags a torn rope and ants
    with faces of sad longing
rose becomes ether
    ether the faint memory
of the antiquity of time

06-26-17

HYMN TO OSIRIS

our cattle our crops the rising river
how many parts of you scattered
like seed in the southern desert wind
we will eat and enjoy the fruits
of what you have sown and pray
to darkness and to the never-coming
rain and to Mummy Nut of the skies
and all about us the mysteries of wells
of skins hung out to dry of palm-leaf
and the white stucco walls of distance
how blind we have been to your dying
annually shifting into the greater red
of the turbulent memory of sand
small we are in our desires our fears
never once touching the really sacred
bowing to shadows of oxen
at altars of honey and myrrh
come back to us one day !
cloudless days of forever
how many halves of you
have we ignorantly devoured ?
scarabs painted on sarcophagi
live in anticipation of tomorrow

when the enormous door will yawn
and waters from the other world
rush to bring back the day
without you sun no longer rises
little stars that decorate the heavens
incised on buried rock
draw their light from you !
why will you not come back to us ?

06-29-17

A SMALL ELEGY : JUNE'S END

the end is persistent and longing
for fields unseen the hand invisible
that takes us over the top longing
persistent as the end is and sweet
marjoram and clover and hyacinth
what bees know and inform the air
all about we wonder at the light
as it forms a maze of brilliance
blinding really the rush of grass
a stream underneath and swirling
skirts of goddesses in plenitude
marble and alabaster and breathless
coming for us to guide us through
and out of the end and the persistent
buzz in the ear somewhere else
cannot recall why who or where
just the sense of waking and falling
waking again in the blue and water
lapping below the bed and voices
outside the window and dazzling
hours without number unruly
wild that we take them and move
through throngs of wind and brush
here and here where a place unnamed
waits ending the day's persistent
monotony but would we have it
any other way ?

06-29-17

FRIEZE : SUMMER NIGHT 1953

"postque venit tacitus furvis circumdatus alis
somnus et incerto Somnia nigra pede"
Tibullus, II, i, 89-90

in the dream version
Joe and I just got back from Mexico
though we never made it to the rain forest
the girls remarked on how tan we were
bronze gods out of Chichicastenango !
the girls—were they girls ?
swung their bare legs back and forth
on the summer porch settee
everything was lazy with a dark heat
swirling unseen beings from the future
seemed to buzz in the dense air
how far from the southern stars !
insect universes swarmed in their hair
giving off a thick odor of musk
and something indefinably rotten
that we'd brought back from the tropics
Joe and I just lying there on the chaise longue
narrating an event that never happened
lightning bolts and volcanic activity
obstreperous claims of the gods
on the once and passing earth
girls ? nymphs ? death-heads ?
swinging their bare legs in the invisible
voices alone coming out of hidden leaves
portents of sleep black dreams
unsure of foot and wings circumfused
somewhere in the legendary distance
of a memory too soon turned to rust
names meant nothing occurrences wild
and blind in the vatic sands of the hour
exchanged vows faces embraces tongues
submerged worlds of black basalt
jade eyes peering through minds
keen to penetrate otherness and time
falling from one heaven to the next
and calling out from a trance
to the planets as they plunged into view
and disappeared just like that
telescopes heliotrope blooms pampas grass
someone placed their lip on the glass
leaving a margin of intense red
which we imagined to be the next life

forbidden motels and swimming pools
highways and mountains of unrelenting dust
art history of senseless rock !
remarked on how dark we had become
entities fading into a screen of shadows
wet mouth sucking wet mouth a kiss
a forever of august nights
if we come back to tell about it
lounging there in the obscure House
where Proserpina prepared a bed
if we ever come back

07-01-17

puella dixit se Venerem esse

sacred and beautiful breathed a
long and winding around grass
the skin lay its distance to sing
how horizons vast are the eyes
can you not be as she in the wain
high above and the rain of stars
and moving mysteriously through
waters of pre-existence darker
than most and lifting the self
up from the bed of leaves night
sighs and whatever else is holy
dancing in the act of re-union
unconscious as stone and deeper
comes day only for a minute light
that shines from beyond thought
she says to be the goddess of love

07-02-17

AN ELEGY : THYSELF

"At mihi Persephone nigram denuntiat horam"
Tibullus, Elegiae, III, v, 5

hanging midway between sky and hell
earth our lawn with its pools and woods
metals mountains and distant fogs
and afterwards when the god of accidence
intercepts the flying rooftops with a hand
the size of ink and night too falls
or gas leaking from a nearby galaxy
rounding out a celestial mere explodes

leaving most of *them* dead a hallucination
in heliotrope and rust wandering from
the scene of the crash the wailing
and bees emerging from the hollyhocks
that line the gravel pathway where soon
you and I and a few others designated
will perform memory a sort of ballet
with a backdrop of enormous waters
and fishes with the electric eyes
of our once ancestors the senate house
corroded from within a great Boom !
alarms that sleep is inconvenient and
lumberyards and the street that used
to lead homewards I am that lonely
today and cannot answer for the sirens
whose shore draws up to the Mayo clinic
as soon as evening shards of carnation
sinking hills and footsteps no louder
than the moon's invisible crenellations
it is a wonder to be here and talking
to the only self one knows *Thyself*
and the whole extension of the peninsula
with its punctuations and asterisks
more like benzene and saturn's disks
listening intently and the fuzz of a bass
shrouding the ear with a melancholy
only Persephone can understand

07-04-17

WEST WIND

the stone I carried
was it ever anything
      more ?
and a woman
appeared to me
larger than a goddess
      a shining
between the rain
and the city that
provoked the rain
others did not see *her*
      as I did
there was more space
      than sky
a fourth element
or a voice written

invisibly in the clouds
that formed like sand
in the west wind
it was the time
after dying
when sleep organizes
      new planets
unimaginable colors and
explosions no one can hear
steeps and slants
that cannot abide
      the light
rock hyacinth ivy
leaf stucco beams
heights of splendor
never before dreamed of
a life gone
in the second
it takes grass
      to become
           frag-
ments

07-16-17

VARIATIONS ON A LINE BY OVID

"en iterum lacrimas accipe, harena, meas!"
Fasti, III, 472

girl ! let your sands out
let the wild take your hair
blossom and perfume sky
with the song of your skin
girl ! you were never more
than a slender frame of air
moon when it is least seen
or lightning yet unshaped
by Jupiter's invisible hand
what is mind but a slender
thread lost in the labyrinth ?
girl ! toss your tears to the wind
forget that dancing thug
busy frequent the Bacchus god
drunk his ivy-laden brow
from India's jungle come
prepares to swoop you into azure
iterated and lachrymose
girl ! your sort is wan and pale
your jasmine like the sands

white moths of dizzy surf
nest in the temple of your eyes
can see no more your life
on the ebb of pearly tide ?
whole oceans make a shore
where your sleeping fails
unnamed birds coral bright
descend to remove your shadow
girl ! you were what a mast
a flapping sail an anchor
listing in memory's cold rust
rudderless a boat steaming
into the murky stygian pool
your prayers the dazzle air
of a noon that can never be
girl ! heed not the mythographer
the poet in his torrid cups
the rhymester or the blind bard
who reinvent you daily
sand tears temple teeth
jasmine pearls dizzy coral
bright sort birds surf
island thread rust & god !
wind blow your hair away !

07-16-17

ATHENA APPEARS AND DISAPPEARS

ire wings gravity & time
it was the goddess who made
me look younger even as I stood
in the doorway facing death
was it for me to shape things ?
flashes of thought ingots
of pure clarity space descents
whirlwind perceptions a word
single vowels uttered backwards
lined up with the other *me*
plurals of myself in great sounds
echoing in the echo of water
running depths beneath the utter
and earth revolving on its spindle
and the axis of the heavens burning
because I could not *remember*
the goddess who clad me
to shine in the moment of mind

to take a step and gravid
out into the endless night
soul fall through dizzy emptiness
perplexed at the many *who*
reaching a hand out to touch
not skin but the idea of skin
winds and seas buffet the bark
skimming totally waves the hostile
darkness that the self drowns
and me the other sightless shade
errant in woods infinite
whatever comes of following
when abyss and flight the same
revolve stupefying stellar scope
whom the goddess spoke
turning a bare shoulder hair
diffused in the cupping air
I am whom you call sleeping
voice like glass in hollows
singing distance of hills
beyond the sun setting
in the bleak and purple mere

07-17-17

EPYLLION

for Slade Schuster

the time angel came running
breathless into the restaurant
stunned we did not recognize her
was the news of a recent death
or a new music fixed in the air
or cloudbursts expected by lunchtime
seated there in our midst drinking
as the nickelodeon turned its pages
her shining was manifest a bright
map of otherworldly light her
was a face beyond description
hair as if created by a lunar wind
gazing around amazed fallen
I am the light that measures distance
longing and the archaic
I am a radio an undiscovered lens
through me speak voices and code
none of you do I know nor your faces
your vital parts how and with whom

you have sex nor why you bear weight
walking or standing and ignore the gods
she spoke as a photograph would speak
trembling the moisture on her skin
ineffable text of the Sybil
her face renewed the air around us
could not dare to reach out
her to be real was beyond our ken
a fixed stare the planets of her eyes
revolved examining each of us
and in turn each of us from a splendor
collapsed burnt by a mystery
falling and falling again through
veils of memory and history
outside the traffic of automobiles
of police whistles of dead children
the riot of asphalt and teeming sun
the blaze of poverty and cities
all seemed to gather into a knot
I am the poetry you have forgotten
dust and echo of verses
? ?
what is outside the unspoken
where cosmic interjections !
unconscious in the steam of operations
hours elided into weeks poured
out from some secret orifice
the landings of so many flights
muses nymphs goddesses angels
winged insects buzzing summers
who after all were we ?
a radio she said and a music
shaped by the architecture of air
and numinous entities with faces
of the witless projections of dreams
we named each other and soon
antiquities of marble and sand
erected whole islands within
floating on seas like trajectories of gas
peninsulas where wars with Sparta
illegal games mountain roofs
naked runners bearing bridal torches
and ululations haunting vowels
symbols of statues learning to talk
and the entire abyss of Home !
exhausted we dragged our shadows forth
evening with its panoply of crushed stars

could angel have been the author
? ? ?
what was next and more numerous
a preoccupation with text and waves
how meters best described
and abandoned maidens and islands
certain feet returning to the shore
a roaring within the Shell
remember what she said
I am the light that measures distance
if we go back to school
what will we learn but ruins
subscript iota a demarcation
a caesura a hiatus in the language of stone
longing and echolalia and ivy
how remote that midday when
breathless amidst us drunk
as if reciting in grass the very epic
a radio and turned the dial to
where it clearly says
partake of me
I am the angel of bread and famine
of moss and the curved back of animals
that bear the weight of the universe
?
if my skin is to be exposed
remember I am just a girl
there are places the sun never visits
I am the configuration of eights
displaced in the monologue of Minerva
who will guide the perplexed
through thread and iron
unto places too radiant to behold

! !
I am the vertebrate Yes
a gesticulation of shadowless hands
placed on the blackboard
where the verb esse takes root
shake my hair shake my hair
I will not always remain here
but
and disappeared in a column of incense
even as heat circled the empty tables
each of us lapsed from the Self
only to awake in some Pharaonic mansion
dwellers in the land of the Dark Sun

or beasts pulling the winch
out of a dry well
struggling to recall
the Prophesy

07-17-17

POET , THE

exalted numinous fragments
half a mind away !
poet , what color
is sleep what distance is
poet , illusion cerulean
gods have lost and seas
a name has been forgotten
poet , you
figment of nerve
fish in the eye
madness , poet
stranger to Thyself , poet
nevertheless and longing
the never sighted island
homecoming of the
poet , mendicant
clad in red a
thing to be avoided ,
poet , from what ?
so many stars crashing
night side delirium
juxta-
      positions of brain
whitening radicals a
fuming , poet
remembrance then
oblivion from this bank
of the river in brackets
the waistline of the goddess
a goddess , poet
which one you choose
opaque hair flung
shot through with gold
poet , dysfunction
sands final asterisks
a few more, poet
then the a what a
inability to think right
judgment in each hand
cups s-

poet , art dead ?
swingshift plutonium
ladder swift the climb
to paradise
the thread that sees
falls down full , darksome
poet , less the bond
a hold on *her*
and light winnowing
      light clouds
the eye , poet
celestial runs the hill
tripartite the stream
below far from the
and a voice hollowing
out of rock a myth
poet , unrecognized
and wings aloft the
grain of sky etched
in thought ,
brims ink
the lost , poet
soul vast as azure
soul , last a long
swerving
      way

07-18-17

FOUR SONNETS

i

the pain my dolorous suffering I
since last met we the small under
and greenery brush light the ice
in my fire dwelling inconstant
longing is you craving my nerves
desire when will the ever be now
tall hills and trees the restless ache
my winds the birds in flight unseen
become just as the loose hair you
in the chapel of time undone gone
had never been but a vision divine
gods untied the left side of heaven
down rush rains a torment called
some say love the iridescent cloud

ii

which is the while dwelling linger
here in this dark mansion hoping
to kindle in your eyes blessed thing
the moment of a past unresolved white
like singing the birds in their small latin
aloft with ribbons and asbestos tinder
that heat stirs in circles my heart a sun
winter budding how like your breath
turned away and walked a steep incline
to otherness a paradise of fog and ire
come back to me by phone if not
by the stygian bark that your shadow
bears far from thought and sleep amaze
that takes me into the obscure camera

iii

what was in your faith but the trust
of lies by the temple door barley cakes
white scattered rice the promise you
meant was it rust the obfuscation
of ores in the pacific rest of skies
now thundered to the west beyond
where met we first in song the honeyed
a belief in the god of hives and lust
just so the winter bees restless yet
frozen in the lamp of your once eyes
what month preterit in the signs
that travel the heavens blind orbits
tracing fires that spurn mountains
where unsleeping the heart grieves

iv

is it depth my clinging flees or
summers linger greening sleet
storms torment the whither gone
great lawns the eye cover slept
in sorrow's deep how ancient the
clasped to other's shadow grieving
the soul its mate laments the hour
parting by colors that never fade
how trails grass its dustless dream
while gods hover great above glass
the fiery arrow the snowy tract
pierce like indwelling conscious

spent to know the never was you
disappeared misty into otherness

07-22-17

CANZONE D'AMORE

what love gives swirling air
in the above tempests porches
from which swing lightning
unfurled thunder in capes
gaping over earth's waters
and love the lip intensely
offered springtime's eternal
shaped a face yes the likes
of You sloping down greens
intertwined with shadows olive
and nectar divine the mouth
runs with love's liquors if
forgetting the least blade of
grass the tall wind takes a
glen a mere a wood an abyss
to know love's other the cloud
that drowns the eye and sees
what more beyond is there
remote as whitening sails a
sea of thoughts self-circling
love's lunar mind if madness
a similarity to sand and history
a progression of notes tuned
to the baffling spheres green
light-shades musical sleep
under root and rock a glyph
much like a woman and taller
than a goddess and veils rent
by gusts and shells deeper as
love winds around the wave
unformed salt and brilliance
noon tides swelling You into
sight a minute only a distance
of sigmas and thetas writing
inside the eyelid love's signal
blinking switches dazzling
sun's pre-birth a flashing a
finger lifted above lawns a
whatever it takes to remove
not just the idea but the shape
of the numeral surmounted

above love's dreaming brow
sweat drops isolated gold
speckling the sheer western
where the mountain and its
mystery at last You fall asleep
within the small cove of mind
an integer of archaic verse
if only love could translate
and leave everything untold
the first the last the only the

07-24-17

TRIONFO DELLA MORTE

swell the eyes shining bright
Nymph hidden in love's grove
come away on the chase roe
small deer buck stag doomed
shadow to shadow on the run
round what water deep whose
reflection does not return
yet sun high the sky designs
winds temper dense foliage
summer greens the empyrean
heat's vivid circles drown
intense in the swarming air
will You be mine for a day ?
Nymph will you come to play ?
bees ants and crickets time
devour sounding loud the buzz
oriental as the palace of your eyes
Nymph why harbor you this field
hidden from the glimpse of gods
these ears of corn and wheat
waving like the secret seas
that turn sailors into phantoms ?
Nymph Thou art an island
a siege of hills working dark
to bring evening's inky cloak
over the small houses of the mind
why cannot the month endure
its famous statuary noons ?
behind which tree hides Artemis
of the silver bow her steely stare
eyes lost in ivory mansions ?
Nymph color your raiment all
hues of the dizzy floral parade

steep the mask in earth's dun
teeming underneath with asterisks
frail roots the dots of memory
gone wrong spirit world night !
forget we ever met Nymph ?
to sleep in the perspiration
of your underarms a tangle
of musk and dandelion wine
crushed in the cellophane of space
how many words we cannot say
mouth only stutters drunkenly
dreams like deadly ivy
twined around the brain's arbor
alert to nothing more than salt
the body surrenders eternity
call yourself what you will
Nymph to me you are *Gloria* !

07-24-17

OMBRE D'INFERNO

what haunted note is that ?
the end of the world just when
light penetrates the spheres
or is it the echo of light ?
the voice not meant to return
ineffable soundless vowels
mingling in cavernous afterthought
what is wont to wake yet sleeping
desires first greenery then rose
blush red life in spirals
come back ! snare drum and bells
footfalls evening's tenebrous glade
homesteads sinking into loam
darker still the place once
occupied by shadows and a
what is that other music ?
penetrating this gassy air
fear of water and rust and coils
stellar mansions empty of form
mythic broken distances
walls strangled by lissome ivy
wrists ankles and hips
locked in a symphony of silence
should the infirmity of matter
should the sheer math of mind
encompass this passing stream

can this be understood ?
a wrong in the shape of a hand
unkept promises and hair
wild map of otherness damp
perfumed blowing in a vacuum
don't look ! love is an alphabet
erased in a dream of zeroes
and to be set beside death
in a row of simulacra
listening for the song of release
drowning rather in an asbestos
of infinite longing
white the missing decade
white the lost shadows
white the last shadows
where the three rivers meet
where the world comes to an end
white the trailing sound
dust in memory
dust in shadows of memory
don't you recognize me ?
shadows circling circling endlessly
don't you recognize me ?

07-27-17

THE FORGOTTEN MOMENT

remember that time coming home
after twilight moon emerging
from its red mansion invisible wings
the whispers of girls on porches
unable to translate what they were saying
some kind of warning and darkness
deception and warmth insects
trading souls in a furious debate
about eternity and its aftermath
it was all about poetry we decided
how to get at the ineffable
one after the other verses in the air
unwritten and mysterious
the shape of the universe at midnight
waiting for dawn the damp-eyed
to spread a new light over the already
dead the many and mostly forgotten
we hurried impervious to their call
baffled by the girls on the porches
who seemed to grow softer larger

like goddesses not meant to be seen
who somehow impeded our journey
home to the island now lost to memory
to the stone and the plum-tree
scraping the stucco wall in sleep
was it then we first stepped
into the labyrinth ?

07-29-17

LAMENTO D'ARIANNA

threads filaments golden stuff of clouds
I dream of an energy greater than *light*
and in the dream I am on my knees
washing leaves to stifle their cries
voices like lattices of blood woven dark
into the nerve of stone even as I veer
from the edge of space into an island
the size of ink floating on pure mind
ether extending like a shadow across
the world of sand and bees immense
as sleep the river that bears us away
am I astonished at this reverie ?
knocking on the door of illusion men
woven from a matrix of distances
streams and rock and grassy knolls
does the cliff have memory ?
is there a place inside water where
statues are born ? am I that thing
desiring and yearning for what ?
nothing and the vast fields of thought
gods at the top of the palace stair
children at best with nascent wings
ciphers so terrible they have to be kept
in urns sealed for all eternity
how do I escape from this dream
washing leaves in a dry well seeing
and not seeing the stranger approaching
hands that seem to talk asking for honey
demanding women and flayed bulls
arenas filled with the ruins of time
cataracts of unspeakable beauty
pouring out of moonstone at midday
what treachery of dress and adornment
betrays me in stalking mirrors
development of horizontal planets
where sea meets its double in wine

prepared for total annulment
and the ships with their mythic sails
unfurling in the devastation of air
and the new god surrounded by throats
singing of seasons and greenery
plunging into the wave like a knife
take me ! embodiment of surf
vanishing forever into the *Bright*
legend of skin and soundless music

07-31-17

AN ACCOUNT OF THE DAY SUMMER ENDED

when the dusky charioteer
asked you to come aboard
why did you accept ?
wasn't the green vale of Tempe
contentment enough ?
to what avail the white whetstone
the limber fishing rods
long draughts of cold dandelion wine
afternoons without purpose
roaming the summer of the mind
you had to go beyond the hills
where no road travels
into the wood obscure
the Library wasn't enough
the shaded well planned thoroughfares
wending in and out the town
nor the meandering stream
where they said Nymphs hide
playing with shadows of the lost
what was the big yellow fan in the sky ?
how did it take you from your mind ?
constantly other in your glances
the world became a simple inch
a distance between tomorrow
and the never vast of space
legends of gravel and night
of the tiny interstices between
the pages of an unwritten poem
longing for the forgotten !
like the day you had to stand
before the class and philosophize
you ate your hands in despair
besought the windows for escape

and in the end downed the elixir
that brings relief and darkness
when you didn't come home that night
when the fields turned to snow banks
in the search for your footprints
then it was the dusky charioteer
pulled up with his smoking steeds
and bade you climb aboard
how wistful your hair
painted in the wind
as you turned just once to look
and never again to see

08-04-17

LUNA PLENA

red tides of insomnia !
silver eyes of the Huntress !
when will I get my youth back ?
ridges of indomitable fury
bacchants riding waves of salt
ungirdled hips of Diana !
when will I get my love back ?
in one golden goblet wine
in the other one more wine
to be drunk without cease
until the skies fill with Longing
to be as ever with the Archaic
unkempt hair of the Goddess !
when will Brother return to me ?
crimson ores of the Mind
legends of unborn gods
rounding out cliffs of thought
childhood in the single blade of grass
invisible footsteps of the Archer !
what is the mystic death to me ?
forever to wake in the Cave
and to be pronounced as One
with the rising Light
who stays up guarding
the left side of Venus the sea-born
and to remember nothing
of that oriental vigil !
eclipses of planets caught up
in the inevitable Black Holes !
when if ever will I be myself again ?
blood of the Poet !

dark moon lifting seas
with a single lever of sand
fornications of untold Waters !
the edge is in the center
and the center is Nowhere !
at war with windows
reflections of mineral Reason
round and round the Hour goes
neither in the House nor out
revolving Insanity !
endless chase of the Divinity !
small animals white beasts ants
hovering in the palm of my hand
will daybreak ever come again ?
it is Never in the cycle of Time
the restaurants are open
the chairs unfolded
throngs of immortals
have come to drink the Nectar !
Wake , Brother !

08-06-17

ELEGY SUMMER

days of immobility
leaf cuts light
like spine of water
hear the splashing
in an ear of grass
as of the gods rustling
in domains of yellow
dust and ochre
eye seared by tongues
of invisible flame
horizons disappearing
in histories of heat
reduced to a bead
of clinging sweat
what memory dis-
allows framed sky
hoisted like a scar
above weaving trees
a scraped stone
bruised in sleep
where dreams stir
in gravel thought
why marble cleft

in talking vast
or on deaf lawns

likens months to
vanishing lamps
no more return
than syllables
learnt by rote
between asterisks
and ampersands
far off to moons
mounting hills
turned to rust
long as waters
trailing shades
into immortality

08-11-17

LOVE IS—

i

love is the bridge washed away
love is bound and gagged
love is the manufacturer's warning
love is the indecent enterprise
love is the obscenity in the stone
love is dying before the last cigarette
love is the hell of paradise
love is the ruinous gift of the ear
love is the pornography implicit in clouds
love is the unmentionable parts
love is what you cannot possess
love is the stairs that don't go all the way
love is illiteracy of the eye
love is a wingless lunar moth
love is the baseless fiction of time
love is the errant sky of Mars
love is yellow by degrees then blank
love is the distance it takes to die
love is the anti-matter of sleep
love is the inhalation of toxic substances
love is on the hunt for human meat
love is devotion to the god of Junk
love is on trial for second degree manslaughter
love is the enigma in the photograph lens
love is the fourth one on the left

seconds later love explodes in powders
skies come undone in a trice
love is the only thing outside the law
love is a fraction of nothing
love is the unreason of reason
love has no substitute like despair
I am at last neither this nor that
a flailing a falling a failing in mid air
dreams are not the stuff of love
everything is questionable
love is the tomb of light
love is the inane longing for the Unknown
love is the dumb capacity for remorse
love is Remorse
love never should have happened
from the first time I saw you
I knew it was nothing but residue
smoke cinder ashes
a knockout kiss unconscious
delusions about seraphim
angelic beings without faces
the bright that never comes
and between bouts of time
cycles of heat and forgetting
lying wasted on a threshing floor
to be licked by puzzled beasts
remains of matter nothing but
love is the dregs
love is the consummate Lie

ii

love is the broken syntax
which undoes the mind
love is the broken syntax
which undoes the mind
love is the broken syntax
which undoes the mind
love is the mind broken
the

iii

saw you standing there
between the two poles
chasing the atmospheres
what greater coincidence
between want & destruction

and your painted lips
faintly parted for voyage
into the unillumined places
darkness the halo of hair
a wraith like unto no other
pallid and steaming both
a painting inside a mirror
of one who can never Be

08-14-17

MEDITATING ON VENUS

what it is waiting for if not
secret kisses while the motor
is still running under a fan
of light transgressions darken
mouth to mouth eyes blind
to what sees outside the
and is it forever to lips
must then pass to Delphi
the tripod the insane raving
chewing Daphne her flesh
like unto a leaf turned sunwise
was meant to spend this life
on the shores of light transient
traversing between souls thought
a vertiginous why not confess
links to syllabaries and rote
air somewhere in the puzzle
darkness fits the key best
long as the way down green
fixtures like knobs of sky turn-
ing whoever is likely to over
dappled texts hold me tight
riverside grown yellow with
upside down by the fire
as the oracle recommended
and the many who followed
the plight of dust and orient
sadness of hills burrowed dun
how trees and mountains
each to the other yield
vortex of dew and zephyrus
because dawn above waters
shadows of the unborn
a voice adjacent to red
and aspersions and commas

great enterprise of clouds
moving like hieroglyphs
across the heavenly slant
feels dangerous touching
when two such bodies
and allow for a vacuum
inserted like a thin mint
into the brain's eerie hive
histories that is marching
sand columns insects large
as we come together high
on the second floor no
wind searing the panes
glass of irreversibility
nothing shines back nor
still waiting for you there
concrete designs early
and the dense sudden fell
through the transept like
everything else erased

08-16-17

SIRENS' SONG

voices archaic longing waters
of the muses singing drowned
waxen sky so noon the heights
cloudless drifting the mind deaf
homophones of salt waves of
mountains rearing misty peaks
to gather flowers *there* beyond
the anything imaginable snowy
colored nymphs legend ranging
feet isolations of brine and rust
distinctions dissolved in light
flaming the and the again tossed
storm until hearing is bright
with loud and disorder universe
liquid statues upraised vowels
immersed in sonant gold hills
distance in three equal infinities
music of ineffable spheres pass
from one Hour to the last
dissolution of time so pale
the faint echoes its marble
lifted like weightless air
into the far where moons

turning red underwater fold
skirts billowing of thought
weaving waving out to deeps
unimaginable sleep the dense
will not wake ?

08-17-17

INTO THE LETHE

golden ichor flows from veins
immortal the leaf imbued that speaks
across and through the ancient sea
inky film of eternity spliced
between ampersands and threnody
alert that once a deity flamed
mountains rearing feathery mists
remember nothing the former void
did you as well ? wending weaves
somber mythic plot masks unveiled
darkest where the sun sped its course
threads of light dispersed the brain
unseeing in its galactic chambers
flung across the universe // did
see as well ? bedside ruddy flares
simulacra of memories eddying
into the stygian pool where hands
submerged ask for their voices back
how did this event occur ? night
swifter than a passing thought
unshaped evolves its chthonic dew
scattered in some forgotten dawn
or buried in the western hills
where childhoods meander lost
was happy once ? skin pales
a thin fix of song then faints
how distant the window glass
evanescent persons of frost
winter-tides rootless the descent
into depths of unrecorded ears
the last and lost a path undone
once led to mind's bright thumb
now as ever unending chaos
fingers missing in grassy twilight
dusky gods // what else ?

08-19-17

KISSING THE STATUE OF DISTANCE

unexpected contact between mysterious
alternate photos compose lost realities
looked a lingering at hair in the tangle
winds rising from the skin's surface
her glance a word from the imagined
past locked in a kiss at once luminous
then dark as a subterfuge of innocence
listing oceans of grass the shipwreck
who lost sight of the moon one night
rocks if they could speak or statues
born with remote ears of prescience
is it love ? wonders running a finger
through the missing face in sleep
dreaming that it will come around
shapeless yet immense with expectation
a day then no days at all waiting
for the ignition to start the following
lamp as if hours or even weeks recalling
exactly what was in the assembly of
words notched for their lack of meaning
tripping in atmospheres swell and bright
come on it says in the snatched leaf
or water issuing from stone alert
to so many possibilities and colors
too much to withstand and falling yet
is it love ? the explosive thread that
damages the universe becoming heat
then what subsides in a wave of
the eye just misses the planet waning
faint as pale and the numerical phrase
becomes enigmatic inexplicable red
defused atoms in the long swoon
this numinous moment of embrace
secret envy of unreflecting glass
when the totality of sky comes apart
clouds the dense stuff of thought
or reading in the street signs a warning
do not turn ! but always too late
insensate roses born in that breath
lips of accidence a case history
of mottled dunes and asterisks
what catches fire is the longing
implicit in the fiercely remote verb
to be whispered repeatedly into its

homophone echoes and chaos of echoes
the nothing more of *is it love ?*

08-22-17

MY SPHINX

"y yo te siento temblar contra mí
como una luna en el agua"
Cortázar, Rayuela

it was a day of insects the first
in a series of archaic solitudes
yellowing dust the world of hills
in absentia the air shaking minutely
all the visible in a state of suspension
largely the reverse of white evenings
the marble history of classical thought
when number and theory collide
silently in the opaque resin of distance
you appeared to me through veils of black dew
a Cleopatra hemorrhaging light
gliding on barges towed by legions of fireflies
through phantom seas of adolescent grasses
your immense shadow imbued
with a poetry of sand and basalt
a cosmos beyond the secret of cigarettes
that lingered in the unrepeatable mouth
you offered in the morning of the alphabet
when nothing else stirred in the ether but
the subterranean hoarseness of vowels
pronouncing for the last time in clouds
ineffable horizons of primordial flame
your hair a tangled blaze of script
confounding the intellect of desert winds
what was there to touch if not the music
that issued from your dancing fingertips ?
can anything ever be duplicated ?
for a moment the world is an emblem of salt
ready to dissolve in your saliva
the rest is the hermetic outline of a kiss
shimmering glass and invisibility of the ideal
but what if you never existed
an entity waiting for the infernal
invention of the telephone
mirage of useless rock and stone
monument to slavery in record heat
endless day of insects unseen target of ants

was never anything but mythic echo
ambulatory beast of illusory sleep
how many times did the dream occur
in which together we mutilated time ?

08-25-17

NEOPLATONIC

mind up the straight to heavens
seeking perfect margins in image
that consists of non-matter
the beloved passing like a cloud
in a mirror like a specter in dreams
terrific semblance to the one
who went before now years dead
can one re-assemble the primordial ?
shadowy substances locked in urns
still talking to the baffled of heart
no wonder upon waking we remain
asleep pursuing the diurnal grief
as if in a moment we could be free
absolved of the human taint
memories passing through walls
bearing statues of grass and dew
who can claim the immaterial ?
as to what is real and what is only
a reflection of things in transit
as to what is solid and what is
merely a mirage shimmering
in the irretrievable summer
when childhoods went swimming
in the waters of oblivion and
what is it about that fulminating
moment that instant coming
up for air that vision of light ?
everywhere surrounded by illusory
beings that seem to move and talk
rock come to breath stone itching
lessons of the imponderable
air floods with minute convulsions
as mountains take wing into
the night phantasmagoria !
and the beloved in her persiflage
oriental and forever remote
a skin of music once heard
that never never comes back
the idea of the circle

but not the circle itself
words

08-28-17

Ἀχιλλεύς

then did the life spirit flee from
the wound surging black blood
nor did memory avail his mind
winged thing frail gone aloft
what smithereens his bones too
ancient as the child he once was
splintered into the dark loam
every part of the natural man
surrendered to a nameless god
wrenching from the dense flesh
an epithet of bleak longing Oh
so did fierce his teeth hit rock
soil gave way to grieving nerve
and in that moment did open
the gates of the House of Hades
to let enter this glorious Light
now dimmed now dull as dust
shadow shifting in deep mire
AOI

08-29-17

MY SO-CALLED LIFE REVISED

first there was the order to enlist
kissing lips-blind the woman in
the photo booth on 40th street
who could never believe what
comes back me in reversible auto
display some fifty years later
in a canary colored car her hair
unbelievably black my hands a
loom the skein Penelope the woof
ancient and the drowned sound
of the ladies in waiting ink stained
then as the ignition turned patient
homonyms for sky the windshield
cleaning for azure ancient marine
everything so like heaven for the
proverbial moment eyes shut my
career in syllables lengthened to

a single tumultuous silent vowel
her incidence a votive cancellation
Diana no more ! naked to the ankle
running through sprinklers amok
in a memory of the Trojan cycle
sand shifts girders cliffs spray !
it is to sleep my rhythms aloft
darkened wefts star gadgets
flying shafts aim an ampersand
involving the story of Rama as
clouds purple thick Dravidian
in essence the female deity big
in her vacated shadow offering
me gift of immortality if only
I would in verses sing her antiquity
labyrinthine joined at the thumb
where space meets its opposite
bent her throat back the blue
vein beating gates of paradise
come back ! what a dream swoon
sounding drum-skins her is a
lavinian shore to me second
chance at love's illusion
in the garage where the whet
stone waits turning its gyre
a multiple of moons ever so
round the slow punctuation
erasures back to back episodes
of tide and genuflection longing
distance the imperfect article
aorist conditions softening hills
I will never be out there again
sun dying on the water's back
so it goes out to sea evermore

08-31-17

A VISION

was it coming down the stairs
or was it going up the stairs
princess in her orphan black hair
something in the air about to shake
metal heated to a fever pitch
concrete abyss of a thousand centigrade
Beatrice forever shimmering mirage
surrounded by cherubim of pink flame
tossing vowels of archaic love high
into the flossy lawns of sky
who can ever forget or regret
having *seen* that radiance consuming
all the suns of the western hemisphere
was it an inch above the dimpled knee
or was it four fathoms deep in arctic waste
something about the hour and its endless minute
about the day going retrograde into
its insufferable lunar dune
all the orange cycles of eternity showering
sands of light about her dazzled head
coronas and nebulae of vast asbestos
ablaze ! ablaze as never before
or it is turning on a single note
a music a maze of strings in pizzicato
wings that take forever to move
through and above and below her shadow
constructed of the million fireflies of Mind
a fever of illegible poetry
ravings and delirium of Dante redivivus
circling above the horn of Africa
disoriented longing lost and blind

09-02-17

A PERFECT LOVE POEM

I remember you from the other time
flimsy bark tossed in the stygian swirl
there are places in the world
where it is nowhere at all you among
them the veils torn the sobbing
beneath the skin the many skins
from where did you come erupting
like a vapor out of a crypt ?
what stone you ask what grief
what rock unearthed what name

do I know you from somewhere ?
all too mysterious the vanishing
moment of love the coincidence
of astral projections and punctuations
enigmas of the undeciphered eyes
looking from the cliff of somewhere else
into the labyrinth of the yet unknown
how many times a week do I drown ?
a hand a conjecture an undefined thought
coming forth from primordial dark
and returning just as quickly
into the temple of absolute silence
it's best to leave the unwritten poem be
to erase the terrestrial vanities
the mistaken ego the wrong turn
the coordinates on the map are in Etruscan
tombs of chthonic deities—can it be ?
footprints that go backwards
into the mausoleum of Venus-denied
how is it your face reappears Sundays
between the clock and the sandstorm ?
what I remember is the phone call
the inimitable voice of the sarcophagus
asking for directions to the Light
what was I to say ?
do I know you from somewhere ?

09-03-17

ELEGY FOR JOHN ASHBERY

and if the universe does end
great conflagrations broken machinery
of the cosmos what after all
is a flower and its bright puerperal day ?
coming to grief in terms of darkness
of ill-spreading hills to the far west
of an orient to be discovered
beneath the brown thumb nail
it's as much a letter still unwritten
as a poem that cannot be conceived
saying goodbye to the promises of youth
bric-a-brac and sidewalk fairs and light
when one is suddenly not who one is supposed to be
in the cracked mirror of that fatal dawn
have you come to this wreathed in weeds
partitioned from the memory of love
abated in the ditches and fosses of time

come on , Baby ! say it all in a nosegay
bury the shadow but not its other
perfumed airs and a music of organ-grinders
the carman's whistle of late renaissance
when it seemed possible for everything
to blossom in its season and order
yet the sky menacing as the 15th century
hurtles its jovian missiles at the high school
now a simple placard denoting *was here*
and the civil war cannon on its hillock
and the lunch wrappers littering the lawns
you were there too being simple
infatuated with the cloud writing
way up there between the cracks
where the gods in their immortal lethargy
invent memories of dalliance on earth
fire-crackers thunderstorms abandoned motels
something about the missing "person"
wig-hat and traces of foot-wear
hugging some sense of the past to your breast
unbuttoned of breath prepared to
lose consciousness for the last time
galaxies and astral nebulae and black holes
the whole swirling mess about to blow
listening intently with one ear cocked
and the other strangely aloof
rushing in the vertiginous sound of sleep
as it rounds its last pyramid
before the incredible history of sand
dissolves in a mutability of light
will this be what you recall ?

09-06-17

DAY-DREAM LOVER

the city on the left destroyed 10 times over
the one on the right razed once and for all
by the horse-taming Hittites
what was written on the envelope
infra-red letters evanescent kisses
stoned on magnum alcohol the mind
athwart elastic ellipses of greater planet
veers towards self-extinction
as ever the map deployed watermarks
strange that you come out in bed-clothes
the motor still running the sun's high lamp
shedding metal of its running seas

you are feast of hell tantric *yab-yum*
what's Sanskrit for "ventilator" ?
they ask marking in history books
important dates like when were the Dorians
or why the eyeless seers of the Vedas
what it comes down to gazing at your swift face
something out of Tartary or beyond
suggestions to move south where the Dead
summer for years on end and there
yes *there* ! make exclamation points so Loud
it's a wonder the cities have any vestiges
standing between rutting roses
and the collapse of the muscovite Empire
if only they had listened to Ashoka
if only they had written to Ashoka
you emerge from a cocoon of heat
all pearls and lunar transpiration
will take me away in the excitement
of gasoline and the sheer solar embolism
what they mean by exploding hearts
isn't that a way of getting into the Mausoleum
and leaving hints that the future is lost
a paradigm of oxide and distance
lay the self down beside the dry well
in old Anatolia and wait for the caravanserai
a chain letter of immense and invisible
characters *feast of hell* the stuttering
lips and craving the initial losses
reported to be in the thousands
and the wailing and lamenting mothers
with their pruning forks and stitching
still it is morning and you waver
before employing the second kiss
dangerous as a century of knives
and rumors are rife that the City-of-the-Sun
has come to its knees that the tripods
have been set up and the raving and
the hills that exchange vows with balconies
and the silt and detritus and foam
you are only a *Mouth* after all
for whom plenitude is a missing alphabet
inured to your passions a cycle
white-caps lingering remote fastness
whereupon they placed machines to the walls
cataracts and siege engines and burning cotton
the conquistadors in their rusted mail
flinging dogs of tar into the smoking air

and picking up the bag of groceries
in your soiled bed-wear you turn your back
ambling an environment such as this cannot sustain
a hiatus of memory up the steps
to a door that has no other side
goodbye

09-10-17

CLOUD-SAMPLER

when you have touched somebody *other*
to the quick and taken the parts of speech
to make a direction southwards to the city
of the dead and talking all wild in sleep
as if flying with winged alphabets
is it a wonder the voice from the quarries
remains untranslatable and the nets
snaring the deities in the sky's vestibule
what else is there to report from
such heights dizziness nose-bleeds
atavistic fainting if you also approached
somebody *other* with your shadow
or to the very marrow swooned in disbelief
cloud-sampler ! the universe is a marshland
a desolate waste of sand and rock
mirage shimmering inside the sleeping eye
turn away from the direct route
burning ruins and the capital of despair
statues of silence and absence !
small houses lost forever in the gloaming
cloud-sampler ! who did you think it was
coming out of the western wind
arms akimbo and as if crying out a name
not yours not the syllables of somebody *other*
but of the forgotten one who went lost
when the immortals declared Light !
what else is there in the wilds of Nature
where else to step coming out of the dream
of one Mansion and stepping dumbly
into the dream of another Mansion
divided between currents of the Invisible
cloud-sampler ! you have no other recourse
but to consult the leaf torn from time
depths and darkness of the Acheron
where somebody *other* waits in vain
to be touched by the afternoon of love
+++++++++++++++++++++++++++++

where have fled the years of the Month
the simple hours in the blade of grass
the steps never to return over gravel
the lamps lit on the other side of the hill ?

09-14-17

FOOTNOTE TO LUCRETIUS

the wave and its corollary silence
imbued heat and its cycles green
will we ever be otherwise a body
and what is outside the events
called sky or the transverse ocean
heavenly cataracts behind the eye
receiving light and shape and !
what do I represent if not
the mystery of water lapping
in the ear or the palace of breath ?
if there is a consequence is it
sand and the great buttress
that surrounds the disappearing ?
is mind weight ? is thought matter ?
where is the future if not
in the fossil vowel ?
and to speak of love in all its
minute atoms and of disease
and its Egyptian molecules
all mothering in the dappled cloud
to ask how did this all come to be
earth and its invisible diameters
fire in the equation of stone
ether never diminished nor increasing
what words express the destiny of space
poverty and inanity of language
where can the foot step next ?
is memory a process of winds
revolving in and out of the brain
as it sleeps its depth in rock ?
if one listens carefully summer
comes full blown out of Cyprus
ripe with the chemistries of passion
only to subside again in salt
ever dissolving from the skin
and to sing what is that ?
do the gods born from the seed of time
lend melody to the mortal rant ?
thunder ambrosia illusion ire

primordial moons circling trials
man's afternoon fears superstitions
lay the head down in a crown of grass
emotions rising from a crimson powder
set armies on the march over peaks
elephants birds of prey howling dogs
is Avernus the next river over ?
is the hole in the dirt imagined hell ?
piece by piece the story unfolds
magnitudes of color and sizes of hour
nothing can be of nothing born !
death in its many rainbows
collateral damage fission and blows
worlds come and go
islands archipelagos ice floes
volcanic activity at the very start
the million million stars of Nowhere
worlds go and come
Venus thee I invoke
FLAMMANTIA MOENIA MUNDI

09-17-17

SECRETO DE AMOR

it's all a dream sometimes sulfur
sometimes grey the town used to be
on the other side of the hill
now the universe has shifted three
to the left of space where the graduates
continue to file by shadowless
still in love disoriented by the invention
of the telephone which keeps lights
going less than before the houses dim
mythical replicas of the unremembered
you will keep to yourself the money
the times you only hinted and got
more than you expected and still darkness
only the red litmus prepared you for
the boats tossing everything over board
winds and sails and unfurled thoughts
what did you think it was reading
the same passage over and over
the porch steps rickety unsafe lamps
just like the stars at the top of the chimney
and smoke alphabets and other personae
come on , if the chance to meet again
and the street fills with tubs of flowers

most likely geraniums and the neighbors
watching as we finally kiss sealing
the air with the great promise of love
or is it simply the opportunity to be generous
planets that coincide with signatures
lapsing into a digression about waters
that run farther underneath than we know
the Acheron for example and the pools
of depthless whatever the fates render
to wake ? what was the name of the woman
in the cancer ward wearing a wild kerchief
a tattoo for a reminiscence and life
the checkered embroidery that comes
down to a choice between atmospheres
a state designed by hunters and
if the next week is any lighter your mouth
the freshet in the mountains the bright
long lasting more than dawns a flake
slowly shedding its falling luster
for a brief hour to be inside your mind
yes ,

09-19-17

INSCRIPTION FOUND NEAR HELIOPOLIS

       the ancient of rock and stone
inexpressible lament
the   who hovering high
    waxen skies and flight
unadorned in *her* lap the head
      fallen   and dripping
slowly again   the whispering
leaves a change   of air
and sinews and the battery
    turning blue inchoate
like lights becoming   and
parting like dark curtains where
    speaking through walls
voices   -ing sighs a wild
wasn't that some   like
a waterfall rushing   ears
bent to earth the mother
    white and incandescent
hands raised   whatever
mattered and pulled tight around
    knees shaking a great
and menacing night   whorls

yellow as dust the archaic
vowel   *my angel*
the sudden park the volley
         rounds of fire   trees
as if shedding identities   careful
not to   shadows bleeding
rustle of wings of   shattered
            as glass effigies
and loud with presentiment and
         pronounced silence
planets hove into view the eye could
      shhh   through windows
looking out on   gravel under
foot   or plateaus of memory
just   to discern which was
         flooding the lens with bright
counting back to the   moment
as they say   running fingers over
the grooves to make a   music !
            tentative as heavens are
searched the skin for a
         listening intently the lizard
wearing masks of gods   lateral
shifts when at once the   bottomless
rivers   took off the top part
sections of sublime   asking
only appeared   like marble
the bare shoulders   an arrow
or maybe   how they return
dreaming   was a former
            pitched tents on
sands reaching down to depths
if it is sleep if it
                 myth of ?

09-22-17

ATHENA STEPS INTO THE FRAY

she was at first a   semblance
out of the car moving stepped heels
ready to cloud the gilt work temple
insubstantial of air high in either
eye the rearing mists of holy precinct
Athena making herself all the larger
laughing in the midst of the crowd
making their eyes water spurts of blood
uncomfortable hearing noises in suits
of meat forming clusters would they
marry and set to the table nervous
out of composure pointing to nowhere
the deity as if suspended jewelry
ringing around the neck wrists up
a prayer the perhaps iridescent love
which was become like a powder
their throats constricted and spitting
the plates and wine-brimming cups
a sea tale broadened a readiness to
equivocate fearing the return a host
of lies turned upside down the urns
looking for the talisman brightness
in a room otherwise dark a fix
her in their beams alert as dawn
dew in the ruddy stalls distance too
grassy and foaming bays come up
to the shore the black keels cutting
water and sedge where lifting his
hoary head Neptune and ghosts
prowling the porch cadavers of
mountains ghosts in the hallways
reaching for destroyed meat red-eyed
how can it ever come back as it was
in the telephone a trapped voice
I love you stepping as if invisible
the enlarged goddess hair a mess
sweep of her broad arms and hips
to relive such moments the doors
swing wide open ghosts entering
angry with stilettos and high heels
where is there a place for peace
hiding in the pantry and alarms
cannot quite recall why they are
here and loosened from the hinges
the great gate crashes in epic dust

poems littered in the wake of time
ships like battered paper cones
the god of winds out of control
nymphs fourteen in number leap
into the cloud-fray phase of rains
legends of fog and crumpled sand
where desist and now what !

09-23-17

DIDO

mortal ennui unending wounds
lasting hours regarding the face
just illumined in the chariot
that racing hurtled off axis into
cerulean depths whose brimming
with light smiled her eyes lamps
burning into the sand-spit of
consciousness error and trial
of love unfathomable distances
syntax of longing it says margins
where the crimson thread frays
a step at the sight unclear as to
her vowels smothered in ethereal
ghosts too swaying like elephants
in the vestibule where clock scars
what remains of the eternal minute
her beside the bedding a pink rapt
in expectation of finally the poem
what it represents gorgeous silent
metered to go off at midnight
with coral and pearl necklace a
sounding inches of dark tell me
her story the whispered leaves
ampersands brightly in the fane
where talking statues sleep thought
its dread around the saturnian pole
a pale more like fade the colors
of the farthest where practicing
the mercy of air night brings its
frank-incense to chambers revolved
isn't it how she passed through walls
a division of number without white
as her pallid each cheek a memory
of rose the aching days of living
will it come to feed again on dark
the absence which is the ascent

to a heaven of blind doves a song
in the eaves a quarter of a week
fast as red circling heat in cycles
remembering who she is to be
coming out of the wistful ivy her
clad in banks of ether and fog
designing flames in *italics* a smoke
of seas billowing in the vacant ear
quarried ruins of the poem a wave
surge and totem of cold flares
her self consumed in a sonant blaze
gold and then the infinite

09-24-17

LETTER TO A GHOST

am I to compose great operas
because I have looked deep
into your face one more time ?
is twice a week enough to taste
your lips the kiss of passing time ?
enough of swift reincarnations
of densities of skin hair and polish
nails and armbands and ribbons
undone in the fluted amber winds
is a cigarette the secret of your mouth ?
wayward youth the decades toll
the empty death of countless years
you return like a nimbus pink
as the dew that settles on metal wars
conflagrations and silent ruins
circle the moons buried in your eyes
like the time we rediscovered blood
in the lengthy silhouettes of dust
an orient that reared its feathery
mountain high over a random sea
destined to bed silver planes forever
listen to me just for once talk !
to hear reverberating the musk
of your now ancient voice in hills
that move with the intensity of smoke
exhaled from the legend of sleep
over and over again the same phrase
in vowels of perpetual absence
there is no syllable that matches
the endless direction of your skin
as it reaches past noon into foreboding

that we will never meet again
unless in the vestibule of hell
hotel with a thousand vacant rooms
where shadows locked from light
dance deathless minuets of love
and an organ-grinder sets his monkey
in search of your enigmatic mind
am I to surrender all the poetry
I ever wrote just to feel underneath
the evanescent fade of your breath ?

09-25-17

CREUSA

*"Ausus quin etiam voces iactare per umbram
implevi clamore vias maestusque Creusam
nequiquam ingeminans iterumque iterumque vocavi"*
Aenid, II, 768-770

looked back but once and lost
to mind and fog the erring step
the smoking eyes the unheard
cry winsome unthreaded to the
heavens a thin and luminous
punctuation meaningless but
for the stop it placed in the text
a where that cannot be located
and the wordless what follows
assuming a legibility of years
where is the sea if not within
roiling thunder-caps menacing
surf feminine in gender white
skiffing the endlessly unknown
shores a syntax without order
night shrouding the small voice
issuing from the briar thicket
vowels of even smaller blood
that cannot be retraced if even
correctly through a maze of streets
darksome porticoes untranslatable
war-cries engine and force of
history laddered against walls
dictated by gods to last supreme
a key a chemise a draw-string
things undone in thoughtless
labor strewn nameless corpses
still talking to the paving stones

anchors rusting on rooftops
dubious dog-cries echoing hollows
clouds come to rest in indigo vats
along the lone and dusty trek
rewinding unraveling porous rock
inside the within of the sepulcher
the wherefore of dun-dark hills
never again to approach surface
faces half-glimpsed veering into stone
the almost of sand and vertigo
reflected in shop windows her ghost
tracing spittle maps of the unconscious
becoming undone like ether in time
immemorial skin ! the muses weep
because the poem has no center
to end when each line comes back
to the start in waters blank as glass
drown then the archaic syllables
in a riot of unendurable silence
going back and forth listening
for the foot the chasm has devoured
what is the allure of breath and light ?
what is there to touch in the unspoken
realm where gravity is without echo ?
life is the labyrinth left behind
life is the labyrinth left behind

09-26-17

THE ORACLE AT DELPHI

I've said all this before
the lunar mansion caught
in the noon tides and the woman
that cannot be possessed and the horses
dragging the sun around the walls
and the dust embolisms and the bird
trapped inside the window and shades
of all the years collapsed into a thimble
and whatever remains of the mortal lie
whatever can be contained in the flame
without burning and the ant-heaps
brought to bear and the streets
of immortal heat and the gods the
three hundred of them sitting eyeing
the doorstep and the stairs that don't
go all the way and the cigarette smoking
the woman that cannot be possessed and

the diamonds around the throat and the
automobiles that cannot be salvaged and
the rust and the brine and the evanescent dew
and the miles of tombstones in the backyard
and the children yes the children still
alive in their echoes and the woman who
can never be possessed and the bad repair job
and the delivery room painted black and
the music ticketed for speed and the the the
and the sky suddenly reduced to an inch and
the awful sense of the pyramids and the
point of dying when the woman cannot
be possessed and the overturned tables
and the lawns turned to ash and the hotel
with its missing floors and the evening
when it all happened for the last time and
what comes to mind when the neon and
the littered junk and the trash cans blazing
and you know what I mean when I say
about the end of time and the days that
follow so countless and the moment of truth
and the stars plummeting into the pool and
once and for all who cannot be possessed
the woman and

09-27-17

STANZAS : ULIXES

rounded the Cyclopean shores
vast a roaring as of seas within
and darkened mile of sky a thunder
jettisoned mind cast from thought

ancient spume foaming ruins
brain struggles to regain its sails
winds from the east weathers wild
spines snapped in two by lightning

seen just once the mountain moving
from its airy peak mists muffled
the cavernous voices from its deep
come running in vacant syllables

man the groaning emphasis
taut between salt and sand the
endless grain planted in the bone
yet to infernal streams is tossed

dream of the nocturnal sun
of rays piercing glades the shade
that passes through eternal stone
and for a moment the stricken light

to the shoals thrown rope a hand
callous fraction bathed in brine
hurting in the tenuous upper air
no place to hold no root to know

fallen from a mythic heaven
the sense of body smitten nerve
raucous the cry of distance
soon drowned in the archaic pool

white grasses summering sleeps
face down in primordial earth
what remembers what forgets
the design of countless stars

voyage to the Island unknown
round cliffs and steaming piles
a shimmering of remote water
a dazzle and dizziness that blinds

have come undone the ropes
and twine the hawsers of delay
from underneath the sirens sound
what no ear can fathom or ken

afar we drift and tally rosaries
tempests come and go like lives
and memories once bright and glitter
now like winter bees lay stunned

return the impossibility flee
surging between the temples
strings the wire carrying images
of talking great and headless statues

ice the blank river–swath winding
down to inconstant eddies swamp
what's buried there what bridal
gift what vanishing afternoon

when home is got the twilight
rains setting behind the sun
no one beside the bed no lamp
turned on no caring silhouette

full circle come the rusted plow
oxen slain for indecent aim
the shadowy figure in the door
mystery of the past nothing more

blind gods !
    fates of rope and sand . . .

09-29-17

"no more war!"

Pietà, donna, per Dio, deh non più guerra !
non più guerra per Dio, ch'i mi t'arrendo:
i' son quasi che morto, io iacio in terra,
vinto mi chiamo e più non mi difendo.
Legami, e in qual prigion tu vuoi mi serra,
ché maggior gloria ti saró vivendo:
se temi ch'io non fugga, fa' un nodo
della tua trezza e legami a tuo modo.
    Angelo Poliziano, Rime, viii

Have pity, lady, by god, OK no more war !
no more war by god, for I surrender:
I'm almost dead, I'm lying on the ground
I'm defeated and defend myself no more.
Tie me up, throw me in the prison of your choice,
living for you will be the greater glory:
if you're afraid I'm going to flee, make a knot
with your tresses and tie me up anyway you want.

09-29-17

AN EPIPHANY

a shot in the dark a green semblance
white shadows on the parapet ghosts
the thing going out like a rosebud
from the gargoyle's mouth in a poem
that is my youth the slender wet thread
strung across a sky hidden in a puddle
how many behind me shouting Wait !
never go through dense the cork wood
without facing sheets of light and behind
still trembling the stalk of death a fling
across the barriers of grass and stone
there rest in the long walk back home
the night when angels burning fled
to a greater music upstairs in the sheets

could it be a page of lightning and frost
has been opened again and lives of rain
come quickening in the broken pane
will not remember any of this around
the gravid moon's pale rambling echo
shut out of the earth's archaic city
larval and retrenched the friends ahoy
just across the street in the shadowy
pines near the houses without walls
lamps and bricks and school letters
crumpled isolation and tears hearing
an episode about the one who stopped
too long beside the unfound river
taken they say by silvery nymphs
damp specters of the absent realms
who will come to say that is not me
retreating from the glass into the dew
some morning in the vacancy of time ?

10-03-17

IN THE ANCIENT

it presented itself to me while
I was walking through the din
sand and sleep the otherwise
strait where Annie was waiting
stooped on the ether of her bunches
violets and hydrangeas yawning
in the morning air if it was new
presenting like an embrace of clouds
to me the already ancient and yellow
she was discolored in a rope ivy
twined around pink floss every
time I looked or the kiss expected
like dew on the rock I sat there
knowing nothing about the south
the direction of the dead or if
itself to me presented like an envelope
memory laden robes around saffron
the natives beneath their stairs
of stars and spilling from her bag
grasses sea-weed anemones a bark
she lifted full her Annie face eyes
still dark with the other time a river
carrying most of Egypt with it as
far as whatever else was presented
a solar disk and tables of mushrooms

I could tell it was older than a flute
playing in the rock's ear or a jet
of clear water proceeding from the text
about the beginnings started so often
and still walking across the street
the big wide one like a canal reeds
singing in their wind of music aloft
sweet as the air that lifted high beds
of pressed flowers ink marks a mind
can do all that and the roadside voices
me calling to tell me the telegraph
come into being just now or yesterday
at the top of the house wing spreading
reddish as the soil beneath the lids
drooping of the eyes unawake a fist
of brain and soiled thoughts the kind
one has presenting itself to me striding
the dust of time as it were Annie fused
to the stalk that goes underneath
to the mansion where the many who
cannot forget have come to rest
blind it seems and mewing darkly
listening for the footsteps of weeds
that are smoking all around me concrete
avenues perhaps I will come to rest
there and the tombstones winged
really for a last time coming back
to where I began walking prairie sod
loam gravel someone else maybe

10-04-17

A NIGHT IN ITHACA

said any fool can string that bow
she , to stifle the weeping in the upper
chamber the well-polished and suffused
how dark it was to become, she by the glass
inviting evening and the suitors eating
everything on the table the lamps hung
by gold mail from the sooty ceiling
in order to listen better and deceive
even those who, the bard in the corner
surmising how things will end the next
hour tightening the screws, she as if
to beguile how they laughed for weeping
yes they too and the chasm where
the gods hide their divine raiment

a light, she leaned over letting slip off
her marmoreal shoulder the well sculpted
the garment flimsy as to entice and
with fingers dainty dipped into the,
appeared beside her unbeknownst to
the Argive troops the goddess larger
than any mortal and shining through
the dust of their eyes encouraging with
her ironic smile a philosophic whim to
live, that is beside the stranger busy
exercising his oiled muscles and boasting
born of a race of heroes on an island
to the west of the Ocean, she in the din
herself become something other than
what she was upstairs weaving on the
great loom and dizzy with fear and
memory even as night comes slipping
out of the silent realms and the stars
in evidence to finish this work, her
graceful as the pearl in its pink shell
aware of love's illusions everywhere
the music by the immense hearth and
the longing in syllables pliant and sad
to hear tell of, rivers that born in Asia
run south and into the salt seas bearing
in their floods images and statuary of
lost deities and of Elysium the happy,
she what was it outside the noise of cars
quarreling engines smitten or ignited a
wave of indignation welling up from the
watery depths or the roiling surf and
batteries and clouds foaming like
great barrels across the already gone
sky, could a moon be a phrase

10-07-17

IMMORTALITY

breath big
as the sky
the tiny rains
infinity between
this time and
the next

text of the
middle sea-surge
waves lapping stars
plunge the body
ungoverned
into ink

pausing to
cross the street
where the school
used to be a
heaven of
echoes

your face
is part of
a song the
rest is a riddle
your eyes
like moons

higher than
the beginning
smoke ends
by trailing
off into
space

never to be
seen again
your shadow
walking chalk
erased by
the moment

just past
cloud gatherers
gods or merely
summers

fading
into stone

doors

10-19-17

THE FIRE THIS TIME

neither angel nor suitor
come down from Olympian clouds
bringing fiefdoms of sulfur and carmine
adulterer in shadowy pantomime
of airs and villanelles declining
nouns of marmoreal ruins
is this in order to certify life ?
smoking morass of the remains
everything that lies either north
or south of the equator in heat
does the ruler of the immortal House
command the shores of light to recede ?
what's real what's unreal great Latin
empire with its husks of death and rhetoric
ashes of sunlight ashes of distance
nowhere to go the failing tides
the grist and drift of poisoned waters
with cancer between the sheets the Moon
displaying its drained aspirin fogs
bone-meal and sewer of the brain system
endlessness of rot going out to sea
red and blue litmus of planet Nemesis
in spiral course to total annihilation
if only could the epic form restore
and the divine hand interpolate verses
and destruction and beatification
were one and the same and the adulterer
in his puce yellow vehicle rewind
the clock of time midnight precisely
every hour of the day and love the
fastidious and out of mind riot
of the senses dollar for dollar
on the market burning as never before
this is apocalypse and serene union
this is negativity of space and Orient !
licking fires of the empyrean acre
upon acre reduced to stubble of Night
when will the one I truly love

emerge from the smoking mountain haze
lunar moth of obsidian friction ?

10-14-17

STOLEN KISSES

a dream these fleeting instants
or a poem that hesitates to be written
billows of black hair riding the wind
gone ! was this what Parmenides meant ?
motion and being are *one*
is the weapon swifter than its target ?
the chasm in Diana's eye !
how revolving are these weeks
without months without calendar years
everything in a single kaleidoscopic gyration
and in the sacred wood who knows
what stolen kisses are being recorded
the man in the gold wheeled chariot
turns back just once for that fatal glance
and off go the steeds bright in their skin
of gleaming sun-substance
over the mythic cliffs—Hippolytus !
the world is an intricate but enigmatic bauble
love is cheap even as cars glide
smoothly over mechanical streets
Saturn glowers in his bullet-proof vest
which does nothing to ward off Cupid's
mean intentioned shafts AIYEE !
let us then to the hyperbolic well
to drink deep the draughts of Lethe
forget the long summer strolls swelling
on the Avenue of make-believe
forget the forget the way I never did
folding phantom lover into the envelope
where clouds and narcissi are born
and opening the door at a velocity
of nine thousand ninety nine light years !
if we ever come back to this place
where the houses seem to totter yellow
and rickety on their totemic stairs
which of us will be the first to confirm
those stolen kisses never happened
motion and being on the verge of space
there must be some kind of drug that
heightens the brain's capacity to devolve
return to me, Lotus-feet !

dark waterways coursing through
sleep's inevitable crisis of powders
shifting the galactic spine to the left
reversing wheel orient and stone
until embraced within a glass of fuel
the nectar of our mouths ignites
all of time and
           next week , too

10-15-17

EROS & THANATOS

"y tú, rústica diosa, dónde estabas ?"
Garcilaso de la Vega, Eclogas 1

inhabitants of Avernus swarming shadows
casting no reflection on the waters
among them me you her them us him
love-sick transients of no known earth
the register of colors now elapsed
like the thunder of clouds without sound
how much is left of the vanishing page
how little resemble asterisks and ink-spots
the flitting personae of fathomless ether
other chasms open their depths to dive
and walls fixed in the dust of polyphony
crash in the sleeper's long deaf ear
light and more light yet never enough
spanning the eerie spectra of Neptune
now distant in the splashing silence
of nocturnal wave and surge cliffs
erected by levers to lunar heights
like sandstorms billowing in script
forever beyond reach of the narcotic eye
where legend of air terminates abruptly
quivering in molecular disaster
nothing remains to infringe nothing
but the evolution of the theory of love
chemistry of the longing heart
physics of the intensely yearning soul
to know the *Other* at last and forever !
walking the shores of Ionia in the never
waiting for Aurora to herald the *origins*
all swerve and bend and collapse
dark and turbulent the questing mind
fierce the skin of song the unending
desire and mutilation and Being !

++++++++++++++++++++++++++
when did we ever meet or was there
never a first time but the always
of noon in the solar eclipse of death ?

10-17-17

JOE READING THE TIBETAN BOOK OF THE DEAD

the farthest is where they find you
unrecognizable in the dream of sleeves
wind and surf of dust and sand
face down inert a pulse still beating
in the rear view mirror otherwise
planets and seeds of air and volumes
of dark matter come through a hole
near the shaft where sound is born
you seemed to be reading a text
margins of red and coriander
and words the lessons of vowels
long and short and the circumflex
just above your brow and thought
itself congealed and lacking shape
like the worm of reason struggling
to have eyes you were reluctant
to rise and shed some darkness where
the event was to take place a long
time ago in the grassy ruins of water
like a city that has been but once
floundering among spears and grain
could hear the groaning of ships
coming on a reef splintered sails
mast and the gone conclusion of oil
spreading over the face of time
what kind of a language was used
to eventually tell the size of cliffs
or hovering keenly the falcon
with its alphabet of gyres tumbling
to seize the apparatus of lightning
sending a spine up the thrill of
day you removed soil and earth
burrowing in the abyss to the side
of the great and mysterious barricade
which is music engraved in the ear
you could no more repeat what
you had heard before going away
into that strange porch of night

the lamps simply girls shining
because of their distance to hold
the ineffable and fading you

10-18-17

THE DATE WAS THIRTEEN DEATH

(Temple of the Sun-Eyed Shield)
for Valum Votan

fortunate the flight and fugue the fell
down swept the brothers held and high
sky limits the incense laden clouds
topaz raiment jade flares in plumes
round the salty mists of distance and
green cormorants chattering parakeets
dovetailed in walls of invisible liana
song making loud the spirit-eye of time
each unbound and spirals northwards
their limitless train furlongs of dust
until which colony prevailed and
musk frozen lakes the twain contained
other beholding in night-sight great
lands heights of tropic memory sound
here and here the dotted terrain of
light the unending and bright spoils
unfurling like sails in dream of waters
come crashing unspotted the prows
black with epic and landing now and
never on darkened sands reefs of gods
the cries of sudden and reverie white
tattooed around the ear of drums
which will be the first unrestrained
to fold death neatly inside the conch
who will dancing blind adore the heat
swelling round and round death
the ivory pleated and hail ! bone-swift
targets of swooping birds crested gold
talons of fire the serpent entwined
will sleeping the air itself burst seeds
scatter like sperm on unspoken rock
and lo ! the main becomes heavy with
and forth spring the ancestors
so , ashes and grey cinders their city
immersed in lakes of basalt and lime
behold the histories of tortoise and ant
limitless pyramids from outer space !

yet death snaking 'neath the skin
earthly and like a girl for the first
her swirling porches of soot and hair
enchantment perfumes legend wild
the brothers ensnare like fireflies
in screens of nocturne and red litmus
approximate the pale worm of death
smoking out of the radiant *Heart*
in profusion of yellow and indigo
fire-water pulque mezcal libations
who eats the corn of death once
eats forever the timeless Harvest !
go we brother and I into the wave
sea-winds darksome shadows aloft
or drowned in inky rebirth
fade and absence
silent *the*

10-20-17

THE SHE-DEMON ANNIE

Annie is the world a step from
the street where whirling lights
a frame takes the western slope
white incandescence of Annie
slipping from view beneath
ancient drum skins the pounding
in the remains of ear the siren
rising from profound seas Annie
skirts the former shores her eye
on the nether zone the music dark
that shapes such masks she wears
weaving or weeping in baskets
brought from the orphanage of fate
orange persimmon citron yellow
bitter air fogs the horizon
as motors of the gods discharge
flares poverty distinctions of
ace and trembling her mouth
a fiction of liquid anemones
this Annie and that Annie
mother of the world demoness
trilogy of fates and moon-shapes
dust of words clouds of sounds
nothing audible in the silence
rushing from one planet to the next
where nothing can ever take place

unless it is the grand Sumerian Tomb
Annie is inscription and blank
various and furious carnival hair
primordial beast-heart vacuous
with nothing to say but archaic
squatting to make water over
the god of Clay and suppliant
arms akimbo to the heavens
opening for a minute only
when will this day ever return ?
Annie is I wonder about last night
but Annie is only echo of Annie
reddish dots violating landscape
can it be she is all over and
never was but shade on stair
flitting typescript of fever
when imagination can no more
conjure then dusky curtains fall
dun hills are gone in twilight
anxious windows fading lamps
wherever she went in powders
green yellow and pale beige
she was still Annie the unknown
lip gloss nail polish & bitumen
ahistorical and vanishing body
rue the day she first kissed me
upside down on a ride to Avernus
was it human meat or angel ?

10-22-17

THE HYMN TO KIPKH

turning automobiles to pigs sashes
red and roundly tied the neck
cavorting like a goddess without feet
into the sanctum where it all blows
star dust crimson agonies a shot
to the prow make sure they don't go
Daughter-of-the-Sun tie-dyed omnium
the fix of pure oxygen and clouds come
steaming to a halt let the Mariner in
love's the price of death the voluble
antebellum pressed face down
in lavender sheets all memory flees
madness to have at her the intangible
nights and days spent in sea-haze
caustic halo and undefined letters

however you read it the sky slips
into the many chasms within her eyes
wanton disregard for the Republic
disillusionment and beast- marriage
her voice the hoarse gutter of despair
for hours her Island turns into years
nostalgia and longing for something
that cannot correctly be remembered
so many transmigrations of soul
animal mineral plant and property
gods of Hallucination and Vertigo
when sea and sand become one grain
and heavens of asterisks conjoin
to the fundamental Idea of love
everything breaks apart here
peninsulas of gas tripartite air
fuses detonating remote star clusters
and especially animals the talking kind
stalking the dense groves around
her Mansion situated in their midst
her we proclaim Daughter-of-the-Sun
blindingly bright stroking spirit-backs
to have lain with her just once !
how doth the errant mind recur ?
cunning we call her sorceress deity
woven from gaudy stuffs purple cloth
hair like a terrain of ink overflowing
caught in that embrace and smothered !
the small red eyes of night probing
encounter only the immense shade
the blank and awful window
the lessened moonlight of infinity
to never get home again !
only the imperfect guide to Hades
with its faulty dream intersections
which she has offered as a memento
the Beyond is this stubble field
ossuary and portico of the Nameless
whose endless dying is a poem
inscribed on papyri of dust
evanescent ever fading

10-23-17

THE FATE OF THE SUITORS

would that we had an end to all our trials
that soon the wood and the marginless sea
all that filled our heads with wonder
craft and pining and the myriad stars above
come crashing around the weary brain
and thought to come from sleep into
another world guided by Hermes
where still shining though transformed
Achilles and thronging around him
brawny Ajax or flawless Antilochus
other Argives dust-drowned who spent their
bodies on the resounding shore and now
without memory
                    cast from the great
House on Ithaca dizzy spinning tales
shall we meet at twilight ?
gibbering like bats in a blind cave
they know not themselves careless
and grieving for the light
we shall count the sands in an hour
waiting for the sun and his two steeds
to approach the eastern gate the hills
gold-tinged a fade
                    our hands
no longer a part of us a frail noise
dice clattering to the floor or plates
meat spoiled honey drenched cloths
did you remember to call home ?
but look now how Agamemnon
the doom-quelled Atreids here too
whom Zeus was bound to love for
many mortal days and yet
           something lost in the head
a rumbling of distances and the sudden
is it lightning ?
                  many of the hand-maidens
too blood soaked and mewing like kestrels
whose wings have been torn
nor our feet where have they gone ?
in the upper chamber the spotless
guttering oil lamps and the loom
enormous with its shadow
that was the world

intestines of the gods !
such is our lot disassembled

vagrant in meandering paths
going nowhere and by sundown
again the countless hours of a day
something of a glimmer
         before endless
night
                  and her
for whom we wagered ?
an illegible cliff
and even the sound of her name
         what was it ?

10-26-17

PROMETHEUS

for whom destroyed the legendary
god-like in stature and booming
hand furled back to the left a bolt
it seemed to defy consciousness
madness the mind employs and love
the prisoner baffled insomniac
counting days backwards to seas
tossed in a minute's revelation
thrust against battered the cliff
climbing into atmospheres dark
his arm the released weapon shifts
in bird-like flight the eye caught
spinning solar flares of memory
can never return home the island
listening beneath clouds wrapped
the soul itself which way to go
walls of sound risen dissolving
what the ear and the small note
confusion of script west leaning
where colors fade and kingdoms
engraved like thought in flares
who will the approach be the ken
savage at first his aim to reach
piercing the god-site rock bright
delivering sleep from its waters
roiling black and steep where
the prow shattered against wave
bussed furiously the divine
intent him the figure written
the struggle to escape tempests
women and the shore invisible
senses piled against the heights

are they muses swarming bees
the crazed yellow flowers bent
awaiting death's still sunshaft
cutting at the neck life so brief
straight the tall shadow of him
wavering in unfounded lamps
glare of time as the wheel rolls
from one language to the next
unfurling the unintelligible
into its horizons ink sunk
can the *other* groping hands
find to shape days that were
or is silence the *it* he commands
meadowing the noon sweep
now forever out of reach
++++++++++++++++++++
the great silent motion
of the sky

10-28-17

DAY OF THE DEAD (vii)

are my knees doubled ?
is my thinking reduced to a red dot ?
the fierce , and then along the shore
perambulating among dead spear-heads
a wave , sun glinting on salt-skin
damp , perforations in the large air
looming with its planets , even at noon
and the sound or roar of warriors
long lost in a volley of language at
times so loud , I woke from a
brief spell of death no less , I and
she both in the flash of the lamp
held in a god's invisible hand , the
, and also quivering in the clouds
strange glowing mask peering
through years of sunset and turf ,
please , *she* , saying cocktails at
three in the grand lobby , marble
spit ancient grass a whole litany
of , some maintain the dharma
while others , unsure of which
text they refer to , enormous echo
lacking vowels the summer edging
its way into twilight , please , *she*
said opening the window of her

heart , were we both at the end
of the game suitable , the edition
with its hours greening a lapse of
consciousness in the sand , naked
each in the sudden tide taking out
whole the indelible continent , a
fissure deepening in the lunar apse
, choirs of snow , faint , distances
fade , the pale , footnotes to the
Rg Veda , you mean ancient ,
coming through dust storms
the origins of everything of ,
virtually the universe suspended
in a glass eye , or am I not the
king of Asia ? what remote is it
what immense longing for the
other , is it ? when I will come home
wearing sugar skulls and being
at one with the mayor of Tenochtitlan
drinking beer and ceremoniously
high ! then will they understand
the revolutions of the universes
plural ambiguously infinite , a
solemn occasion with no feet
to stand and a face turned to ,
all directions are one , Brahma
and his lusting concupiscent *Eye* !
Madre de Dios !!!!!!!!!!!!!!!!!!!!!

(Joe seven years on)
11-01-17

DIA DE LOS MUERTOS (vii)

(epilogue)

traveling down Thirteen Highway
with Muddy Waters and a Sanskrit suitcase
the largest section of sky the biggest
azure whitening right down to the
and here am I listening to all
the Beethoven quartets performed
simultaneously in the last second
of Eternity ! you down there
in the state of Hiawatha freezing
in your imaginary lake moon and all
the triplicate version of death is Great
the summons to attend the funeral

of Valum Votan sweet weeping Jesus
living the alcohol and peyote dream
is it Thelonious Monk on a rooftop ?
watching from a heaven of bitumen and
coral and the backdrop of boomerangs
and the total illusion of drugstore
clockwork and girls timed to go off
at precisely midnight and three !
I want them all and always
perfumed and masticating Toltec *chicle*
when was I ever more difficult
than Now ? listen up *hombres*
I am not the herbivore you thought
just a melancholy beast on the edge
living on sand and dust memory
it was a while coming around to this
eating rope and lye twisting clouds
through the left eye and singing !
you will of course telephone Mom
let her know what religion is all about
Egyptian fly-trap mnemonics
and the Pyramids ! what a devastating
secret dancing with a charade
as if night could ever end this darkness
am I going to supersede myself ?
sitting in a circle with blind gods
trading marijuana cigarettes
and actually Laughing !

11-01-17

PRE-SOCRATIC

vita umana altro che procella dei sensi
  che sei ?

as to what is the matter of the world
whether the portion toward the top
where air is less dense and the light
that sheds on the peaks of its rocky
summits is what they call feminine
the southern spaces and what is most
puzzling ether and peninsulas of gas
men quarreling the subject of water
eddying around the large land mass
it is called by some Gaia by others
where the small entrance near a
dark recess to Hades come talking to

the Master of the dark realms why
it is not resolved this fashion and shape
hands cannot form no more than mind
the vast empyrean outside the senses
yet do humans go on storming idylls
fraction after fraction and what Zero !
below the emerging ice blocks rage
and jungles and petroleum rivers
obliged by tortoise and snake to run
through and under the cities of sand
runes and scripts and numeral sizes
whole systems of thought in the letter
red idiomatic collision of vowels wild
and to imagine beyond what can be
only exhausts sleep and the formidable
dreams that occur on the moon or else
what more we go delving do we into
distress and the epic verses deriving
from some dimly recalled incident
automobile accident involving alcohol
or the teenage fantasy of living forever
while driving straight on into danger
the sheet metal wrapped around the
brain and isotopes and molecules
and all the deranged elements of what
they call life living as it were in a
quarry like statues not yet born
*human life other than storm of the senses
    what are you ?

11-02-17

ON THE WAY TO MENDOCINO
ONE FATEFUL WINTER DAY

"Cómo cansa ser todo el tiempo
uno mismo."
Julio Cortázar, *Rayuela*

so we were zapping up the coast
north on highway One night-time
even at noon and years of water
furiously lapping at the fading cliff
margin wherever we were going
nothing held the bleak winter air
culminating in a horizon lasting
no more than a radio song minute
everything was Blink ! glass rain

shattered egos lifted by the collar
into a sooty heaven of utter despond
knowing yet not knowing each other
driving a wheel right into the fort
where the Russians are said to have
argued over the purchase of sky
who could smoke the most cigarettes
or whose name came to mind first
and what of memory the fault line
field and meadow crashing in a rush
as if a dispute between gods red
and white and the ambiguous birds
wheeling overhead invisible sirens
a warning that the continent was
on its way to oblivion redwoods
unseen shopping malls concrete
the sheer enormity of the infinite
staring us in the face like a wave
bounding out of the raging surf
no wonder we went lost in the dells
listening for the rocks to open up
somewhere between the season
the Ohlone celebrate as death-wish
and the vertiginous flashing second
of the unforgettable movie screen
centaurs talking clouds dust-wheels
time itself unspun on the yardarm
piercing the mists around the motel
where we were doomed to spend
the rest of what seemed our lives
++++++++++++++++++++++++++
is what we read between the lines
not earthly passion but a maelstrom
a whirling of unremembered planets
of lost traces through the dense wood
in search of Beatrice the thirteen
year old epiphany in sandstone
a time of day in oblivion
an enigma
fade ?

11-04-17

LOVE POEM IN AN ANCIENT KEY

in the hyphenated vocabulary of the gods
what is the escape route what is the fate
of those abiding like shadows on the steps
souls forever snatched lives forsaken
et cetera goes the ancient theme
yet here and today with greater losses
earth itself the endless trouble-spot
were you and I to live again together
and heighten all the light we shared
to carve inside the withering air
our hair our names our mouths
would the path lead down instead
of upwards with but scarce a glance
at the perfect but foreboding sky
will the next hour be the darkening
when imagined the ships pull up
to the wild and listing shoreline
is the crashing only in the ear ?
should we sleep like bending willows
the summer long dreaming otherness
to keep the burning ring outside the mind
yet listen now and evermore the fading
clouds the unknown plural air
what draws us into the pale like smoke
and winds our bodies into invisibility
around a rope of rushing water ?
is it because your face is a geography
of what can never be fully known
your eyes enormous pools of rock
where is to drown if not inside your skin
and then come running unnamed gods
footsteps that tattoo the enormous wind
with the roses blooming from your lips
the smile of utter vanishing !
will there be a next time as infinite
as the time when first we met ?

11-05-17

YOUR HAIR

if one could say where Asia starts
and where Asia ends then maybe
one might have an idea of your hair
redolent of cigarettes and fragrance
of blue lotus blind mesh of darkness
ensnaring the multiple moons of sand
if a skein of it could wrap around
all the light that has ever been
or even a few strands of it coiled
around the goddess named eternity
what evidence would there be of
anything else in this enigmatic universe ?
thick masses of it lush and damp
fill hands of air overflowing wildly
causing tempests to rage above the seas
and the sheer texture of it raw silk
woven illusions of the great color red
turned to black like portals of the sun
and horses indwelling at the root
fiery and mysteriously charged to fly
bearing with them all the weight
of your endless hair ! my love
when will you let down the other half
the hemisphere of colloidal ink
to match the missing hemisphere of night
when it is time for the Hour to end
when day has nowhere else to go
but back into the Stygian pool
your hair revolves around the loom
like the massive water that fills black holes
and comes forth again a million
light years before our birth
do you laugh if I take what I can
of it to strangle the myriad cupids
that dart crazily through my eyes
how can you walk with such mountains
waving and weaving stupendously
involving the secrets of your body ?
the cosmos is at an end !
if today were anywhere else
your hair would blot it out
combs pins ribbons seamless years
my fingers lost forever in its density
my life a single drop distilled in the oils
that feed on the obscure puzzle

of your hair your boundless hair
enervating useless totally beautiful
shimmering fatal shaking slowly
in the winds it has created
now and forever blowing away
the face of time

11-06-17

TWO UNRELATED LOVE POEMS

i.

VANISHING MUSE

so-called power of love but fragments
figments fictions loosened detritus
from the Himalayas already miles
into a foregone future yesterday
mango groves filled with longing
passion-fruit unblemished cheeks
eyes perfervid wide open lasting
minutes before blinking dream-shut
who will that be peering mid shades
hallucinatory mornings haunted
by what can never be the poem
written in asterisks and sent up
to the seventh heaven the miracle
of clouds shaking it out in powders
linked sky to sky the arms of a god
lower to take in human form love
anticipation frustration despair
that a next time will never be again
that tomorrow was the yesterday
when idle rumor spread sheets
yellowing and withered over town
numbers could not be reconciled
traffic came to a drilling halt
whoever was sent to go shopping
would never come home again
and so the story goes lovers ditched
in side-streets of total amnesia
kisses sewn to angelic phantoms
embraces unbidden like tattoos
painted on a disappearing skin
You I know in the wreckage midst
half here half gone half nowhere
impatient to start the minute

that leads into the labyrinth
and *Me* loco weed and oblivion
holding on to the gassy substance
known as the great dementia
stop all atmospheres shuttered
windows of the brain smashed
legendary inkstones blind bees
raging to return to their glass-hive
and somewhere in the miles of hair
lifted like a ruined & dark paradise
into a roaring sea of oxygen
the name you used to go by fading
fragrance of cigarette and roses
how pallid the memory of time !
yet again and again you vanish
behind the triple doors of absence
footsteps whispers silence

ii.

THIS IS THE POEM YOU WANTED ME TO WRITE LAST SUNDAY

sounds like gunshot in the air
visceral aerial tides at mid-morning
when behold the screen door yawns
wide and the appearance of *her*
fresh from the wafer of sleep
a hundred years in the making
without makeup just those eyes
it's You , baby , the *it* of the bright
everything else just blows ! I'm
high just thinking about how
you'll stairway yourself into Being
nothing modeled nothing brewed
just the section of heaven at Ten
when distances become pure metal
shining prepared to take off like a jet
racing down the street frantic to fly
you and me in the glass of Zero-time
something invisible something nothing
pearls of radiation stud the atmosphere
either you are cloud Nine or I am dead
to have at you somewhere in history
between Bolsheviks and Vikings
Bang-Bang ! you lean into the void
and take what's left of me breathless
unthreading the woof of my soul

burrowing like a transformed language
into the other side of Me ! Gone !
mexican hat-dance brilling wildly
on the burning sands next to the only
yes Pyramid and the junction
where the pharaohs take opium
to *Remember* ! me and you already
leaning deeper into the void red
and crimson and violently blank
eyes shut worlds away from sleep
how to wake ? how to shake it ?
here give me that tongue !
nothing left to say nothing but
the and the again
Freeze !
this is Forever !
houses streets cars trees
air above all and sky sky
the luminous as much as
we can take in a single minute
before it all goes
before it all goes !

11-07-17

INEXPLICABLE HEART

I look at you and I fall in love
I look at you and I fall in love
I look at you and I fall in love
the human inexplicable heart
exploding racing out of time
to reach what it is the eye *sees*
perception is illegal and red
the world is only air and gravity
illusory trees leap into nowhere
leaves spell out destruction
waiting as always for the rains
and I fall in love with stairs
with empty bottles with bags
filled with detritus of romance
any reason to *look at you*
delirious for what is within
patchwork cloth cast offs
cigarette smoke hanging there
like a riddled enemy flag
or to touch even a hair as
it arrests the amazing wind

that circles you like heat
is there anywhere else but here
this fetid dog-air street
where miracles *I look at you*
have nothing to do with doors
or the smoked windows that
peer out into the mind's abyss
and I fall in love no comforts
but the madness of denial
everything is combustible !
start the motor let it run
until the mouth can crave
no more its lost winged soul
I look at you and I fall in love

11-08-17

RETURN FROM PARADISE

for Bob Ness

world shadow beast-dream
how many faltering the steps
across what waste fields lost
in error the spent soul fades
how the music was in the air
loud then a mere echo of what
legend of the missing ships
of the islands of pure absence
never was what it imagined
to be in the lingering atolls
where mind clings to an *Idea*
everything in a rush passing
through sieves of memory
golf-links abandoned barns
summers like a hail-storm
pounding heated metal roofs
the nothing the incomplete
zero the cipher suspended
in the month of no days at all
sheer circularity of space
when one another we faced
green then red then whitest
of all the illusory long-lost
what was it you kept saying
moving from shadow to shadow
something dark and distant
is it today again already ?

++++++++++++++++++++
is this reality ? whet-stone
in the garage half-empty
whiskey bottle and overhead
long fishing poles waiting
for a day in the sun // reality ?
walking the long side of
second street past magic shop
past greek restaurant mystery
across the street from hospital
where we saw light of day
tripods oracles mantic omega
moving further down to
an avenue then the root
beer stand and the music
from a car radio top-40
hot asphalt girls in roaming
wearing just lipstick and
farms hundreds of them rolling
toward a small lake where
fish and polkas and blistering
grandpa's chevy rattling
gravel unmarked roads
to where the Indians routed
dumb pioneers in Mankato
and back again a solving
sands gravel dead leaves
must be change of seasons
sky all weather and azure
clouds to count before sun
down // reality ? is this ?
coming slanted through glass
a reflection from millions
of years ago clay pits and
dinosaur tracks and trees
birdsongs and catholic rites
the self crossed in lightning
++++++++++++++++++++
by evening scared to forget
what was it like before
the light ?

11-09-17

"UNFORGETTABLE, THAT'S WHAT YOU ARE..."

what was it ever if not
illusion and deception,
born-of-the Sun , Joe !
the world 65 years to
the day when we discovered
its kaleidoscopic surfaces
reverberating tumbling
going back and forth
on the radio dial songs
promising love forever
not hipster journeys
through drug-riddled heart
to become in no time flat
rejuvenated first glances
on mobile dance floors
holding the shadow of
passion the outline of
desire the embryo of
death in your night-
arms swaying willow
at the waist and steep
down the ravine kissing
while heated automobiles
raced sand to its sleep
illusion and deception !
how did we know which
window was Perception ?
before tomorrow was over
the day before celebrated
you ! exalted-peyote-head !
it was down in the slough
it was with the blues band
playing beneath the lake
it was nowhere near the east
nor the eternal southland
where the dead swing
perpetually intoxicated
it was exactly on the margin
that separated me from you
some unmarked hour of time
minutes before your hand
lifted the atmosphere
in a great retrograde
signal to the missing *Sun*

and you became
Unforgettable
       too

11-10-17

BEING WITH YOU CONFUSION

if I am confused I am talking to you or
it is a dream you are a reality or a delusion
I am listening to you talking an illusion or
a hallucination opening up the robe and
what a figure the moon is rising up your
throat watching a thin blue vein pulsing
confused as I am whether it is a window
or the air which is turning azure I know
that I love it when you approach across
the miles of time it takes to descend
ever so slowly first your feet then your
legs and from the knee up I go crazy
the steps become something voluble
wavering surf on a sea of confusion
it will be later before time gets around
to touching your hair the skein of it
revolving around my thoughts confused
as they are to name what it is I feel when
of course you are there for only a minute or
two the hemispheres divide and continents
formerly known for their watery masses
implode which is called a kiss a fragrance
or something similar to the tide pool
where colors involve what it is your eye
sees being taken darkly into the hour
when night finally consumes me confused
still thinking to talk to the columns of
wind and the storms start up in smoke
your mouth impossibly at the center

11-11-17

SALVATION

radiance of living in this one moment
what is the rest of time ?
surface of air intricacies of sky
are we prepared for landing ?
is life worth the risk ?
one look and automation takes effect
from the head down no pronouns
the masses of hair disguise planets
hitherto undiscovered where salvation
is a single unit of mythology
otherwise the two of us are left alone
on this unguided spacecraft
in search of the perfect way out
nebulae of madness and dark matter
crazy formations of hands
probing islands of desire
almost unbearable having to experience
this rush this world we never made
how can we be saved from ourselves ?
how is the plant kingdom at fault ?
how is anything at all possible ?
the distance in your eyes
is it equal to the longing in mine ?
what it comes down to is the street
the quotidian geography of expectation
lunar devices sirens wild acts of devotion
emptying the bank of its currency
retiring to the jungle in stolen cars
naming you what you are not
absolution in a pinprick ?
how many deities are watching ?
I cannot bear another minute
clouds incense signals smoke
which is your signature dissolving
in the morning aura
silence but not salvation
from ourselves

11-12-17

MAYOWOOD FOREVER YOUNG

"me and Marlon Brando and Pocahontas"
Neil Young
(for james balfour, bob ness and slade schuster)

i.

stubble fields the endless yearning
oblique extensions of memory and history
out of the fluttering lies of text books
when were these lands ever free ?
driving over and over the routes
now turned to bitumen and asphalt
where sacred the deer and buffalo
champed on nostalgic may-time grasses
taste of mint and heaven combined
in a sepia version cinema rolling
across buttes cliffs and bluffs high
above the Father-of-Waters dream-
serpent cascading through burial yards
profaned by the maps drawn
to artificially demarcate counties
townships and tracks of the iron-horse
brings us to the small streams and pools
that never were in some undesignated
childhood an echo or subliminal murmur
before high school graduation closed
the circle with fading photographs
what goddess left her knee in
                the gooseberry tangles ?
who was the first to be felled
          on the highway going north ?

ii.

interminable hollow sundays bereft
of the light of a winter day
listening for something in the hills
the western winds the soughing
unconscious and whispering snows
face down in verdigris anxiety
the self mute and vagrant walking
the alleys that separate clinic from hell
with movie theater blues why go home ?
round and round the same empty block
automobile graveyard dirty ice
looking through drear bar windows
broken neon sediment flashing

on and off fluorescent alcoholic faces
that could be your *Indian* , Joe
juke box pool table hassle (Heart)
endemic vitriol adolescent cynicism
collar turned up and ready to vomit
right into the spoiled orange twilight
flicker flicker
what a long lonesome way it is
disconnected skies pine trees cursed
where the slope indicates a missed turn
greek restaurants illegal motel rooms
down there where South Broadway
runs into great albino oblivion
I feel all choked up, Ma
I just can't go on with the lesson
my fingers are falling off the table
there's no room for the music

iii.

is it a wonder to ask why they go away
who have never been here but in yearning
the massive occlusions the tombstones
by silver lake a fading path
that once led to the Manitou spirit home
corn shocks bent in the vast blue flare
where the beyond is a nothing of space
we will all go there one day
to join those who have never been
it will be a struggle to remember why
to set stone against stone to mark
the way to the numberless stars
we will lie on our backs waiting
for the small white deer to come
and nibble at our fingertips
turning to one another dust and ashes
what smile what wan expression
will manifest in the gloaming
shoulder to shoulder on that cold turf
near silver lake by the headstones
erased the names they used to bear
closed the cycle of photographs
beyond recognition the scar of sky
that we too we were once as clouds
shifting distant shapes afloat
fading hues and echoes
gone

iv.

latin exams / flush with sea victory /
augustus eulogized by virgil / hexameter
scansion the / virtually all collapsed /
watching rise the smoke / dido's pyre /
delenda est ! / snake and tortoise and
golden sands / the ganges / notebooks
torn at the spine / geese in alphabet
overhead // to mayowood / the reckless
waste / on either side the spreading
foliage / the sound of distance itself /
to gaul with caesar / counting the several
belgiums / jocasta they say was a real
bitch / come nightfall and the snows /
foreboding in the reverse index / a
chat with the Higher Being / a demon
dressed in asterisks / a football player
gone gaga / autumn nights in mayowood /
the television has just been invented /
jackie gleason and ed sullivan / the brothers
mayo enshrined in a corn-husker / ! /

v.

all is hush the little players
in their diamond birth suits
laid out on the sprinting lawn
hard by the pool and the paddock
where withered buffalo stare
this is the future
the great rerum natura
the whatever it could have been
frost bite and tendonitis
walking home in the frozen
looking at the immense lake in the sky
Ojibway and *purple rain*
how far !
        come into
my teepee
lay down thy sweet face
on this here lonesome iron
listen !
        vast the edifice of air
the rest is talking and more than
enough of *their* tall tales
to the northern woods
beyond the deep mines

back to the winnebago
        death house

11-12-17

THE NEXT TIME I SEE YOU

you will be neither home nor
asleep in the clouds recounting
what it was you saw in the other life
the one before I opened the red door
to discover you both awake and in
trance unable to recognize in me
the avenging angel of ennui
the next time I see you the floor
beneath your feet will be pure helium
aloft your corporeal self will be
in an attitude of perpetual prayer
desperate to become atheist
a mystic of hair blacker than ink
no one will extend a hand to pull
you down to earth and least of all I
testimony of astrophysics and denial
come on , *Baby* , it will say in the language
of statues and nodding to the deafened
street signs passing you in surprise
you will be even less the self you were
the night before blowing the candles out
the next time I see you won't be the last
but it will be a riddle and an enigma
that you ever were able to pass
through life after life incognito
still I will recognize you the next time
I see you somewhere between
this series of moon shots and the next
and listening carefully to the oceanic surge
I will hear you whispering phonemes
of love both unendurable and wild
there may be no next time I will see you
there may be just oracles of sand and wind
or simply a great hiatus in which stepping
deftly from the planet of absence
down to the planet of longing
thousands of asterisks will explode yellow
and bright red in the sleeper's ear
you will be invisible or an outline of shadows
the next time I see you if there is a next
time will tell if there is a dream

of you appearing in a sequence of eyes
taking photographs of your impossible
re-entry into the noosphere
my gorgeous and ineffable *Ghost* !
if there will ever be a next time

11-13-17

SONG : I AIN'T MISSING YOU AT ALL

now am I prepared to go afar
weary of sea-combat the restless waves
if I touched the plectrum once
it was to sing you your fair face
eyes flashing that belong to the living
when night touches down on western rocks
I wonder where you will be laying
your shadow your worldly robes
how was it of a day without explanation
I fell in love with you knowing nothing
of the exchange between light and dark
the garbled text of the planets
oracular and devastating
which was the sign allotted to you ?
immense and floating galaxy of thoughts
no sooner sighted than gone !
yet there was skin and a mouth and
all the secrets the distance of a body holds
enigmas of the infra-ray
the solar expanse of your smile
vanishing as do all things into the One
yet am I about to be off into the waters
that circle above and below earth
that bear the souls of men
from the boneyard into spheres
inaudible but gorgeously sweet
memory of you untainted
whom I touched with song once
with my plectrum

11-13-17

THE VOICE WITHIN

I have been made great and shiny
the power to move among the various skies
and to have this voice which is neither mine
nor that of the god dwelling in my heart
but the echo of something from beyond
resonating with the origins of Chaos
now am I greater than myself
the outside of clouds the inside of clouds !
with me move the mysterious Ones
who have been ever the grass and stars
that inhabit the fields of longing
Yes ! I am either Chaos the music of all
or the spent force of Gravity scattered
throughout the houses of the Zodiac
nebulae are my thoughts asterisks and
the tiny red dots that punctuate dreams
I cannot understand that this is myself
and not some hospital room in 1939
nor that for days I am a bewildered abacus
summoning to mind questions of eternity
a moment later and I am in Etruria
the hills are enormous and brown and withering
and there are calls of nymphs and fauns
demons who want to tear me apart
to have at my heart where resides the Divine
still I am walking moving among the minerals
among the unforged elements of Nowhere
is it love that causes the soul to depart ?
who left these marble temples in *Ruin* ?
flight from the daily into the *Noosphere*
who is it propels me to shake moving here
and here and here and here forever ?
to take flight as love does from the mind
amidst the names of so many deities
all forgotten and consigned to the dump
and who am I to seek continually moving
shaken to the core looking for the Enigma
the thing that resolves in the end Nothing !
I am itching to be *Other* to be unexplained
to shift from calculus to immemorial sands
love that sets the orbits roving absent of form ?
that empties the Cretan jars of their emptiness !
is it hush all over the stoned ears of Bacchus ?
silences of noon the closest thing to death ?
what is this enormous entanglement

this skein of night-black hair wrapped
tightly around vocabularies of the Archaic ?
makes me walk through rock and stone
as if they were pure air this impiety *Love*
vomit sputum mucus piss shit & sperm !
the many who are already dead *alive !*
they revoke *Light* the all consuming
I am with them their pallor and sorrow
uncontrollable weeping of their shoulders
yet do I move through and past them
I am Mozart the four evangels and Echo
I remember nothing of what this means !
tomorrow the secret will be revealed
nonsense shibboleth and hobson-jobson
language utterly in reverse high and gone !
is it because of *Annie* stirring in the depths ?
is it because of *Annie* being *Annie* in the dark ?
is it because of   *Annie* ?
I remember nothing of what this means !
poetry is the deathless syllable alone
and all the dust of time reconstituted
shiny and great and powerful I move
shaking the axis of the cosmos to bits
++++++++++++++++++++++++++++++
I am become nobody the sleeper under the bed
the child within the murmuring shell
dreamt in the irreversible tides
moving out forever into the deep
lunar evocation madness disembodied self
voice at last of the divine within
     ineffable

11-14-17

APHRODITE REDEFINED

hagiography of your shadow
cave-dweller of the heart !
is it no wonder I walk bewildered
down streets of anonymous anticipation
numbering the days from zero
to the day after Never
how can I ever know *when* ?
illogic and unreason be my guides !
nothing is ever as it should be
whenever there are worlds redder
than the hiatus of the last Unknown !
yet you open a door and the air

darkened by Pandora's secret
lightens up ghosts of thought flee
ruined edifice of brain stands shaking
whatever the eye realized yesterday
is a mirage in azure tinctures
sky blown away by its own proportions
where are you hiding that illustrious *thing* ?
last week there were sand cathedrals
monuments of ether statuary of silence
and today there is but a single trace
a damp print on the windshield
but no voice no whispering
only the motor idling by the curbside
anxiety of molecules in disrepair
future of bodies to remain nameless
the subject of love pinned to its arrow
what wild weathers of ink !
to attempt to read the *Illegible*
cornerstones steeped in oracle
what deity is raving in his cup ?
by the time we meet again
it will be ancient a land of wrecks
rust in fogs circling a wounded sun
what of your timeless face ?
what of the cigarettes of paradise ?
what identity will you resume ?
life after life we skirted our selves
touch and indigo and broken gold
peninsulas that no feet ever feel
islands ! where the soul lies suppliant
to the *Goddess* and her alone
dew-draped radiant in imagination
you the very myth of my mind !

11-15-17

MYSTERY WHO SHE IS

exalted *One* ! darkest side spindrift
moonflower tide crest spotted waters
writing is only a form of sand !
poem is the unaccented syllable
of the unrepeatable archaic sound
and she is at the center of Nothing
being written being pronounced
so loud in the vacuum of the ear
that none can understand how it is
that her name will ever be known
counter tape of air and cloud shape
intricacies between lost memories
echoes of hills buried in longing
illicit consonant surrounded by ink
serpentine signature indelible *Red*
reincarnation ! of whom of whom ?
paradise is just a broken stairway
heaven is the unfinished cigarette
burning its entrails in a glass omega
nothing can ever be corrected *OM* !
nothing can ever be rectified *OM* !
no world other than this buried ocean
no ocean other than this buried earth
moving as she does through deeps
through mottled transgressions of gas
through elements of fifty past lives
alone hers is the reorganization
the foil and target of the single *Eye*
all stone and rock all cliff and steep
what is it that sings through quartz ?
when she emerges from Oriental pearl
a fog of fire her deathless black hair
and skirts of thought disintegrate
because she is stepping through smoke
eliminating one by one writing systems
clay pits gravel mire marble quarries
it has to be death in a silken zero
it has to be dying every time grass
and the missing fingers groping grass
and the evenings no one can recall
the thousands of hours waiting for her
planetary errors mistaken comets
a house for every word she has forgotten
a small oblivion in the parting of her lips
you say she cannot be numbered

yet look ! she is the very last letter
of infinity repeated like an isotope
drawn across the blackboard of space
I saw her in the doctor's office today !
she was every woman who yearns to *Know*
but when I turned to look again
there was only the agony of a magazine
littered among the two million feet !
now there are lawns and expanses
where the dead search for their cattle
slopes going westward toward the *Inevitable*
harbors of north with ice of continents
but nowhere the symbol of *Return*
a remembrance of eternity
it is in her glance when Sunday opens
or it is gone before the following week
what is mystery if not her absence ?
what is mystery if not her absence ?

11-17-17

NARCISSUS & ECHO

"saw Narcissus wandering around
in the outback and got all hot . . ."
here among grasses lost the mind
listens for the purling stream pure
illusory where images refined soon
dissolve darkening in the sun's wound
am I in the eddying atmosphere but
a color some petals whispering dells
where is the vale the small glen or cove
hidden where my face repairs to cool
what hears the unbent ear in loam
hooves or serpents secret sounding
other worlds spent in torn veils
beneath and still call the waters
by evening felled reflections twilight
glimmering a voice my ears retell
do sleep then nerves by heat frayed
dim the distant noons of rioting light
will I again return to the liquid glass
my features reveal to none other but
the driven self of unrequited night
in exchange for whom I cannot know
me divinely spelled in Echo's lament
shaking slightly in dense summer leaves
shadows wrapped around word-relics

what comes back through black ivy
what reaches me in day dream shining
what bright vowels what resplendent
diphthongs doubled ever more remote
caught in a web of murmurs and *rumor*
itself spreading distortions of my name
Echo ! bring me back to myself tonight
Echo ! why weave you this gorgeous stuff
my body's gravitating disaster longing
because you have no corporeal image
because you are the evaporating soul
of every song you chanced to hear
your immortal mouth repeats sweetly
as if pouring into my stoned ear
trance monotony of love's stammer
it is never a rapt hour of eternity
only the insane trajectory into pools
deeper than the archaic Poem
ECHO ECHO ECHO ECHO
just once my hand touched lily moist
the skin of your waist before nightfall
shaking the massive inky wind of your hair
you slipped away into the mountains
what's left for me but to remain clasped
to the echo of my own reflection
drowning in drowning in drowning in
loss of my own reflection fading
in soundless depthless waters
weightless unpossessed
tattoo of ether
                 and endless light

11-17-17

MYSTICAL YOU

the poem about the legend of the
is what follows sublime it is white
flame pouring from the ethereal eye
the sunless doubt of a day in paradise
beside the myth *you* are the nameless
a quote from the thunder of the gods
a refrain underlined in total silence
to hear it repeated in mindless sleep
to wake greening on the other shore
hapless the image of wandering grass
a hand from clouds takes the remains
who cannot recall this is the song

a mystery to translate and redefine
you similar to the fade western hills
and flowers too sprung where *you*
stepped pursuing oracular destinies
zero times fragrance & luminescence
of pure beauty sun-adorned dew-
stained alba mysticism asterisms
at noon when the *Invisible* becomes
You transfigured and immeasurable
mountains I give reduced to shadow
waters that have no source night-swept
this earth and the gone other one
darkness in layers of years spent
looking for *you* chasm and abyss
light in the form of a single arrow
sands I give that are the size of ink
and directions too and winds and snow
all gathered in a single red knot
what is to be done about yesterday
like all fictions cancelled by error
or love finally how is it defined
doubling the rivers it empties out
into the center of nowhere precisely
where *you* wake above the stairs
below the clouds afloat in a space
that has no known origin mysterious
unlit the vacant stanza of a lyric
recited by statues at their birth
++++++++++++++++++++++++++
meaningless cycles of heat and
revolving around the inane core
life and afterlife and breath and
the light that adheres to the eye
unseen and unwritten texts of air
forces of ungovernable chaos *Fire*
inch by inch that takes the soul
away into some other dimension
there where I will find *you* exactly
as I placed *you* a thousand lives ago
breathless shimmering the *One*

11-18-17

TWO SPIRITUAL POEMS

i.

ANNIE'S HOUSE

I never get near it but the magnetic needle
goes wild pointing in all directions at once *North*
there is nowhere else to go but straight up
or worse straight down into the *Dark Kingdom*
traffic is strapped to a single immobile belt
angels of rusted metal hover over the freeway
ignorant of the manifold human error below
thunder claps of pure light snap sky in half
clouds sulfurous bituminous iridescent heave
into the windshield and an eerie silence
takes over the radio emitting lyrics of despair
if I ever get there it will be in another life
another time another dimension totally gone
many are the dead beside the road in flowers
playing invisible instruments inarticulate
yearning as only the dead can for oxygen
and there is none for we are at the center
of a Black Hole a massive reversal of sleep
awake and not awake myths in disarray
language at the very root of the back-brain
ceases operating as if merely as if identity
has finally ceased to mean anything
except for Annie who must be waiting
somewhere in that labyrinth of rooms
moving through that dark maze like waters
that have settled on a lone mountain peak
waiting for hours and maybe only minutes
briefly alone with her great hair and a mirror
that reflects nothing back but a shadow
her eyes will be there and her mouth and
a cigarette always a cigarette like youth
smoking its mind out in sheer will to live
briefly alone with untranslatable thoughts
about a peninsula in Asia or a hospital appointment
not knowing how many previous lives are resident
in her or which previous life in particular
spreading like ink will seize her soul everlasting
amen it says in fine print below her fingernails
amen it says in the comb forgotten in the sink
her children will certainly come to stare
there will be no one there not *this* Annie
nor *that* Annie nor the *other* one who will have gone

up the heavenly stair into rooms empty of light
to look for compass and magnetic needle
sure that she is in that obscure place *North*

ii.

LOVESICK BODHISATTVA

beyond the expected a bodhisattva stands
penultimate among the dead statues
a signal his embossed right index finger
is there something troubling the atmosphere
where have all the automobiles gone today
his face spreads soporific in the direction
of south where Dravidian tribes paint Shiva
in glossy reds carmines vermillions
depictions of death as an abstract painting
mottled hues of celestial aspirations just
squatting there overweight eyes half shut
knows something we don't know in the middle
of the road that loses itself in the jungles
of sanskrit literature miasma of undergrowth
liana weeds sandalwood and flowers massive
dark like eye-shadow wilting in the fetid sun
doesn't look up if we question where to go
what to do how to pray lay down the body
release the soul from its anchor give up
smoking and jazz and all the other worldly
barely smiles nodding heavy with opium
his once elegant bronzed face tarnished
verdigris the hundred previous lives
have worn hard on him he seems to waver
squatting there on his heels in that dust
ochre and overrun with insects elaborate
many with wings and some just drilling
into his skin tattooed messages about *Nibbana*
for a second he extends a right arm forward
the hands weighted with expensive jewels
around his neck enormous pearls like sweat
flash momentarily it is simply the great *Ennui*
the buzz of a million oriental gods now blind
flitting between diseased trees and green-rot
sky is only a symbol a distance measured
in his drug-dilated pupils a thin blue streak
consulting our berlitz-bibles for the right phrase
we find nothing better to say than to ask
forgiveness in a dialect already lost to ears
he no longer hears everything is archaic stone

porous rock caves streams all but dried out
lizards scamper between the parentheses
that barely hold his vast body in place
noon already the stillness pallor death-hush
only a quetzal bird preening in the baobab tree
sounds its echoed mourning like heated crystal
ready to break into a pair of hemispheres
the world ! here for a minute only before
the act of total enlightenment destroys it
it was in Hotel Memory that I suffered
love's torment a single night once
and have been lost ever since

11-19/20-17

CHARLES MANSON DIES AT 83

*"hey hey my my
rock n roll will never die"
Neil Young*

"what you see is what you get"
mouthpiece of the gods !
music born of the eastern steppes
carried to Santa Monica on live wires
red hot translations of Saint John
Beast of letters and time
revelations of the never-to-come end
Fire must be addressed first
then *Blood* and the Mother of God
stripped to the bone of her sanctity
America is like this broken finger nail
my heart is in the Mojave desert
my heart is in the Mojave desert
I am the victim of illegal body transfer
wherever the prairie has flowered
I have brought *Mahabharata* !
you may strum your guitars all night
you may record your favorite love songs
you may daydream your lives away
but today as never before I transgress
all logic all sympathy all purity
forget them America ! serpents
weave their trance around my brow
sneak attack on Hollywood !
a railroad box-car will take me to *the* Music
waves lapping shattered pier-heads
dumb moonbeams salt spray *Brian Wilson* !

flower children with store bought names
I have escaped from collapsed Mid-West
I have worn orphanage on my back
I have paid no heed to Ogalala warning
there is a movie running in my eyes
about cowboys and *Svengali*
when I tell you all women are mine
I speak the Truth ! I speak the Truth !
still I am victim of illegal body transfer
heaven is the cemetery of love
animal waste voodoo powder jazz
I'm digging those good vibrations
America is jiu jitsu claustrophobia
America is bad used car deal
America is rusted knife in the back
from my command post high above
the Grand Teton I survey death
Saturday morning cartoon carnival
out of whack *Road Runner* wins !
and coyote poor coyote do you know him ?
it's President Gerald Ford that's who
the final hour has drawn nigh
something inside has gone wrong
they all look at me as though
even I were human not a monster
          nevertheless
ME CAGO EN LA MADRE DE DIOS !
"what you see is what you get"

11-20-17

BECOMING MYTH

flowers once the name of gods
whatever is beautiful running wild
grasses weeds great brush-fires
skies that rush to greet the inevitable
greens of smoke and lyres echoing
in the impossible hive of stone
or you with a summer of bees
swirling to compete with your hair
moving as flame through quartz
shifting as dawn through chaos
red to blue to undying alabaster
the stuff of statues or after-life
choose a form a shape a style
endure as Persephone underground
shades of a shade in tranquility

where only boneless shadows
tread bemoaning a memory
of light that might have been
long meadows before dusk
where small deer come to pause
before trees of the Archaic
enigma imbued in the foliage
rustling of primordial speech
giving to the darkening air
illusion of meaning and sound
what takes place on the moon
what happens in haunted shoals
to be suddenly transformed
like Daphne into an altered state
crowning atmospheres bright
radiance from another dimension
recalling almost nothing of what
it was like on the other shore
mingling of intellect and loss
you were there among naiads
shaking dew off the skin
as if vanishing with the sun's
heated legend of horses aloft
passage of unbearable beauty
giving to your being a height
a dizzying cycle of passions
becoming one with the *Other*
a recitation as ancient as thought
to become to originate to *Be*
in this instantaneous world
whirling cinema of remembrance
and oblivion a body of lives
passed from poem to poem
given over to a fragile hiatus
questions lingering texts
floral patterns inked in dreams
descending always descending
bathed in cloak of mystery
myth forever what cannot be
possessed shining irreversible
approaching but not approached
signs in the hills of an accident
a voice from the psyche of time
rock-bound sand strewn
honorific pronoun that
once engaged turns to dust

ever more distant echo
my gorgeous one ! where ?

11-21-17

"YOU CAN'T HURRY LOVE . . ."

resurfaces through tangled memories
confused years interpolated gone lost
hotels on the coast and thumbing a ride
to get past the present into a confession
that what possibly happened didn't
but the heart aches terrible megrims
wanting and wanting more than recall
allows and the recent incarnation yes
takes place third from left in radiance
a shining a bright air an intimation
that stalls the motor windows down
meadows of the imagination great
spreading miles the opening mouth
to darken a whisper a word suffices
an ear bent to the loam amazing soft
where the rush of incidents occurs
the cigarette and the photograph
with the cigarette still burning high
the upper right corner of heaven
turning sepia with years like leaves
withering brown avenues disappearing
between fast comings and goings
phone calls promises to meet again
stone abrupt cliffs sleep trying lamps
morning comes the last moment
of time or it's yesterday renewed
birds ! dynamites of fate ! is there a
secret to the immeasurable grief
that passes from life to life ?
try me again, Baby , days are
growing briefer the flame a candle
flickering at tunnel's end
when was reality ever more illusory
was matter darker and less tangible ?
mourning voices usher in the clouds
listen ! all along the Great Highway
the sound of sea-wings beating against
the enormous surf endless endless
echo of your voice across space
and then what ?

11-22-17

THE HEART IS A TORNADO

exalted One ! the heart is a tornado
exalted One ! I can no longer give
there are threads of stone there are
nowheres of sand and iris and death !
for once the dictionary that gives meaning
to words for sword and hive in *Archaic*
is at a loss trying to define *you*
exalted One ! memory is a hotel of smoke
collapsed floors and cries of dust
how is it the moon has no windows ?
there is an astral projection in my eye
there are metals growing out of an x-ray
shaking leaves ! I cannot remember why !
coming home is no longer a possibility
there are hills where thoughts are buried
intricate as the fossil fish of time
electricity has its own history
magnetic portals open up to hearing
legend and its black ivy ! *omicron*
exalted One ! you remain undefined
a thin water that has no plural
moving through parian marble
to become a statue ! night after night
the world has no identity
everything remains unexplored
exalted One ! where are the signs ?
a planet and another planet
inexplicably red revolving in the mind
I cannot be as I was before I met you
grass and evenings outside of space
there must be another way to burn !
here is the folded sleep of crystal
and beside it the *shining*
and the two thousand directions !
there must be another way into it
small hands ! the mystic palms
painted with henna and singing !
exalted One ! as I was before I met you
squatting on the curb smoking
exactly what you saw in the rubber plant
or scaling the garden wall a lizard
moving inside out of itself
skin tongue darting pupils
liquid resonance of the sun !
can you have more than five personas ?

it is all beyond my reckoning
number and its futile debate
with rain and punctuation
flowers darkening in their ocean
miasma finally of the *Known* !
exalted One ! as I was before I met you
diaphanous sandalwood of death !

11-23-17

BITTERSWEET

it's been quite a year so far
moons to the number of thirteen
all occurring in a single day
fallacies of diction and reason
was it as recent as last July
when the sky fell over your house ?
months become interchangeable
let's face it and streets and cities
monsoons coming out of August
only to boomerang back into June
how many times have I gone to the bank
just to discover a dead season
leafing through the ledgers
it wasn't the possibility of love
though I ask myself exactly
when in the month of Mercury
at what hour or minute of the day
did we transform from what we were
just instants before into what we are
now secret bodies in ideal gyres
not understanding how or why
light falls differently on the leaves
clouds impose luminosity instead
and traffic shifts at wrong angles
into a distance composed of ink
love's magnet draws metals
from across the cosmos
and the stygian stream purls
just behind the magnetic chaos
years are curtailed in brevity
of time and space into grasses
sprung up on illusory lawns
the moment you stepped
from the curb you lit up
the other side of the world
are you then a different One

than before a satellite of love
borrowing your crazy ellipse
from the erratic moon ?

there is no dawn like yesterday's
everything pulled in by a ray
this is not the way it is
this is not the direction to take
this is not life as it seems
there is only one *Other*
there is nothing but
and the great fall through
and the full sense that disoriented
there are continents of dew
there are quagmires of deceit
there are illusions and delusions
that somehow define what *is*
there is everywhere a threat
there is everywhere a
whatever you want to call it
falls apart shattered
not what was not
but what can never be
not memory of life
but memory of a dream
shower you in lotus petals
adore your lotus feet

11-24-17

THE LAKE OF THE HEART

"o mente che scrivesti ciò ch'io vidi"
Inferno, II, 8

passed through the narrow defile
more asleep than awake the dun hill
to the side seeming to fall as I stepped
into the crevice the depths that stared
before my entranced gaze all but
stifled in the dust softening remains
of the light from above how heavy
the head and the brain stunned by
all the losses and the senses dulled
keen the shift of mind gone brown
memory already a tapering glow
a thread unraveling and unseen
my hands the legend of touch of

whatever had once grazed the tips
like erasures of dirt crumbling
against invisible walls of the dream
what more beyond what abysmal
that was life a corner of rock seen
through a darkened lens a shape
seeming to sift through powders
searching for the ruin of thought
and nearby barely shimmering
the lake of the heart waters deep
reflecting nothing but night's fade
go no farther a voice of distance
a bare echo issuing from sands
weary the body plunged weightless
a shadow of lingering a whitening
emblem on the other shore wraith
beckoning a small hand a flower
promising what to wake again ?
behind where there was a city
vast incommensurate wasteland
to pass through it repeatedly
renewing shadows of opaque hope
will ever see *her* again the wan
fragile consequence of love's wager
tombstone littered with anemones
entire sky eclipsed by sun's silence
when there is nothing left to say
watching from afar the last egret
lift its lithe shadow from the surface
to disappear like a winged asterisk
how much else is there to suffer
regrets pentimento purgatorial
small skies where punctuation dies
forget everything that went before
the accident of passion in the mills
why is the asking never answered
roads overturned trees widowed
a month of four days quiescent
followed by instants of Beatrice
in reverse waiting for the motor

11-25-17

THE IDEALIZED *ANNIE*

fossil bound numbers of the pre-historic
moving adjacent houses into a ditch
pile-ups on the freeway years in length
snaking in and between the wreckage
the idealized *annie* provoking smoke
in vast rhetorical nebulae evanescent
isn't the day before supposed to happen *now* !
equivocal noons by the thousands heat
in cycles a headache posted on the wall
summoning insect tribes of lost summers
in the basement where the body should be
drinking cold dandelion wine out of
small skull shaped tumblers the ghosts
the mighty who were strewn across Europe
in the epic time of the Fourth Crusade
relate phantom narratives about *annie*
irrational and hallucinatory on a moon
nine yards round and twice as intense
can she ever be about the dancing lights
the signals and flares that monitor the cosmos
a parallax of feet and strange indentations
many and multiple her descents into chaos
or crossing the river Lethe tied up in red
her distance becomes the only Flowering
and everything else is oblivion and death
sacred vessels pouring their emptiness
into the immense craters of the Archaic
spatial representations in tiny snowflakes
solar flares like tongues of the Beloved !
the next time you ask me for a cigarette
or want a ride home in my rickety chariot
don't expect me to turn into the god Apollo
I am not one to shine lights on the opaque
mine are the bouquets dedicated to *annie*
lotus hyacinth narcissus and rose blooms
incandescent as puerperal fever high
tracing multiples of the number Zero
back into the forge where Fate is born
burning in six volcanic essences alive
and with a skin singing the infinite wave
what else but the fused and many identities
of *annie* the forsaken the street born the
intimacy of brick and mortar in a ray
and speaking to the Light and warming
in the pre-dawn supposition of the Tomb

array of lawns capsized and reverting
always into the great stellar revival
that occurs when the mind is a distant
thing an anachronism a wordless game
of shadows on the liquid walls of Hades
is it because she has nothing left to play
but the radio of all lost lyrics a shift
in the spectrum of thumb and brain
aloft she is before daybreak and there
she stays though dark takes her knees
oh *annie* when if ever ? when ?

11-26-17

SMALL HANDS SMALLER RAIN

the number fifteen is great
after fifteen thunder becomes indigo
after fifteen the mystery of lightning
opens the seven mouths of the Nile
after fifteen whatever happened in the myth
when green phosphorus took the earth
can never be translated into anything
fifteen is greater than zero by a hundred
fifteen is older than Beatrice at her death
fifteen is when music sprang from
the daughters of Memory into rain
I don't remember any cipher
more marvelous than fifteen
yet I wander in and out of the woods
looking as ever for the entrance to Inferno
somebody told me it was after fifteen
but before any following number
fifteen is when people turn into grass
sage and wild both on the slopes
waiting for the inconstant rains
to pour out of the tiny hill in the west
fifteen is never after the dance
holding tight the waist of anemones
why do we look for just anyone ?
fifteen is the mystery at the bottom of the lake
the face submerged in light
the very thing that keeps me awake
why do we think just anyone is waiting ?
fifteen and fifteen are nine hundred ninety nine !
the subtraction of any digit from its whole
is the accident of chaos
fifteen is nothing if not the stairway

that simply goes nowhere in the mind
all numbers are secret
but none more secret than fifteen
why can we not find the one we love ?
simply put fifteen is on edge
the gravel strewn driveway of life
the fifteen that never gets past fifteen
and when the gas is ended
and with it goes the remainder of sky
far to the left of the photograph
showing fifteen standing on its own
between the two angels Gabriel and the One
who can never stay still
who will never grow up
fifteen fifteen forever fifteen !
in the footfalls of Dante
do we ever get over a lost love ?
after the last fifteen
the rains smaller than hands
and the poem inside the rains
if you listen carefully you can hear Persephone
who has always been fifteen
cry out for her friends and mother
especially her mother

11-26-17

ADIOS , AMIGA

a final last full of endings some
more than others the beautiful leaves
carnage of color traced in your eye
maybe no more the stolen embrace
breathless and panic looking about
the neighborhood on edge alert
to alarms and the insane heaven
wrapped like a kerchief over your brow
come back ! up the stairs into dark
turn around ! gone into the opaque
of another day on trial all hedges
toadstools slippery dew-stream grass
rains commence their long dialogue
it's more like jazz in fistfuls wet
lopsided then sudden and eerie
noon with its fossil fish gone wrong
you can smile through it or laugh
raucous and hoarse your cigarette
waiting for the right note & BANG !

riffs on longing and smoke rings
a brace of geese in the autumn sky

11-26-17

THE FOUNT OF ARETHUSA

is Sicily to blame ? parched earth
fields overrun with weeds and parasites
the largest share of sulfur the smaller
of insect kingdoms gone to rot beneath
and herself the goddess of bucolic
a liquid narrative punctuated by light
from no known source the heavens
opening their four o'clock apertures
what hasn't been told you can guess
the optative and future modes theft
of shadows knees extending evenings
far to the right of photography &
so much like hair unwound loose
over the immense lunar shoulders
of the fountain arcadian longing
can sing bosky threnodies anon
each shepherd his own dying tells
spinning tales through grassy weave
how distance comes into being and
enormous clouds of desire roseate
centaurs approach shying from guns
what ! come to drink the translucid
with its bottoms of other worlds
staring back in trance her wounded
gaze surrounded by naiads bluish
tinted their eyes burst with asterisks
burning sites of antiquity marble foam
rushing middle seas the shores erase
and calling as from a secret abyss
poetry unravels its perfect vowels
time will speak to no one here or
myth turning dense black with ivy
skirts the shapely thigh a snake
and poisons veins invisible the high
bright a moment then and agony
performs an arena of troubled thought
horses racing to reach that noon
all hush the violent silence of time

11-27-17

KISSING DARK

who that is wonderment seizes
aching to know the voice it is
speaking large silences of time
into the waiting ear this end of
nowhere and bright again sky
washed of all its purgatories
thunder when least expected
striking the clock off the wall
heat radiating joy is why she
envelopes of later than when
sudden how evaporates air
smitten as I am by a second
why shields cover only so much
and death's tiny wrist snaps
in the middle of the reading
about the pursuit up country
beautiful fern and lattice work
sun probes and willows shaping
poetry's other bank her face
it means assuming sheets
spreading light across highs
cheek bone and the split
between hairs kissing dark
in the event of rain rising up
so many the passages written
on the back hand of water
can slip just so much paper
before fingers the opening
of music the capital of ink
and staining calligraphy red
shiny as the fire in her eye
as it takes in first the ocean
of *Being* then waves lapsing
across the greater sand of
fierce isn't it how she dances
fossil electricity moving shifts
keen through the absence
and what can I delving sleep
with a finite zero fade ?

11-28-17

THE LANGUAGE OF MADNESS

taking with her she does language
new to heights sublime the One
and efforts to reduce to a syllable
all the phases it takes to pronounce
it's all a daze excitement fornication
the pluperfect tenses of passion ovoid
sentiment of having seen everything
not just once but three times already !
as she does the twenty five dialects
of reason that is no reason at all
punctuation of the air at boiling
and the fictive noon of dead horses
still racing a career in dreams
how can the door ever open to space
if the Beyond is already behind us ?
come to me , Darling , vagabond
night with its errant red fuselage
is at the window offering cigarettes
and a ticket to the cloud circus
together we can annihilate distance
breathing will be a thing of the past
that's what I say to her who is nowhere
if not in the arcane manual of dots
here it is here and there is no there
located in the middle of zero Two !
whatever we think or say is nonsense
Brahma reclining his four big faces
watches her move in every direction
without taking a step from her shadow
Loud ! the invention of silence in echoes
Nirvana is the day before yesterday
death is just a mistaken encounter
on the street between lovers unknown
to one another if not for the Masks
she is one of them she is the Other one
which of the many can grass hide ?
jasmine is the vowel in the middle
flanked by consonants of black hair
dense and ineffable the rest is aphasia
longing for geminated yellow moons
nostalgia in the parenthesis of time
she can never be uttered correctly
who is the forgotten syntax of noise
chaos ! the repetition of chaos !
she is the fugitive vedic idiom

it's as if the Mahabharata had never
been written and Radha-Krishna !
she is the temple with forty-one doors
within there are fifteen labyrinths
but only one exit hidden forever
to learn to speak her is a Mystery
to live without her—why !

11-28-17

A SMALL COSMOLOGY

of what use is the firmament
with its millions of galaxies
glittering in the back-brain of time ?
is not all the same as nothing ?
the world satellite of the unruly sun
and moon pearly suburb of earth
what are they in the fiction of mind ?
gone ! bickering Venus bawls
wanting her Adonis back and
unspent comets rage in miasma
the cosmos is that infinitesimal
reflection in the pupil of your eye
comes and goes with sleep
waters of untold depth stirring
even as you walk unconscious
from one house to the next
in the dizzying perplex of lives
how is it you have come *here* ?
one and One are never the same
illusions of three become bright
surrounding like a halo your head
transient figure eight in shifts
taking by turns the color red
and transforming it nightly
into the enormous noosphere
which is human imagination
it is one thing to smoke a cigarette
and still another to climb the stairs
paradise is no consequence
but the ritual of unknown words
uttered hypnotically by the *Other*
first there was only sand
littering the origin of space
then as green fluttered its wings
and air became light and sound
how different *everything* became !

there may be more tomorrows
or the end may simply conclude
as soon as clock strikes midnight
you have no choice but to sing
using your hands to conduct the stars
in their fragmented yellow course
through the mysterious Beyond of fate
not ever knowing the why
the when or the wherefore
it is that you appeared to me !

11-29-17

C*R*A*Z*Y

crazy how we got this far
nothing in particular about the number
nor the signal at the end of it
nor exactly how it all added up
a voice a hand a rush of light
breath like smoke in the ear
going crazy in the small circle
zero could be a possibility forever
or the way the chord hangs deaf
from a cloud that has no sky
being crazy is the nature of the leaf
or the disorganization of the statue
absolutely formidable this mind
which is the state of flux undone
whatever can be seen is beyond sight
what is the exact and precise summer
when ciphers of grass mounted
their raft of dreams into the Bright ?
never mind that we never met
being with each other here and now
that is the delirium of a lifetime
crazy is the distance it takes
to travel from the farthest star
to the house next door the empty
crazy and more than that a door
and behind the door the bedlam
of the various and undifferentiated
voices that activate the brain
what is to know if not You ?
so it says repeatedly on the marquee
of the afternoon cinema of madness
which we frequent not together
but separately in separate lives

counting backwards from aleph to zed
until by chance in the dark
in adjacent masks we meet again
crazy that we did not understand before
that there is no going back
only a perpetual water of depths
unsounded and immutable
such as life is when least expected
a dream of fading ends

11-30-17

NIGHTINGALE FLED

"murió mi eternidad y estoy velándola"
César Vallejo

woods opaque and distant islands
with palaces of dust and the *ays* of nereids
what else is worthy of memory if the nightingale
has fled and darker still the day of rebirth
to wonders of a sky carved out of pearl
impenetrable and so far away only the dead
can understand such longing for white
great blanks of time ! out of the oracle
issue the nascent cavities of grief
each with their language of shoulders
each with their dialect of migraine
how can there be a philosophy of eternal
return a metaphysics of cloud structure
the very composition of the mind !
cages litter the dawn of earth and enormous
the shadows of all the things now gone
who is it that reiterates the passage of noon
into a twilight of vagabond afternoons
rife with lies of passion and decay
how is it that if only a minute has passed
entire years fly through the sleeper's eye
have we not come down to planet Gaia
to separate our statues and learn to speak
yet all is deaf and crowns of ash
vast assembled waters come crashing
off cliffs and reefs once the domain of light
nowhere is there a place to settle
rumor of cities built ten at a time
one on top of the other with bodies of Cyclops
consuming the fire and bricks of air
I was here once so it says in stone

and flinging my arms like wings
so what ! here and also here is a *presence*
chthonic the mystery of some vatic thought
will there be another day such as this
when loss is a victory and emptiness
what a grave error was made
when choosing between flight and breath
the sun was denied its course
plunging the vedic horses into darkness
what was it Echo cried ?
love no more the vacant form
no hands remain no heart to hope

12-01-17

A PHONE CALL

here put the little mind to rest
it was so sweet of you to call
between these roadside flowers
and the longing rain and the image
of those naked souls in a row
head bent trying to make it across
and your voice with its electricity
no amount of time can ever erase
so generous each archaic vowel
poured into the stoned ear just now
and yet these trees so near so far
do they own everything in the sky ?
put the unsettled thought to bed
let the thing in the window darken
listen next to the wild west wind
as it beats its hundred tiny hands
against the tempest of your hair
what rivers are racing underneath
where are these torrents bound
like night their swift energy disappears
in the infinite second of their passage
there are arms and legs repeatedly
asleep in the vacancy of the *Sign*
shoulder and knee tied to grief
accidents from the day before
that in casual disbelief never end
sweet of you to call across the depths
dreaming grass flowers by the inch
across the road and a body of water
where your syllable first appears
with mysterious lotuses floating

blue and red like faces haunted
by what they've seen far below
in Pluto's eerie tragic kingdom
but your call ever so sweet as earth
as the moon that clings to earth
circling enigmas in the fundament
when will the time come of *never*
when separately what we call bodies
will catch fire and turn air to *Bright* ?
your call the sweetest ever & I turn
from the present of the pronoun
that calls itself the One to the past
of the pronoun that refers to None
put then this small mind at peace
gather brief the flowers bent heads
in the wild wind whose tiny hands
like rain keep looking for your hair

12-02-17

Two crazy Poems written under the Influence of the FULL MOON

THE UNPROMISED BRIDE

whom to sing today even as earth
comes crashing around the ears
anathema to nation states !
each is the number of sand and rain
none are the ciphers that circle
endlessly the sleep of the *Other*
bow now to the incandescent form
to the shape of the sky in descent
to chant the billowing out of seas
the incessant and fragrant wind
that blows across the hidden continent
where what has never happened
will happen just one more time
marriage of the *Unseen* to the *Unknown*
the *Bride* already a rumor in Greek
a record of unwritten myth
even as the elements turn to chaos
abysmal proportions of darkness
that envelop the Body Politic
away with diplomacy and war !
the *Bride* a signal in red litmus
whose approach conveys illusion
of shadow and foreplay of clouds

let her sign in invisible ink
the peace treaty between warring gods
Minerva and Mercury and Pluto !
while what has happened just one more time
has never really happened
merely the hallucination of memories
corrupted by the dying sun
was there ever an Occident ?
oceans Yes and the great Stream
that goes round and round fictive earth
and the drowned of multiple reason
whose last will and testament
was to remarry the *Bride* unpromised
yet all is sleeping and dross
planetary accidents and delusion
houses empty of anything but ink
overflowing double and triple the effort
to return to the paradise of *What !*
she will be smoking her cigarette
she will be making out of the stairs
the enormous effigy of *D*oubt
for the many there will be no waking
but for the One the unconditional *Bride*
whom today I sing the ineffable
who walks the other side of dreams
never anything but Imagination
unpossessed and Impossible
is there a canal that divides
eternity from its hemisphere ?
that is where *she* is immense
in the distance of her hair
wild mirage at the beginning of time
whom I sing and sing and sing !

12-02-17

LOVE POEM # TRILLION AND FIFTY

it's the full moon or centigrade zed
it's the House of Hades the decline and fall
it's in the sky four hundred degrees west
and five hundred fifty degrees south
it's nowhere at all unless in stone and rock
saturdays are unusually deaf and righteous
if only there were an entrance to the tibia
it's regarded as One by the senseless
and as None by those who cannot pray
footsteps always lead inwards to the soul

arm brace and splinter folds heights of zero
bleeding from either side of the bed and
the bride of Dracula in hydrogen and sepia tint
writing this poem over and over in stanzas
polished with mercury and prussic acid
this poem with its botany of illusions
this poem with its oratory of Yes !
backwards as eyes are sleeping in this poem
anachronisms and bell-clappers shouting
symphonic variations for sand and wind
blindly forging into the epic ivy and
bacchants aroused by zippers and hinges
jovian clouds in striking shades of blue
lachrymose cellars the plaintive stain
what can compare to the poem and cenotaph
the you in the midst of the other You
and so many directions to choose
and no place to hide from insect variation
how is it to dream displaced from rhyme
and to reckon each and every verb inept
none can describe the adjective of Force
the destiny of asterisks abandoned
to the tongueless beauty of Air
everything in the poem is an exclamation !
a perpetual riot of nets and pins
silver sandals of the goddess Thetis
waters of immensities of space Beyond
rushing always rushing to evaporate
high on love potion number nine
speechless as a statue in hypnosis
a cliff or a steep or a step of gravity
only to fall forever fall away fall at last
from the leaf and its door of rust
all colors *Fffffade* away beside You
cornelian and beryl and jasper *Pearl !*
think it's over now
poem ,

12-02-17

FOREVER IS *"YOU"*

the first word that comes to mind
    is *forever*
it's in my cup of distance
in my ear that only hears silence
it's the *forever* that precedes death
next to you what can *forever* mean ?
another word is *longing*
it's in the parenthesis of light
in the breathing of the leaves outside
in the totality of the day that never comes
longing is the you of somewhere else
it may finally mean *Angelica* !
other words that follow are
rust collision cigarette mimosa lark
stairway pearl lotus heat and circle
do any of these convey your presence ?
there is only *absence* the shape of time
it never returns it never goes away
absence and only *absence* is you
formidable moon of other skies
shadows of music in roaming clouds
asterisms and the rule of logic
bent by waters where you have stepped
Muse and Nymph in *absence* only
substance is just a numbing zero
matter a philosophical *absence*
what is there to understand ?
mineral and ether and grass
what can they define if not you
being and not being in a paradise
that can never be described
it is a syllable pronounced in stone
a myth of statues in confusion
somewhere becoming conscious
and losing all sense of reality
marble hyphens ! smoke
how is it you are only *ineffable*
beyond any dictionary
a pictogram of thought
going lost in a labyrinth
forever

12-03-17

HOW THINGS STAND TODAY

in which mysterious words take on
even more mysterious meanings
were I to take you into the secret hold
enigmas and a darker music a history
of sand intricately engraved in light
would the artifact of breath take new form ?
trembling beneath your skin a rosary
of burning pearls to remember this
confusion and your face emerging
from a dream where memory combines
with smoke a morning later after time
has been dissolved in a red powder
would anything else matter ?
except for *you* shimmering mirage
distance like a raiment of ether wrapped
around your shadow and what speaks
moving as a spirit of light on the sea
immense notions of space and darkness
would anything else matter ?
how can you be explained ?
at first there was a casual imbalance
of geographies and mountains shaking
rivers arrested in their sleep
a myriad of voices beckoning the heavens
to yield their porphyry moons
shedding somehow a luster on your face
issuing from the cigarette briefly lit
between your fingers in a story
about incomplete stairways and heights
what a complex of emotions !
nothing can ever be the same after you
there are densities of shoulders
& weeping in the sidereal corners
there are vacancies on planet Pluto
and homophones of the sun and its satellites
that can never be rightly comprehended
there is finally a single illustration
of the remotest ocean giving birth
and tempests of flame and isolation !
the heart is only so big !
the rest is a simple footnote
to the day I met you

12-04-17

THE LAST TROJAN WAR

set old Priam in the four-wheeled cart
a herald at his side and god Hermes
disguised as a strapping youth and down
to the shore where the hollow-bellied ships
listed waiting for the call to pull anchor
Achilles in his tent brooding over Patroclus
so the movie version would have it //
the menacing dark breakers surf high
how many troubled flitting the souls
gone greaves splintered left as carrion
birds of omen and mangy curs scrabbling
for the remains // Hecuba grieving
out of fifty sons nineteen left then those
too especially Hector for nine days
his corpse left intact despite all efforts
Achilles mean spirited dragging it
round and round the tumulus where
his lover lay buried and Athena and Zeus
and Poseidon quarreling and bitter
the winged words // didn't they fly
like spirited ants darkening the air
mottled as faces sullied with tears
flowing non-stop down the unfinished page
a classicism coming to be marmoreal
yet riddled with defective gods Yeah
the verse stuck and stopped here
and there lacunae dreaded silences
where circumflex accents crashed down
on the littered sands *"you animal"* // a
painting in the air a shattered cloud a
vexing oracle to be wounded finally
the shoulder or ankle or the hip released
from grace the untimely // -stant echoes
adrift as far as Mycenae the lion stone
threatening tragedy
. . . arise ! the my ancient a hose spraying
Asia in a minor key the tortoise shell
origins of the Lyric   !?   // as
such see 'em crawling under cannon fire
skies burst open the awesome
yellow and crimson ampersands !
imagine just *imagine* Kassandra raving
on the steps // armed with the strength
of illusion sword spear javelin *Boomerang* !
swinging red-eyed his bloody ax *"you animal"* !

vomited all night long the young men //
it is never the next day only dust the
pulverized sun struggling with the reins
gone awry the cosmos from its Ionian beach
and Dawn bleary unfocused from a bed
of drunken squalor // who will inscribe
these banknotes with honor cataloging
names the lost without purpose and
the brassy sky tumultuous with //
Diomedes and Ajax and
// silence filtered through stone
"She who sits astride the waters"

12-05-17

FORGET YOU ?

forget you ? how could I forget you
having enumerated the hundred cities
of Crete and flown the Aegean posthaste
to raise the banner above the rock
where did you put your Name ?
we live from secret to secret
on the banks of the River Lethe
there are no days at all only hours
a fleeting passage through the minute
that follows the destruction of Chronos
we reveal ourselves in *Signatures* !
yours is the one in flowing red
sleep ! an angel with immense wingspan
hovering over the clepsydra whispers
how will you get up again and walk !
step back from the Waters and breathe
if just once to accept the rushing Air
three concentric circles seven heads
and ten crowns ! everything is Gone !
first there was echo and its grammar
of grass and foliage and dewfall
then you took a step through plurals
issuing from a legend of trees and cliffs
smoking in the midnight of day
brightest in the whorls of noon
where the primordial sea eddies
its dark steeps in fictions of antiquity
be brief ! the pink coral of your feet
and your intermittent shoulders and
the lark interposed in the sigmas of your hair
how many things are not to forget

and the street became a chasm
and the automobiles went plunging down
and with them so many souls *the Night !*
cataplasm and vertebrae and madness
wheel yet to be invented and bay leaf
to chew and chew until sightless
the renewed *anima* sees again what
Apollo promised in the book of winds
still you have gone lost in the woods
astray a murmur in stone a small print
like the hands of summer in their heat
dissolving as ever into the azure
but forget you ?

12-05-17

ΈΚΤΟΡ

brought back to the city midst great wailing
and of the women especially the moaning
not dust-caked his slain flesh but all dewy
fresh as the first morning of spring yet dead
he lay on the cart drawn by mules up hill
across the river Xanthe whom Zeus sired
and through the massive stone gates
even of Helen bewailed she who twenty
years now of Alexandros illegal bride
would he had been slain instead yes of
Helen too bemoaned bawling her eyes out
darkness instead of victory and Andromache
widowed of bed and pained to the quick
mourning as well their ill-fated son whom
she foresaw tossed like a dog from the walls
how she made moan and high pitched her cry
like the color red staining the night sky
enough to make even Hermes turn his back
for who knows what wind would fill the sail
taking her across the waters a slave
swiftly and Kassandra vying in beauty with
Aphrodite   smoke raving mad
stomping on the oracular step mind-spent !
many the men whose fathers brothers sons
he had slain now waiting to take aim
great and smoldering the ruins
and of Hecuba's fifty sons by far the dearest
so tender even to Helen was he in the
now shadowy palace
Hector you was so good to me

```
                        cigarettes and moons
littering the deserted beach
                   rings of fire remote high
and dawn           the fade
                         their masts waving
in the furious         ships
                 stolen girls
ransomed and slandered and abused
War !           for nine more days and went
to the woods to gather kindling for the
pyre and over much the populace wept
their cheeks ruined with tears

separated the white bones from the still hot ash

              incense clouds
```

12-06-17

STATE OF EMERGENCY

"e vidi dietro a noi un diavol nero"
Inferno, XXI, 29

in name only silence the frequent and
we stop at thirteen and is the girl
still a woman behind her plural hair
or is she in wife only a substance
a vagabond consonant in disguise
rising to the occasional heights
at the top of the ladder to smoke
remembering dimly the horizon
that once was earth's last boundary
sequence of fading red vowels
who will save her from the daily skin ?
to resume pushing the limit past
fourteen and inches away from hell
shopping for cosmetics and lingerie
meant for a goddess she filming
herself in an attitude of despair
can that be anyone I want to know ?
the phone comes into being ringing
off the wall and all that jive
her voice a jazz of foggy distance
hello vulnerable pliant saddened
painted air sailing through her eye
it all adds up to forty three years
eighteen months and a hundred zillion

days ! time the multiple thief of knees
counting backwards the thermometer
at zero degrees centigrade blows !
bringing her back down one by one
from clouds of passionate oblivion
until at street level she imposes
a shadow of regret and longing
on passing traffic headed for where ?
come on , Baby , the signals are off
red is not green nor yellow the high
you expected wearing that syntax
wrap-around eye shade magnificent !
tomorrow is a microphone or a migraine
a doctor's visit to the crematorium
to watch a polyvalent childhood
incinerate with its nails and violins
smoke ! hidden mirrors a secret life
poems received daily like explosions
or tickets to the hair-dresser of paradise
I know *her* now idiom and breezes
taking by surprise the earthly surface
underneath all is labyrinth and stone
whispers *I love you* in sixteen languages
touching for just an instant eternity
that hour long month of existence !

12-06-17

ASLEEP AT THE WHEEL

what is it about You ?
always the question that can't
be answered the hair-style the
what is it that I can't stop it
thinking doing saying dreaming
about You incessant paradigm
flowering in the back brain
as if plural heavens bursting
could reveal anything Real !
your voice ? the terrible distance
separating Thursday from Sunday
and all the infinite in betweens
there is no addition or subtraction
there is no punctuation between
the stars no guidelines for falling
from Midnight all the way down
to the incessant daily grind
who can say why You were invented

why You came to be up *There* ?
listen ! can we put an end
to the calendar of months ?
suppose there are fifty moons
a week and every moon
has its only hour and the minutes
don't exist either nor *this* year !
when was the first curbstone ?
where was the cigarette burning ?
instead of a shadow You
there are many others of You
but only One without a shadow !
myth of forgetting to Be !
legend of the telephone in love !
OK , Baby , it's just a make believe
thing a suppose I don't exist thing
a forever idea about You thing
and afterwards all the ruins
on the way home the broken
the wrecked the ravaged everything
why can't I get it straight
you're just a bunch of syllables
sent through a wire into eternity
and me ? I'm the *dot dot dot*
of a secret code for the insane
trust me ! I don't know anything
about YOU !

12-07-17

MORTALITY

I remember the tomb
and being in the tomb
being born in the tomb
and Joe was there too
it began to snow on the hill
it began to be cold and still
darkness could be felt
like an old damp quilt
wrapped around shadows
who was talking never clear
who was taking us forth
what day it was winter
and the first light to see
the other things indistinct
the café across the street
and the tomb left behind

but never out of sight
walking to learn and speak
at least two languages
one of the dead who live
far to the south in jungles
the other of the living
who claim the sky
but can never possess it
left the tomb but never
for long and the light
like a drizzle at dawn
seeking to sense the shapes
the moment of silence
the Loud and being !
how many days it was
they were shifting
the bread and the shoulder
the way to become Big
certainly years were nothing
before we went back
to the tomb Joe first
and I just waiting

12-07-17

UNBEARABLE

the wind has blown the moon away !
Muse ! that's my mind being erased
and Dawn has yet to rein in her horses
life the unbearable moment of light
coming to be and in a trice vanishing
forced to live and breathe and take
the consequences as they come rushing
what is a poem in the imminent dark ?
what is love most tender in face of night ?
Muse ! what speaks in the grass archaic ?
is stone itself a record of time ineffable ?
leave us this break in the relentless hour
to involve if briefly the heart in its fade
of sweet illusion and grief and yet and
abrupt the cliff and steep the waters
roiling in the starry wake we yearn
to drown heedless of the cloud-sent hand
angels of marble and blind in their descent
shatter as well in torment of surf and wind
is it a dream we shared that faint escapade
when light filtered through the salty air ?

lip to lip the taste of eternity in a sigh
what was the Trojan war in that failing ink ?
driven by wild passion of paper and leaf
all of space seems to open its schisms
Dante and Vallejo each with adjectives
burdened on shoulders of plangent humanity
come and go on the apocalyptic screen
flashing instantaneously behind or beyond
whatever film of light keeps rolling deep
sigma and tau and houses of omicron
Muse ! what brain in my flawed memory
keeps reciting the daily verb of inaction ?
come then you and I into this missive
to write what has never been heard to say
mouths in search of paradise in havoc
swell the boundless waves surfing higher
than thought can bear the *Unbearable*
of every passing moment swiftly darker
than the day before if shining metals
have their sway and plunging
how can this poetry
there is so little left
and smoke and
ethereal
sublime
the

12-08-17

YOUR VOICE IN THE LEAF

it was a voice a remnant of sound
echoing from some distant fragment
of unfinished words of an oracle
or was it only you on the other end
of time solitary vagrant like Persephone
was it grass having a dizzy spell ?
did the stone's spinal nerve ache ?
leaf that trembled in my hand
torn from its language and sobbing !
so much memory in that single syllable
broken in its half and weeping in its other
woods labyrinthine and soundless !
you hidden there amongst vowels
that cling to fragrant spring breezes
yet goes round and round the hiatus
the punctuation that separates life
from life and budding in the consonant

the sound that makes *red* resound !
I know you must be in there crying
into the phone of random poetic matter
chords unraveling rays of light
clouds burst in the sleeping inner ear
rains and more rains and a sky !
listen as I might to that shaking green
reading in the weaving twisted veins
a text of silence and misapprehension
to bring you out of that hyphenated spell
to give you shape and form of light
whole as a depth of immobile water
your voice your song your heights
no longer enigmatic & incomprehensible
but clarity of mind bereft of thought
mystic resonance of the Unseen
beside me at last the untouched Soul
the body of the body without shadow
in my hand the trembling leaf
the transformed *You* tears like rivers
furrowing the continent of myth
and memories of the Moon !
but your voice torn leaf trembling
in my hand whispering lotus
no end to the silence

12-09-17

BRIEF HISTORY OF THE ORIENT

begins with a discourse on the vanities
the body no resilience the effort to be
despite the obstacles of air and silence
later when the stone effigies rise and walk
moving as through curtains of light
fragrances too wafting from sandalwood
an incense stick held in the opposing hand
delicacies woven in the flowing hair
a model of skin in an attitude of prayer
somewhere to the south of Mount Meru
nothing can ever be completed neither word
nor full sentences nor syntax carved out
of pure nothing happening along the route
where silk and the damp pressures of sight
come along with me it says underneath
the enormous bell-like pagoda of the ego
intimations of sky rubrics of sand and silt
a city perhaps or a mahogany engraving

pictograms for *eating sleeping dying*
put another way details that elude the eye
deafening resonance of temple bells dust
dusk din dumb as the elephants erect
on their passive margins trumpeting a
way to heaven a way out of the shape
of becoming and yellow lattice work
and immense cave paintings full-breasted
the women bearing fruit and deep pools
in their eyes and who will bed with them
coming to the other world of darkness
underneath all that solitude and longing
kissing and the hot breath of smoke
issuing from the profundities of the One
a palm leaf inscription ages long and
with instructions about living in hell
at peace with the deceptions of time
come be with me it says on the edges
where the waterfalls embroider sleep
and ice and other exotic commodities
dreaming it is never the hour to wake
learning and unlearning the script
where it is written with a scent of cloves
that all beings are united in living rock
and later on still when the airplane
and the telephone connect illusions
the continent will finally shift off its axis
and slide into a ghostly netherland
unburdened any longer by desires
and with whom will I then spend
a life in the hotel of merciful death ?

12-09-17

THE HIGH HOLY DAYS

laughter in the labyrinth high as winter
in the Bermuda triangle *I'm in love*
a votary of all the goddesses whose
names begin with Alpha the casual
stoned and beatified walking avenues
that refuse to exist and tip my head
to the plate glass shrines tiny Buddhas
they're all in love too especially today
in honor of the holy sky and the clouds
and grasses that levitate longing for
yes just longing for and on my knees
I kiss blessed cement & its chalk circles

orange and puffy brown and yellow too
listen for the wind rush out of the sewers
and magnificent trees palm and banana
rising out of the manholes and traffic
mechanical automated digitized running
like steam over the imagined populace
shopping for holidays that have no name
puzzled that there are no more stores
just torn magazine pages fluttering
like leaves in the dry ochre wind of *love*
where is there to go anyway ? to the lake
to the place where sixteen swans gather
or where ants ruled by terrible *Minos*
who judges all manner of dead underground
parade licking their sweet evil mouths
how marvelous it can be all of the cosmos
once it's tilted totally askew and empty
for emptiness is the condition of the *All*
even today I wander lost with as a guide
a language manual that asks questions
for me when I get to the street corners
and no one else is in sight but for shadows
imperious irreverent elusive deceitful
who never give the right answer since they
have no body ! where is *Annie's* house ?
and the air points everywhere but two
large hands the shape of thunder Boom !
deafened by this knowledge I reel
transformed into a circle of zeroes
I can never go there or forget ice cream
and steak sandwiches and candies
green as traffic lights and sundered from
the whole I list an island forlorn and
desperately trying to recall the why of it
the purpose of waking and walking out loud
talking to myself in dream rotundas
yes and yes again because in a minute
the phone will ring and the invention
of *Annie's* voice laughing in the labyrinth
will teach me to fly higher than ever
into the irreducible azure
into the vanishing point
into nothingness
Zapped !
I'm in love

12-10-17

RAY OF LIGHT

radiant as are these final days
no money can buy nor eloquence
diminishing the fine light that
keeps us anchored to some small hope
as if the histories of Florence and Pisa
or the recondite painted shields
of Homeric myth could buoy us
for still another new year one fraught
with world anxieties and polar melts
raging fires and decimated cities
if you but accompany me
through this shadowy earth-time
into some other dimension into
the pleasure dome or Pandemonium
where poetries large and small
diffuse and unintelligible only heighten
the delirium it is being one another
inside and out upside and down
how many persons are possible ?
is there a limit to the amount of sky
it takes to create an eye ?
look all around at the oncoming dark
how it enlarges whatever is hidden
the heart's small tom-tom POW !
and besides that what is there to take
from the void other than a ray of light
sliver of moon shaking in its ague
take the gold out of gold !
absence is just the reverse of space
what's to mistake about vanishing ?
masks dancing in an invisible ballroom
yearning to know what's behind
who's the one smoking tempestuously
why in charades riddles remain unanswered
Sphinx ! you are mine forever
later when time wearies of its dust
and only a few scant days
left to the once Roman Empire
Tiberius ! Saint Helen ! Caligula !
where does that find us ?
as ever one to one in a missing house
nerve and episode of hiatus
lingering and longing to replace earth
with a higher order of lyricism
odds are we'll never make it

to the next traffic signal
so much aching in the distance
between here and now
immortal as that may be !

12-10-17

RENUNCIATION

renounce you , Baby , in the shopping mall
in the place where you try on shoes
those bright red ones with five inch heels
enough to kill a guy for sport !
not for a million bucks would I keep you
for another day not the way you wear
that hair a thousand miles long
the size of ink and twice as deadly
and another thing , Baby , that phone thing
you keep buzzing around your head all day
those voices actually talking loud
inside your Brain ! jeezus how many
are there and are they really gods ?
who can compete with that ?
homophones of sun and moon your eyes !
and that cigarette , Baby , enormous
smoking for days on end invisible
skyscraper of white paper and ash
do your lips really caress *it* ?
what about the vows and the small craft
warnings and the isometrics ?
prodigious landscapes of tombstone
incomplete statuary of the living dead !
if I had another day to live
would I spend it with you , Baby ?
where do you keep your thighs ?
how much time does it take
to put those Byzantine hoop earrings on ?
plethora of fingernail polish
and just whom have you put in those ashcans
if not the cosmetics salesmen ?
come on , Baby , admit it love's
a small commodity on sale at Christmas
and remaindered for almost nothing
after the Persian new year
how can you expect to wear it
as if it was a hub-cap for the head ?
because you employ the hyphenated
vocabulary of sleep-walkers does that

make you a miracle of post-modernism ?
inches go by and the weeks still lack
a full Sunday not to speak of the months
out of synch with the Mayan calendar
yet you keep gazing into the mirror
expecting the year to end !
I paid an acre of rhododendrons
and took you off the auction block
I paved the street in front of your house
with jasmine and agate and ampersands
and you still haven't learned to speak European
mistaking Etruscan for Basque !
renounce you ? why should I keep
this window and not that window ?
where do you hide that legendary waist ?
after during and before the flood
what did I see in you ? Bang !
isn't this America oncoming traffic
on all four lanes ! Boomerang !
this is it , Baby ! tomorrow will be
no different except for the fires
the ones eating up the coast line
blocking our escape route to the Dead
how will we ever come to terms
not with one another but with
the heavenly stair ? cinders and azure
renounce you ? how ?
drowning in the pool of your eyes
depths unperceived lapis lazuli
and infinity going on and on

12-11-17

THE POEM IN YOUR EYE
IS THE POEM I CANNOT READ

since the last time things have what ?
calmed down turned blue grown dim
a slender stalk weaving wavering
between verses of silent starry
you'd guess a world has changed
burning as ice does in the far north
or galactic upheaval in its month
with fishes electric and distant
penetrating the recesses of your eyes
seeming to be then to disappear
flashing indistinctly something bright
alone along the last dusty path

whenever that was and you at the
top of the steps turning once
bending to send a kiss wayward
into the lost morning air the shine
of fade dun the wasting hills erode
sun's ancient flame scrolling light
how once the flowers blended grief
their passing majesty a wan relief
colors run into loam like small rain
grown grey in its long solitude
nor echo of beyond the circling arm
around the incorporeal shape love's
immense but shadowy existence
longitudinal tragedies written deep
in the soul's vacant hemisphere
a wonder that what I can read
is not what I see before me nor ever
wasn't that a time when first looking
you proposed a heavenly ritual
mouth to mouth breathing sky
a thousand seconds in an instant
the letters of the Greek alphabet
seemed to fly forming clouds of words
nebulae and cosmic meters drumming
across the background of the invisible
if another day comes imperturbable
non-existent hourless immeasurable
gazing even deeper into the anima
taking shape without hands way
back there in the depth of your pupils
realms of insuperable longing
how much between each shoulder
is there of the indefinable You ?
waking if there is to be a second time
if the script has not become disorganized
coming back to earth in a statue
searching for vestiges of memory
sure that we were both here before
in front of this ruin of thought
will what I once saw in your eyes
return as a reflection a shadow
aching water of decomposed words
fluid chaos of mortal desire
blank !

12-12-17

THE SOUL ITS SHADOW
& ITS OTHER

on the fringes of life
where deepest the cut
        of experience
the soul emerges puzzled
by the abacus of light
does light go hand in hand
        with shadow ?
is there somewhere else
        to go ?
look at the picture book !
map after map of the body
great contours called *love*
special bays and valleys
hills rising from nowhere
the sun in its orient !
the sun in its occident !
where else is there to go ?
shadow eclipses shadow
light devours the moon
entire nights without life !
only the immensity of space
the egregious encounters
of body and body : *You*
everything is an enigma
grass and the absence
        of grass
soul wants to elope with body
shadow wants to eat more moon
legend and myth : *Mountains*
caves grottos Nymphs !
soul is in everything it seems
and body is only a dream
shadow a derelict of reason
detached swiftly from matter
great is the water of Being
where all finally drown
faces assuming faces
        of the *Other !*
coming up for air
and sky eternally missing
and azure the color
        of the soul
and hematite and gorgeous
relics of temple deities

marble and tufa and weed
how is it *You* are abandoned?
neither east of the shadow
nor west of the *Other*
somewhere in between
where the soul emerges
dazzled by the abacus
        of Light!

12-13-17

YOUR VOICE

it must be your voice
I can't think of anything else
that captures the stellar dusk
the quietly approaching haze
at the end of twilight winding
down over the distant seas
beyond which Hesperian hills
quench their color in dim ochre
your voice the siren's echo
the net caught in the massive
damp hair of the nymphs
the cradling resonance of grottos
the inescapable hint of sound
in the mountain peaks of night
or the unremembered words
of someone behind a screen
in the midst of a court dream
about fluted silks that talk
and amber poured into urns
afternoons in the quiet
of an island lost from its moorings
beddings and tapestries soft
silencing unwanted rumors
of affairs and siege-works
dust storms aroused in the ear
lips murmuring against lips
in the deathly hush of love

12-14-7

CONNECTED

what does it take ? the human eye
reaching into distances no shoulder
can imagine no hip nor arm no ear
as far as the hidden waistline on shores
sand burning remotes no face shaped
out of airs and oriental steam afar
beyond the beyond where song roots
and the human voice becomes angelic
sublime nor thigh can foresee nor
knees redundant in their continents
nor stepping out of depthless waters
the body composed of whispers and
grass and the never before felt heat
that circulates when the brain is asleep
is there but one body ? and one eye
and one horizon coming into contact
with the other horizon the invisible one
and beneath the sentient zone and the
furthermore who can say what relates
who connects to whom in the labyrinth
where the body dissolves into the body
and nothing remains but a history of light
syntax of enigmas if one can remember
what it was suddenly standing in fire
pounding in the ear a distant thunder
a summer of lapses and lightning
being and not being in the *Round*
the great circle where the disconnected
joins itself to hemispheres of gold and ash
and the Soul emerging from the hiatus
strives to regain the one body which
is the other body the one inhabited by you
can you remember why ? the human eye
takes in what it can of light and space
connecting what will never be touched
with the enormous error of consciousness
just so this morning you appeared
a nimbus of powders and gloss and hair
months collapsed into a single hour
and the hour itself but a grain of sand
falling effortlessly into the place
where eternity connects with never
you and you again connected to all
the infinities of your burning Asia

and I on your four margins connected
as never before to the *Unknown*

12-15-17

SILVER BULLET

more fleet than an ampersand of mercury
mind and its unbridled horses of thought
imagining you the silver bullet racing
to find a heart to wound mortally a bliss
a location in the center of the outside of time
a space replete with icons of the *Invisible*
multiple the identities of the Unborn !
silver bullet in its trajectory of passion
derelict and mordant aiming for the vein
that leads in and out of the human summer
heat and the puzzling cycles of its month
the unrepeatable sequence of a day inside
the Only day that can possibly be !
what is it about gunshot in the ear ?
powders red and fulminating scattered
across the universe of the unseen Eye
here is the star of the afternoon lesson
here is the other star the sound of distance
glitter of jewelry in the brain's bric-a-brac
where do all roads go if not to Hell ?
there are houses without rooms only Light
darkness in the keyhole of the Unknown
silver bullet puzzled as to where to go
where to shift in the luminous never
that proceeds from the first of August !
Speed ! illusion of Inaction ! intangibles
skin which has no property and song
musk and opium jazz of the Nymphs !
silver bullet ! silver bullet ! silver bullet !
hyphens indestructible and perpetual
one says you're mine two says you're
Ecstasy and three says you're *Nowhere*
what if yesterday was just a decibel
away from the music of the Spheres ?
there is a small hiatus between moon
and its absent hemisphere wherever
that is in the silent oceans of Being
everything is silver ! the story of Helen
pre-Socratic philosophies of Ionia
unspeakable information about Breath

and the ever enigmatic duet of the Soul
two says you're Ecstasy !

12-15-17

                    "Io sono Aglauro che divenni sasso"
                            Purgatorio, XIV, 139

rock now one thousand years
rock now one thousand years
painted to match heaven's bright
the yard where pass courtesans
of brilliant hues ageless as diamond
skin the reflection of archaic water
rock stone sand bluff and steep
faces like a dream of knives
entering repeatedly curtains of ink
voices wildly fluorescent behind
where gods scheme for mortal wives
bayonets of lust knuckle bone dice
carpets as large as the city of Troy
silence deceit massive underground
that honeycombs the nascent mind
who is sleeping these thoughts
who is unable to wake to lamps
hanging like mimosas overhead
and the chatter of priceless insects
ribbing of flutes and drumheads
dripping faucets carmine fluids
who is turning in a bed of words
unspoken in hiatus hyphenated
dead as the verse of unknown bard
carved in gravel runes and daggers
magnificent beauties ready to embrace
who is drugged for life and raving
remembering just once the Other
silk and velvet gold and amber
umber traces in ochre hills afar
echo and echo again the dim return
syllables vast and empty thundering
alone ! miasma and torment of seas
draining all color from vacant sky
monotony of life ritual & statues
still and faceless on quarry's edge
pick me up ! hold me ! haunt me !
who face down in his own distance
struggles to revive a phantom self

shimmering eddies a gone mirage
whoever she was ! whoever she was
rock now one thousand years
rock now one thousand years

12-16-17

CIRCE TODAY

and as for You lotus blossom
impoverished relic of water
dancing in your plural shadow
either blue or definitely red
Circe of city streets
no island yours nor groves
of dark enchantment seething
how many nights unslept in You
dreaming other worlds of smoke
stairs and curbstones goddess
in other names a form shimmering
within the daily animal
text of undecipherable runes
distant body of the *Invisible*
section by section of a sky
carved out of mutilated rock
whatever language you use
the ink has run dry
over its phonetic decay
made savage by your mile-long hair
you remain beautiful as a cloud
becoming big with rain
purple darkening the west
with concupiscent shades
imminent drizzle and longing
impermanent as dew on stone
what muzzles come to lick your feet
what transformations of being ?
to be indifferent to You ?
drown the soul first !
weeks mount to years and years
become ageless eons of light
still the daily animal
suffers its daily death
dog stag boar and sparrow-hawk
the woods teem with their spirit
leaves once the voice of women
trees the bodies of so many !
come to your mansion as I do

seeking hearth and home
You I find multiple and absent !
dangerous and lunar your essence
invades the darkest thoughts
mortal equivalents of space !
nothing is to be considered
nowhere to go and die
in love with the archaic You
bewitched by the *inevitable* You !
endlessly circling the summer
inhabited by You
wondering when the next time
                       will be

12-16-17

VERTIGO

it is a world of *this* lying down
with *that* not the world at all
some twigs a path leading nowhere
other branches leafless dangling
out of nowhere it is not *that* world
talking as if it were not talking
taking a path nowhere to a
place that is not there at all
some grass tufts weeds a ravine
snow filled or not just a melting
we have just met and are going
to meet again the next time you will
be me and I will be no one again
when we meet is it tomorrow ?
force of habit creates illusions
matter and non-matter that fill
voids when we meet the void will
cease to exist if it is yesterday again
look at the sky abrupt as it is a
piece of painted concrete with
clouds floating fleecy white mirage
suffering it to be and to become
within and without us you and
I again on the edge of the world
of suffering because we are aware
being born and growing and sense
of things all around us coming and
going disappearing to sleep alive
in dreams only the same as dying
next to each other the light at

first small and the motion of
air as we move on the precipice
you will alternate being me and
hold my hand and touch stone
moving beneath and the abyss
which is being conscious below
the mind as it suffers itself to be
looking at me you are and I am
looking at you each with eyes
redundant with light will you
reach out into the light then
will things come into view beside
one another it is dying to know
or simply dying having known
who is *this* and who is *that*

12-17-17

annieannieannieannieetcetera

how many times annie and how often
the same annie is in and out just
as fast as speed of light a maze
of annie in hair and robe and skin
appearing in morning mask of annie
repeated as a solar spear repeats
itself in the lake beside annie
or is it another annie beside another
lake repeating its annie in a ripple
eddying out to the sea behind the
mountain in the middle of the city
where the so many of annie go shopping
in windows of fruit and lobsters and
tins of sardines in oil that annie
marvels isn't it annie on the steps
annie with a cigarette with more
than one cigarette the smoke in
curlicues spelling annie high in the sky
where the annie clouds gather fuming
for storm of annie and rain and large
blasts of air that shake the city of annie
so many misunderstood and punctuated
annie on the phone or in the dark
metaphysical and beautiful without
make-up or waiting for the doctor's
report and the science of annie
which is a puzzle annie crying or
that great laughter and gathering

light and the scheme of history
winding down into bare rock annie
with or without music in pink
absent as always of annie where
to present a new annie next to
yesterday's annie or the version
in the poem about her voice or
the one about her hair remember ?
annie could not be other than
annie the drifting skin the lift
into heaven on broken levers
just an inch from the paving where
in small pools annie's face recalls
a dream a system of sleep in red
and the waking annie in a density
of time on other planets where
the unknown annie strikes a pose
annie is epic poem in two syllables
is an invention is fever is annie
duplicated multiplied intensified
moonstruck annie whatever cannot
be defined is annie enigma and zero
cipher reduced to cipher minus
annie et cetera annie in trance
annie singing doo wop doing
astrophysics annie just about
anything including mind theft
crazy annie can't get her out
of my annie mind

12-18-17

THE NEXT TO LAST LOVE POEM

quantum mechanics ! universe atilt !
wherever you look the egress but not
the entrance and the cinemas of flame
the unending nights off the screen
hand in hand lovers entranced by
what death has to offer by way of steam
sugar-skulls and woven grass crowns
everything is forbidden ! telephones
cigarettes stairways prayers ! ha !
do lovers go underground deathless
realms snaking streams of pure smoke ?
princess is walking in the fourth dimension
her shadow needs a fix *anger !*
where oh where is lover boy in this mess ?

labyrinthine conjectures as to light
windows boarded up by gods of envy
princess is a siren whose voice melts wax
smoldering her face burns through *space*
love is a tango love is nuclear fission
love is derailment of the mind !
don't ask for reason don't ask for truth
love is a blazing lie a false concept
a detail in the unwoven fabric of air
love is the language of sediment and vermin
love is a failed socialist state
something you never want to go back to
unless it's to see princess one more time
walking that fourth dimension blues
love is mania for electrical outlets
love is Money ! love is desire to Lose !
princess don't care she's on the prowl
up and down the effigies of time
moving as a wind out of Purgatory
over rocky recesses and abysses
dark otherness encountered Once
love is certainly not Poetry !
love is a limit to breathing
a fingerprint in concrete illusion
cosmic dissolution ! Nothingness !

12-19-17

THE LANGUAGE OF DISTANCE

at a distance it keeps being this thing
and if I am talking to you through *it*
if there is jazz and morse code vibrating
across the long distance wires what *if*
is it a matter of principle that I envision
you as the hiatus between worlds lost
and forsaken drowned or boomeranged
across the eons of language to hear *it*
beatific syllables words half formed
like hands emerging from clouds soft
without contours yearning to hold *if*
only once the imagined you a realm
of enigma hair and nail polish moving
as vowels move between classical statues
at a distance greater yet mineral and animal
symbols dotting the remote heights *if*
mountains could be identified or lakes
elevated by levers to the seventh heaven

where music is born in a great silence
pushing back from Olympus and Ida
waiting for gods of eye and light to appear
or the errors of planetary systems *Bang !*
you sleeping dense in a hive of asterisks
a dumbfounded whirring in the left ear
why don't you wake and talk to *it*
or even farther down the line before time
or the uses of electricity or steam mills
is a section of air dedicated to you ?
are there formulas for evoking phantoms ?
is there a place in the distance of distance
where the past becomes a single unit
a red equation inside a clepsydra ?
of all the burning worlds which is yours ?
all possible means to summon you
have been exhausted & you are still *it*
fragment of door that opens to infinity
speaking in enormous monosyllables
to the multiple and non-existent beings
who come and go in the fiction of mind
++++++++++++++++++++++++++++++
once , a long time ago
at the top of the celestial stairway
you , radiant and speechless silhouette

12-20-17

THE LAST MUSE

or else there is nothing absolute
not even the sky with its running texts
of endless enigma nor for that matter you
iridescent for the moment in your see-through
being breathing like glass waiting for reflection
a symptom of grace the twist of your mouth
coming to terms with the deity of absence
you are there and not there a plenitude
of puzzlement unsure of the following
minute's chaotic future a metal of
red fragments making air a sudden
and opposite element a silence louder
than the crashing of distant planets
in the dream of an ear immersed in sand
whatever else it is and the possibilities
can only open up vistas of sea torments
of mountains capsized in arms of dust
what else ? plains leveled by locusts

devouring earth's countless punctuation
while you disturbed by so many errors
in time and space where do you turn ?
is it because they never gave you a mask ?
what is the proportion of grass to distance ?
will there be a last time to cancel doubts ?
running over the histories of other worlds
nothing really seems to make sense
comets perpendicular moon-shifts bright
orange constellations reverted to mineral
myth and grapheme like signatures etched
in the ruined statuary of an incomplete epic poem
the one I was writing to you in my sleep
you appeared as the Muse the very last one
on the precipitous margin of a page
that has been erased from the chronicles
everything else now is a fade a phantom
letter in an occident sunk in its own disease
you emerge as a footnote a hint an ampersand
speaking some kind of Egyptian remote
yet gorgeous in the desert winds
that come rushing out of the vortex
doors open and shut then darkness
surrounds you disappearing
into a desert of lost voices

12-20-17

THE POEM

to write a poem the poem to you
three parts passionate one part longing
take the body and shift it out of space
the poem begins only when time annuls
itself by fifths a modality of sublime
when you become the inspiration and
the only reason and then the body
out of time as well and elevated
by glass ropes into spheres of music
that can never be heard you lean over
and through the poem even before
it is written or thought of or conceived
you not only are the poem but also
what it is not an exercise in annihilation
covered with hyacinth and jasmine left
out on the street overnight to gather
moon and scraps of star and early
warnings about the poem to be written

as if it were excess of emotion of blank
madness clouds wild episode of aromatics
air and nebulae spinning around words
to bring together to compose to arrange
but it never works that way a sense of
erotic just when the metaphysical poses
its problems a headache an enigma
you interwoven in the lyrical shadows
counting from zero to zero in Dravidian
or is it like Dante ready to mythologize
Beatrice heaven after heaven exploding
deep in the heart's disquieting ear or
you involving what should be the poem's
theme its core its whatever you just make
it work like a round of disjointed syllables
one epic thrust after another which are
kisses one two and three ! Bang ! opus one
comes into being on a series of lotus leaves
shapes of things to be aquatic and dark
your face moving across the ages of time
right into the poet's imagination stunned
tries this way and that to make it happen
zoom lens and microphone to capture
radiance of the moment whoosh into skies
of never beyond and back again on earth
looking for the next line and the one after
always there with your eyes spaced like
verses of pools depths and intricacies
what is there to finish this poem unless
it's the act of love the river the flowers
over there on the other bank the Light !

12-21-17

O*B*S*E*S*S*I*O*N

does it mean to be besieged ?
to be bereft of Wit ? seduced
by perfumes that don't exist ?
addicted to women named Opium ?
to live in the frenzy of outer space ?
to forget simply to forget ?
who is the self ? who is the other ?
to wear unpaired shoes to a funeral ?
to place diacritics in *her* hair ?
to read and reread the legend
where it says sleep will never come !
are their places on the map

of the Void that are not there ?
is it coming around every day
to buy flowers and then sell them back ?
to whom ? what does the writing
at the bottom of the tub say ?
will water be the final answer ?
is memory reduced to a single event
that keeps repeating itself
somewhere else ? it's crazy to go
on as if there were no calendar
only days and days without name
there can be no Yesterday !
it has always been Thursday
only Thursday on Mount Olympus !
sometimes a poem occurs
five letters per word and an ampersand
to conclude the incomplete thought
I am having about the One !
afterwards there are hours so blank
so intense so sand-filled
why go on ? violence is in the Noun
that doubles itself to become meaningless
look around ! walls and more walls
see-through categories of Love
engines that start by themselves
before self destructing
is it always being on edge ?
looking into the precipice of Being
then jumping ! when does it stop ?
can it ever end ? or is it just a dream
of something without a beginning ?
I can go to the ropemaker
I can place myself on the list of the exiled
or there can be triple moons
for each of the heads of the Hound of hell
or it is a drugstore with cherry coke
and a girlfriend who sits waiting
for me alone !
I'll never know
I'll never know

12-22-17

BODIES OF LIGHT

so many of them unformed brilliant
love's intellect in spheres circling radii
and to listen to their conversation
music ! a language of zeroes and ciphers
sung at decibles too pure to hear
not angels but higher entities performing
acts no mind could ever envision
yet come to earth and meld into human
actors or statues waiting to be transformed
imitations of the shadowy but divine figures
crossing great tracts in Dante's Comedy
one of us could be among them bent
on becoming at last the Other the One
or No One at all in the enigmatic dream
of life yet this numinous metamorphosis
this floating mirage of staged lives
performing on water and sand and rock
you and I ! what does it matter in the end
a purpose drilled into stone a sonnet
or a sonata caught between glass panes
flitting phantoms in reverie of flame
blazing creatures half sleep half mind
waking and not waking to storms
flickering on the moving screen of experience
history the debacle of human reason
the this and the that of the everyday
conforming to nothing and the bric-a-brac
and nuisance of trying to figure things out
while all around us these vast illusive
bodies of light radiate their expansive
shadows their punctuations of fiery thought
informing and destroying the informed
in a single instant—what is there to know ?
light waves light years light everything
beside one another in a bed burning with
the Unknown and spilled out in all directions
I know *You* ! I know *You* !
passages of darkness night bound illicit shapes
swarming insect-like in the back brain
puny and intransigent ! other lives come
and go other destinies snuffed in a trice
oceans of light pounding against the door
who dares to open it ? faltering grammar
of the inevitable as a rush of batteries
charges the atmosphere with lightning flashes

summers lit up like eternal noons
ready to self incinerate beside the pool
where mythical ancestors floral or animal
rest their reflections for a momentary eternity
we are at once in Mexico and Nepal
Buddha ghosts and Aztec serpent dancers
shake the air with their violent hair
up and down we go on streamers of light
I know *You* ! I know *You* !
afterwards there is only an immensity of what ?
repeated and aggravated rebirths of Flame
way out there past the origins of time
a light and another light coming to be
in the vertiginous silence before memory
I know *You* ! I know *You* !

12-23-17

WEIHNACHTEN

"Voi che'ntendendo il terzo ciel movete"
Paradiso, VIII, 37

the famous singers have done their bit
all of history in tatters at their feet
what's to know about the oncoming dark
of the night that no other night can follow
lights flicker on and off amid the tears
who's to say this isn't the last performance
who's to say the world outside is still there
the doctors in their arrogant white smocks
teeter-tottering between Aristotle & Plato
what do they know about the body of doubt
recesses and well-springs of human sorrow
the treble distinctions of heart and knee
rounding bends of dolorous & windy shores
I went ahead and gave that woman all my money
I thought it was love but I just wanted to own her
evening sets its cold steel locks on fragile hills
avenues twist and wind into nothing world dust
whole abysses of sky whirl above gyrating
in faint yellow tremors before vanishing forever
who last glimpsed the falling summer star ?
when did anyone ever really reach the lawn ?
crushed in the ear's tinfoil a chorus *Am I blue ?*
eddying reflections in the deep-set mortal pool
was she really a Beatrice to illumine my mind
the last and only of a sequence of undying loves ?

take some lines from Hesiod's *Works and Days*
creation of deities out of rock air and fire
steam fitting cloud press lost in atmospheres
destroyed long before the waning tide of breath
stamping feet on winter soil the deathless tone
come back no more horizons erased of gold
numb mountain crests frozen in their myth
alternate continents now sunk before Memory
and will not quit this fold and keep moving
forth toward the Third Heaven in search of
exactly what not known and sleeping in fits
waking to other times having offended Minerva
and long the journey errant and to fall off
the radiant spheres into
                      longing and grief
her not located here nor there not reciprocated
heart's dumb entanglement mistaken for divine
not my rusty companion
                      world's dearth
emptiest night of the year and the burning
from afar   dross and inaction
heroes dressed in rags their bones
scattered on the vain littoral   surf
surging high and salt   relics of the gods
driftwood   signatures in black sand
shifting into Mercury and from a remote
      voices within a parenthesis
seraphic will end

12-25-17

PHOTO-CELEBRATION

For Bob Ness

photo-reminders of the dead in their
living veracity alert to light and air
hugging chosen ones and staring
death in the face for decades it has
been the same birthday celebrations
highlights of a trip to Yucatan
posing always posing dead already
before the fact before history can
have its say a footnote to someone
else's album alluring bright High !
who was that third from the right ?
who the stranger without a shadow ?
how many fingers did the guest lack ?

no one ate the cake they just stared
how many wives down the line ?
there is nothing living in celluloid
and even less in a downloaded frame
enter as many houses as the dead can
they are still the one someone has
totally forgotten and shoved away
dog-eared in some messy receptacle
remember Joe ? who ? you know
the guy with the flute the Prophet
the New Age flim flam man you know
his picture was on the Wall Street Journal
when he did Harmonic Convergence
Joe who ? the Mayan guy who went
by the name of Valum Votan and
said 2012 would be the turning point !
well he never made it and they even
spell his name wrong and side by
side with erstwhile poets and other
crazy Mexicans he gets lost in the mix
shimmering nevertheless in his white
Gandhi clothes preaching the one
and only verdict on Time !
that's Joe who I mean the one
the totally bright and High !
mi hermano

12-26-17

BLACK MAGIC WOMAN

is the math all about the money ?
which side does Cupid stand on
when he aims his deadly shafts ?
you as ever on the other end
of time talking hustling crying
what's to believe in the sky ?
where do clouds go to die ?
whatever is beautiful is you
whatever is beautiful is you !
repetition of the formula gets
you a place on the edge of the moon
lopsided falling into the abyss
do I own you ? will I take you
out to the Last Supper breathless
will the pavement rise up and strike
you wet on the backside of the head
will your cigarette last an eternity

even though the skin you possess
is the least fraction of an inch
in the long range run of time
legends and cycles of smoke
eyes that flutter in the red
hair the episode of infernal ink
wrapped around like serpents
in the history of hip and thigh
dance ! draw circles around
the mind space out drop dead !
come back my lovely thing
ask me over and over if I can
the motor is still running
planet Mercury is in the morgue
planet Uranus has migraine
whatever lease we had on life
whatever rope they gave us
to either hang or toss to the waves
what does it matter as long
as what ! do I suspect
you won't last the century
that the debacle of your fate
tied however loosely to mine
will keep you buoyant
once the threat of love
undoes the sepulchral lies
that keep the heavens afloat
look at all the flowers
look at the waters and heights
mountains ! everywhere
planet Venus submerged in a tub
full of fuchsias and marigolds
put your hands up
you're under arrest !
One is only a number
and that number is you !

12-27-17

THE ENIGMATIC

tender the leaf emerging from the phone
silent the door behind the talking wall
immense yet distant the tree of heaven
that spreads its shadow across the spillway
other voices other vowels indistinct murmuring
through the pages of an unopened book
what silence are the hovering darks
are they wings you ask nightly the foaming
stars fields of brilliant burning distance
so long ago it has always been never now
lost in a bark navigating mythic waters
of the unknown magnetized to the One
rent soul the hiatus of so many paragraphs
written in occlusive inks transpiring
which of the many skies will open its chute ?
on either side planets Y and X mysteries
of the zodiac glide trembling past view
if you still have hands reach out for me !
so it has ever been a maze a puzzle some grass
across which shadows search for fingers
and bodies errant maps of meat and fog
seem to hold discourse on dark matter
take me out of this elysian Park !
which of the many substitutes for the Name
is yours and why was it not revealed ?
++++++++++++++++++++++++++++
we are not about anything today
except for enigma the invisible tangle
on the other side of your voice edging
its insane way into the emerging leaf
the door its shadow the talking wall
we spread our lazy selves beneath
heaven's distant ash tree and sleep
an entire afternoon of eternity inside
a megalith the shape of a sea-bottom
what hazy borderless nothing mystic
secrets within a single spear of grass
the great rotating sun burst in a needle
space an errant casualty of thought
beside the you-and-I of the ineffable
too late for the wedding too early
to be buried on the pounding shore
just heads away from the crimson inch
be mine forever ! it says in moon-bloom
crescents orange dilated fresco pupils

the talking wall ivy around the tongue
phone invented for the drifting ear
please please me ! our crazy selves
senseless in the original tuscan text
fused to no particular canto of Inferno
blossoms of memory plead for more !
++++++++++++++++++++++++++
step gingerly off the parapet
it's a long way to the next *event*
I am you are we is a
red is inevitable it wears you like
gossamer //
the enigma inside your mouth
is nothing less than cosmic
it says we are in the orient forever
lazy inanimate sprawling wordlessly
not a sound

12-28-17

THE INNER YOU

it isn't what you see or
how you're seen the veils
are rent invisible skies
clouds in the eye passing
summers that never existed
lawns and fields and hives
mountains just inside the
bee's retina and countries
drawn on no map with seas
and coasts and islands bright
stars and moons and planets
like mansions of light and stone
the rock the sand the cliff
the ever churning tides
all within the inner you
the one you've never seen
unless in the poems
you've yet to understand
the ineffable Esperanto high
egyptological caves & queens
scorpions basilisks that blind
deserts monsoons tsunamis
terremoto of the beauty salon
where you crop your hair
nightly insane with musk
I know the you who cannot be

the vertiginous lamp behind
the running motor of time
you inside the polar wax
the insect craving to freeze
the you and the other you
and especially the inner you
folded one inside the other
in orange peel and balsam
purple at first then hyacinth
and borderline red and mad
the succinct verse in marble
that reappears after hours
as a fluttering wren's wing
something in the air above
the flight of water through
the needle's apex or the sun
itself reduced to a microchip
worn inside the skin of song
alive alert shining through
both eyes dense with flame
or else the simple pools
where small deer stop
to drink and drink again
their own reflections
eternal as the instant it
takes to give back to sky
the intense and one alone
the inner you ablaze
dazzle of all space
darkest you are
when shining through
once twice then smoke
gone to no return

12-29-17

THE DREAM OF LANGUAGE

asleep in languages cloud vowels
tectonic consonant clusters
red shifts in epic hexameters
the empyrean star flung light years
untranslatable hyperstasis of sound
words that don't exist rudimentary
case systems aboriginal declensions
the eye at once the transmitter
of meaning yet confused lost
in its own maze of idea and silence
a dream a wanderer in pelts
a stone diphthong in the right hand
a subsection of sky eerie yellow bright
just above the dazed mind
is it ever midday on this trajectory ?
a bone text in the brush archaic rune
upended half buried an oracle
a formula in cuneiform dialect
summoning the armed goddess
to shatter forever the city of Man
mutilated bric-a-brac of syllables
barely formed in burial mounds
tumuli sand shapes ant heaps
origin of writing in voices
mourning the rent corpse of Osiris
whose unrecognizable pieces
scattered over an evening meal
are transmuted into pictograms
to be devoured ritually in trance
then does the river overflow
and the year-end devastation triumph
hollow the languorous souls
that meander in mire and miasma
looking for the gift of speech
prayers to Monkey Gods
who have intelligence
and can articulate Thought !
illegal syntax disjointed tongues
long and sonorous verses
hyphenated spun out of control
sent spinning into the void
detritus of human communication
labials palatals and gutturals
priestly invocations
to deities of silence and murmuring

waves beta and alpha
toxic brain particles of meaning
hands extended to the sun-letters
to learn to pronounce them !
humus of memory on an island
left behind so long ago
and the sea rushing up
to take evening from its sky
the last a lilting a small
+++++++++++++++++
they were sparse and smoke
a legend each a unit
making sounds
deep in the grass

12-30-17

THE MUSE MNEMOSYNE

the smaller letters stand for you
a mere ideogram of shadow a
relentless forking of the ways
where a river once mighty and
stood asunder both feet planted
in the delta of seven mouths
insisted on being a simulacrum
madness in its paper version
crumpled up in the right fist
making way toward the mountain
what the larger letters cursive
and belly up stand for Queen-
of-Heaven once so much dust
inkwells like eyes in the fastness
where sky reaches out to sky
once in a lifetime to encounter
you here between these sedges
pronounced exactly like Sigma
only with more heat and emphasis
the others blind and puny racing
their minds and jabbering in Latin
4th century edition what can you
palm leaf in hand like a wall
imposed upon this immense sleep
come and go statue of evening air !
exactly where red becomes ether
inhaled deeply before the stone
comes toppling down into empty
you will relent leaving behind

a husk of reminiscence a dry shell
with multiple indentations pink
and sovereign in the absent ear
afar distant seas slash their beds
a roaring from the eaves of time
raging in the smallest coin of salt
you will go knowing nothing of
the past that inhabits you like a knife
a curtain of bath powders surrenders
your silhouette to the roman senate
what you have been besides vapors
a syllabary of hilltop sounds echoing
distance the imprint of memory
entrails of ivy isoglosses of fern
face to the loam a terracotta hand
makes firm the wind around you
before all else plunges into dark
yet you wet and intense behind
forest murmurs and bird-song
a legend of pearl and tiny jewels
coiling around your definition
all remote the wild assonance
of hair wrestling with night
what remains of you after
the storm rain spouts trickling
sand in the forgotten ear
wondrous bedding in grasses
whose hush hour has come
you absence a shadow of air

12-31-17

THE DEATH OF THE END

a new year's day poem

it had to happen
the end can't last forever
flowers are fair game for
withering noons and snow-flakes
on the window pane gone
before they begin
what does a child know
of day's end other than
it happens under the stairs
where the god who makes dark
waits for his end to come
my brother's end came

soon enough even before
like a snowflake he'd begun
ends come in serial forms
in statues blinded by the sun
ends are all around us
death-in-life photographs
in gestures mysteriously
caught upstairs when
no one is really looking
and the tub fills with steam
and sky after sky unfolds
end after end of light
this day of all days
is an end in itself
the beginning of nothing
glass and vapors and heat
sudden night a dazzled end
chance encounters
with traffic on a wrong way street
I'm at an end with you
even though we never really
got started despite the flame
insects we are ending
in the luxury of burning
wings of dust ending
in spiral topographies
of smoke and annihilation
end it all !
end the whole fucking thing !
on this day which is no beginning
only the end of the beginning
ending in hour of ennui
in the end of thought
in the end of childhood
in the end of the roman empire
Heliogabalus and Constantine
turned to stone
staring with eye sockets
into the future of ending
and on this day
when there is nothing
left to end but breath
ending over and over again
in hospitals where it begins
and most certainly ends
the end is in my eyes
the end is all that I see

the end is Krishna
in whom all things are
the end is in Krishna
outside of whom
nothing else exists
ending ending ending
this is not new year's day
it's end all day
the day of all ends
end the whole fucking thing !

01-01-18

THE HEAVENLY STAIR

first of all there is no such place
the woman you thought you loved
is stone ! her beautiful moon face
colder than the wastes of outer space
wherever you turn the choirs upended
at the top singing gorgeous Monteverdi
are nothing but digital simulacra
ephemera of the passing moment
earth left behind below the bottom rung
is a simmering dump in a colloidal sea
the voices of mortals distorted
on small crystal radio sets of 1929
was it Dante who measured this abyss
this passage from madness to insanity
in rings of eternal light ?
but the woman you thought to love
is stone ! whatever she says
is a sequence of pathological ampersands
promises composed of thought decay
the heavenly stair you saw in her eyes
is a mouth chain-smoking cigarettes
until the last one burns through glass
ashes lunar detritus moon-mad !
don't climb those stairs !
watching from the distance of sleep
from the elevated peaks of Mount Ida
from the mythic graces of cloud reverie
you know there's nothing there
you can hear the claxons of human traffic
the blare and grind of human emotions
the intoxication of love at first death !
look again ! streets leveled by deceit
avenues folded up into small rugs

cities by the dozens reduced to scrap
small flares and arrows bent by heat
that used to point the Way !
but the heavenly stair ?
the beautiful ascent to the third sphere
where Venus and her acolytes
bathe in essence of infinite !
shimmering illusions that feed the mind
that break down the daily threat
that inure the brain to decomposition
the heavenly stair ? mangled
like the heroes in Tartary
inane and empty of memory
but the woman you thought to love ?
there was an instant of warmth
light proceeding from the top
of the Eye
is stone !

01-02-18

DANTE SHIPWRECKED

rains of flame love's inner beings
come down night's endless flow
darkest yet the other side the land
no one has ever glimpsed but in sleep
and tales light up stories woeful
about cast off and hero and death
in the same field wrestling for a lamp
for the switch that turns on and off
the heart's burning engine alas
not you nor I in that pale scenario
nor the poet who entranced ascends
to other heavens blazing ethereally
to visit the Love he has never seen
great rock and stone and sea
tempests that roil the midnight wick
attached to nothing the vagrant *soul*
blind within his text of deaf longing
is tossed and sent asunder in waves
recordings of silence mills of boom !
what other ear can ever discern
when skies are rent and why
fulminating summer motors tear
across vacant pastures of light
far above in the sublime reaches
where only Zeus aloof in his disdain

stretches out for his infinite siesta
yet errant *soul* his book of thoughts
and memory of One he saw alone
in vergers of nascent poetry afar
within the labyrinth turns and turns
and mocking voices ricocheting echo
distances that don't exist
star signals cuneiform flares
alpha and omega writ in burning sand
the air implore to make a way
for this poor Dante this passenger
whose animal was slain in dreams
where is there a place to rest
where a statue with whom to speak
of the awful waters that naught convey
of shipwrecks and senseless grottos
of Sirens and naiads wreathed in green
whirlpools violent atmospheres of
marble and quartz ablaze the ire !
is it you or I slain in trance
sent to visions otherworldly aflame ?
do we wake sea-wracked and spent
mouths filled with ancient sand
what is there to narrate of what we
have never seen yet felt to the bone
universal grief and nostalgia
rust of the ages and death-knell
washed up on Lavinian shores
pocket poems bleached lace chaos
listening to radio song of the oceans
spin out across the galactic mystery

01-03-18

THE ELEVENTH HOUR

for Sharon Doubiago, who asked

time's up zero times zero
the hour has yet to begin
as a consequence of the mountain
and the grammar of the mountain
how many handmaidens does it take
and counting sand drills and air holes
how many will survive to start the hour
and the hair in the upper left corner
and the girls all twelve vestals
candles on their brow and combs shining

tortoise shell the lyre singing it's time
and the hour never like noon at advent
nor the moon coming to its own beheading
just south of the orient waxing bright
redder than the reds of Spanish gold
autopsy of time ! needles running riot
backwards into the silent sands
hands lifted up from the weights
pointing to the great ampersand of the sun
which is racing to its destiny
on the outskirts of Sicily mansion of the dead
if the hour ever begins and the walls
and the long narrow gangplanks
and the pyramids mysteriously erected
overnight behind Taormina's ruins
a lesson must be learned as unwinding
the enigmatic atmospheres of the Volcano
and fires meant to speed up the hour
and soon too soon the midnight Mass
intoned in cataleptic 4th century Latin
Isis herself the weaving wavering linen
of the night skies burning coldly
planet after planet in her wake
and the dog-headed Anubis at the gate
this is the final countdown of the Wheel
from crevices in the parched earth
voices speaking a Punic dialect
great weeping for Dido has done herself in
and sister Anna bereaving the hour
and the other mistakes of celestial topography
the enormous yellow seas of the Underearth
and the pomegranate and the mouth
it feeds and gorgeous in her skin
Persephone ! who better knows the Hour's
grassy brevity the nodding flowers
meridian haze of acres of poppies
lush overrunning with crimson
weeks it takes for the hour's last minute
to consummate the Month
mysterious oneiric chthonic
everything pales
Gaia falls out of orbit
splashing like summer skirts
in the deathless pool by the quarry
just outside of Agrigento

01-03-18

A HELLESPONT BAEDEKER

this is the place of the talking tombs
here is where Hecuba was turned into a bitch
her barking heard in the breezes of the Hellespont
but as for us these urns these potted palms
hotel ruins baths become mud and mire
the frescos tell of a distance in color
so remote we can only imagine the hazards
and return to our routine of escape
and chilling accounts of near-death
winters that keep us isolated
loves that have gone askew in the ether
here beside the talking tombs the barking
the nuisance of having to translate
everything out of this foreign script
the deltas of mourning the immensities
and subterfuge of myth misunderstood
can we but turn to one another
for some kind of comfort for a warmth
long denied us by the adverse fates of Troy
and that barking and all but inaudible whistling
someone panting at the door
metamorphosis of humans into plants
flowers that appear as letters of an alphabet
illegible by light of day
we wander these ruined wastes temples
brought down by a single rain statues
appealing to us for alms and mercy
conversations of the coming war
of terrorists who hold captive the Orient
we ask what year is this what fatal month ?
the decision to make red paramount
to burn the sands heaped over the tumuli
to wear masks whenever possible
beautiful the days when first we arrived
on these ravaged shores ESPERANZA
the name of the ferry boat
and yet disembarking what was it
a market overturned with rotting vegetables
a hotel with no address taxi drivers mutilated
by a desire to drive non-stop to heaven
and above in the fictitious sky dirigibles
bearing numinous names all aglow
and that barking insistent whining
could not get away from it and the talking tombs
the suspicion that it was us after all

locked inside looking for a key
for a lamp for a residual word
ominous days for tourists
who have lost their tickets home

01-04-18

LACHRYMAE RERUM

saw this shadow sitting on a rock
there at midday by the roadside
nothing but the sun's loud silence
accompanied by a chorus of crickets
the broad expanse of fields burnt
by time spreading out everywhere
looking closely I saw it was Joe
been sitting here forever waiting
for the sun to move just one inch
to the west while I smoke this cigarette
a small flare between the shadow's
long yellow fingers and a crackle
as if a bit of sulfur had fallen nearby
nothing stirred in the dried leaves
drooping from the willow to the left
and from way down the road
a distant thing seemed to move
swaying side to side an ox-cart
perhaps or the infernal chariot
if there is a tomorrow if time
ever shifts itself from this rock
then I'll have learned something
about smoke and eternal recurrence
but for now I need to rest
tired from so much memory
still discharging in my brain pan
I can still see Mom waving goodbye
through a lattice work of light
and the clouds that Dad used to paint
whenever he got really drunk
which was often enough and
the cigarette kept burning though
he never put it to his lips
there was a somewhere else
in the shadow's vacant eyes
a remoteness of dead islands
of cliffs rising from the mists
of Nymphs drying their hair
with long shocks of corn silk

of weeping especially weeping
as if shoulders had lost control
it couldn't last forever this stasis
this immobility of knee and thought
kept expecting Joe to get up
like he used to and sleepwalk
right down the stairs to sit in that
great leather rocking chair that
belonged to somebody's grandfather
*and a few more things a small
what ? of the girls I knew and
some I even married the one
I loved the most I never saw
her the one to the far right
in the undeveloped photograph
all of us skinned shins and elbows
running down the gravel pike
and her freckled face and pigtails
calling out a hundred times
for us to stop running to just
once turn around and look at her
why was she crying ? who was
she in the end holding what ?*
by then the sun had reached zenith
no shadow was anywhere cast
only the rock in its solitude
in a sea of burning light
*all languages are one
life is the same as death
there is but one mystery
eternity the
immobile*

01-05-18

THE VOYAGE TO PLUTO

what degree is it on Pluto ?
can we fly there ? or do we need
to go to sleep again counting
numbers that don't exist
am I bewitched because I heard
a voice on the long distance wire ?
section by section of cloud nine
just evaporates leaving us naked
perched on the very lip of time
the husk and bore and drill
that work us over in dreams

the challenge is to identify
in the mirror which of us came first !
colors don't matter it's the myth
the cyclone of gods and retributions
mankind in its own purgatory
judicial process of grass and totem
deliver us from what ! how far it
all is in the history of the Eye !
is there a sixteenth century on Pluto ?
just yesterday we were walking home
from school reciting rhymes and ciphers
who was the poet who created chaos ?
why was it so difficult to speak like
statues in the marmoreal meters of Vergil ?
kicking up yellow and orange leaves
we sensed there was an end not just
to the day but to events on Pluto
searching photographs in our minds
for persons we were supposed to imitate
being here being in this shadowy world
remember the tree that grew out of
the concrete on the way to the library ?
what a tale to tell all leaf and branch
winds and storms of distant seas
heroes upended or turned to beasts
talking nonsense to the Huntress
daughter of Latona sister to Apollo
how do we get to Pluto if not
through a sense of bereavement
grieving for the losses almost daily
that leave us finally on the outskirts
of that brightly painted map of the skies
tempest of stars comets and remote
flashing lights of intelligence
Pluto dimmer than ever faintly red
x-rays of music pale the last sound
frozen rock circling senselessly
outside the gyre of memory

01-07-18

CHASING SMOKE RINGS

looking for you lately and
what do I find ? rumble of
rain storm clouds and black
lightning and porches rushed
with ominous winds a tempest !
do words describe this rage
of absence this being nowhere
when the world on all four
corners is alive with shadows
furious mad reflections of
otherness of indescribable
yellows phantom greens
where are the heights ?
where is the incandescence ?
up and down you go unseen
a silhouette an outline in air
no one knows where you are !
where the seas go crashing
against cliffs and planets
the celestial topography
lies wasted a ruin of sand
and spit and warnings about
exactly where the burials
will take place the monsoon
predicted to erase the city
the one inhabited uniquely
by you somewhere in the east
where bonzes tortured by flies
and immobile buddhas forty
of them line up waiting for
the express bus to Lumbini
each with their evening paper
stories about your disappearance
the silence of Mount Kailash
on the longest hour of the week
you missing among the bamboo
among the wattle huts of Bengal
wandering in teak forests looking
as ever for the blank persona
of your being the illegible
text of your invisible body
who can ever touch it ?
why are there rattan screens
surrounding your dreams
and the place where you slept

now a depth of archaic rock
your hair the faintest memory
in that forbidden zone
are you nothing more than
a wreath of smoke a pale a
fade in all vanishing space ?

01-07-18

MY LITTLE QUEENIE

advance ticket sales to the contrary
my little Queenie's nowhere to be found
is there a drug that gets us to the moon
without knowing where we are
flying is no big deal even without wings
houses lined up for vacancies to burn
groups of prospective renters in rags
skid row is a great place to live !
artists delinquents pachucos horse thieves
a whole medley of mortals alive
who has ever seen my little Queenie ?
inches below the surface of skin
miles perhaps to the next railway junction
shoes and spoons that litter the alley
that leads to the tiny entrance to hell
an abandoned gasoline station a small
plank tossed over a polluted pool
the Sibyl herself dangling inside a bottle
no longer able to articulate in human
what is the world trying to tell me today ?
are there no forges or convenience stores ?
here is where the great temple to Minerva
stood piled marble rubble and ivy
snaking its sinuous way into the mind
vatic voices seeping through the cracks
are telling me something about little Queenie
abandoned by all her husbands
left to mend for herself in Arcadia !
who walks the asphodel fields by night
who spurns light of day seeking caves
daughter-of-the-sun ! coppertone
allusions to snake-skins that adorn her
movements among the zodiac houses
to change direction to destroy North !
each is every meter a measure of absence
totality of all rhyme schemes is Zero !
is poetry the scribbling underneath

the darkening fingernail the twilight ?
the god of junk has declared her his own
my little Queenie traversing the infinite
disguised as mobile-homes and detritus
hurricanes tsunamis and eddying tides
all have borne her image somewhere
moon relic of an archaic and former tongue
babble and frenzy of the brain to know
what's behind the schizophrenic mirror
if that's not where my little Queenie
hides conjugating high school verbs
in and out of the stucco remains of time
it cannot be ! she's the totem Sign
wearing all the black hair there is
inky labyrinthine endlessly at fault
processed air-wave report to Saturn !
when was there ever a disease like this ?
ruthless mortal schemes to annihilate !
and from afar lilting cavernous song
painting atmospheres of never-again
my little Queenie moored in her hive
abuzz in the reversal of all sleep
one two three the traffic signals
and suddenly the furious rush
from tomb to Etruscan tomb lessons
of the underworld and figure eights !
what is above has always been below
there is a hill with no sides in the middle
beneath that a trickling stream the Styx
my little Queenie forensic evidence aside
has never been dead ! light of light
unseen among the countless Invisible
she meanders through dark matter
shrugging off rumors about her Life !
my little Queenie ! my little Queenie !
come out wherever you are
time is up and nowhere else to go

mmmmmmmmmmmmmmm

01-08-18

THE NATURAL HISTORY OF ECSTASY

from the fortieth floor the elevation
to heaven seems a done thing
lean out the window and kiss the sky
grab a passing cloud unzip the lining
jump and you're there high dazzle !
world is a curious passing dot below
ants termites and bulldozers charge
making a beautiful ruin of everything
gods the size of midges look for a pyramid
to climb and reclaim the heavens
sun and moon like ornamental fobs
go on and off in a trice then sleep
with its half a dozen islands drifts
from the place where it used to be
wrapped in mountain grass and fog
to somewhere new on the edge of time
whichever planet comes into view
first collides gently with the amorphous
ink of sleep and everything starts up
again and again leaving you puzzled
as to which body is yours and mind
what does it matter ? drizzle and
fiction of mirrors you look and look
what an amaze this otherness !
how many lives did it take to get here ?
how many lives did it take to find you ?
it's hard to be simultaneous and nowhere
or to know just when to get off this life
and hitch a vertiginous ride to the next
who is the secret *you* circling dizzy
simulacrum of the last and former life
this unrepeatable crown of light
you effortlessly wear as you pass
like an angel from one dimension
to the next which is always the last one
there can be no other place in the cosmos
rebirth is never a possibility when
there never was a beginning !
how did we get here front to front
mastering the abacus and sand clock
furiously investigating the Hour for
a way out of this labyrinth of instants ?
look over your shoulder ! red and more
red the fusion of dream and trance
the shape of the *Illegible* transforming

into summers of impossible alphabets
heat and warning and sea-tempests
enigmatic hieroglyphic subjunctive Olympus
with its famous dozen gods ablaze rioting
how to destroy ? they want *You* !
hasn't all this happened and kept happening
every time I see you carrying weightless
the world-form of the Imagination ?
myth compounds myth in its Hesperia
in and out of burrows and heaps
the plurality of your persona Stuns !
it is nowhere near yet it is always there
the marvelous underground where ecstasy
is born and takes shape and sleeps !

01-09-18

SAINT NOTHING DAY

buried deep in the outback of the ear
is the secret of silence that loud rush
of light that both precedes birth and
supersedes death the instantaneous
moment of irreversible photography
when all the universes compounded
or in single units the size of an eye
come together in a mystic wedding
a conflagration of the sexes as One !
how is it we overcome the ritual of ink
inscribing fantastic but illegible verses
poets ! where are the words to describe ?
what is the one myth that keeps recurring ?
where is earth and its hundreds of seas ?
is the city you inhabit the Destroyed ?
why do you keep coming back to this Day ?
a year circulates in a single grain of sand
but two years ! when has that ever been ?
there is a picture book somewhere
there are houses inside it that cannot be
and animals that feed on thought and
so much that cannot be imagined
poets ! put your minds to sleep forever
take your hands off and offer them
to Diana and to Minerva and most of all
to Hecate of the Crossroads and let them
sing ! and the shoulders and the knees
and the distances between them Holy !
there is no body but the uninhabited one

there is no Soul at all but the fleeting
glimpse of a wind emerging from the south
bearing with it the enormous fictions
of space and time and all the in between
poets ! there is nothing to celebrate !
put an end to the chasm and the hiatus
embrace the abyss and become full
after tomorrow what should there be ?
organs of light multiplying themselves
Big Bang hypothesis and the never-ending
going in circles ad infinitum even as
poets ! you stand there trembling ecstatic
on the witless margin defined by the Muse
I am becoming and becoming Other
without memory and unable to forget

01-11-18

HYMN TO THE GODDESS OF THE UNKOWN

I see you as twilight as dusky azure
I see you as vanishing copper hue
I see you as skies verging on insomnia
I see you as mind's definition in Red
edges fade pale shades into moonlight
farther still skin passes into ineffable
blank and submarine and distant
is the meaning of love *iridescent* ?
you're never there when it matters
all the movie theaters are empty !
I see you as ink looking for a shape
I see you as night not yet come to be
there are entrances hidden from view
where your face emerges transparent
yet darkening like an unseen pool
I see you as a tree a rock a stone
places where light is born ascending
black glass poetry prism endlessness
all the shades of bright filtered dense
what is it all around that shatters ?
how are the many come to echo nothing ?
you vanish in the imperceptible sun
that dawns over the drowned mountain
I see you as the most archaic thought
I see you as the moment of ignition
deep within the myth of eternal return
the body without a body transcending

hills and woods and the everyday field
flowers imagine you are their goddess !
small streams offer their reflections to you
asterisks ampersands and question marks
punctuations that divide the air infinitely
yet unperturbed you step through clouds
dim at first than roseate and fresh as dew
feet and hands and something else above
your absence is the greatest ornament !
noon is forever in the disappearing moment
chimes and ladders and opalescent grief !
wherever you have been a wake of white
striates the boundless waves and darkness
which is where you rest your emptiness
love is liquid indigo poured into your ears !
listening carefully the nymphs *Understand*
scattering everywhere they destroy space
statues become alert cliffs break vows
hush of immense meridians multiply you
moving and not moving through crystal
diaphanous intelligence of the Spheres !
I see you as rosebud hyacinth and lotus
I see you as painted screens of the winds
yours is the touch that cannot be felt
breathlessness and the end of everything
I see you as the rainbow of invisibility
you stop just long enough to seize
with your dappled fingers the sands
which are the decomposition of memory
enough of you ! the one and the One
silences of the unwritten Poem !

01-12-18

SITA—BELOVED OF RAM

if I could steal you for just one night
turn the world into an envelope
full of drifting sand and grass
follow the thin crimson moon
into the decay of yesterday's promise
skyscraper higher than mount Everest
basement empty of life and time
steal you and never take you back
unload you on the other river bank
decompose your memory in small shifts
of red and blue and listen to you
demand for more of the same

eyes lifted to the developing planets
on the horizon to the far left of space
never sure if it was today high noon
or merely the hour of low tide
on some undiscovered martian sea
could steal you for just one more day
bundle you up in a car trunk
and drive to far off Sri Lanka
where monkey gods honeymoon with lotus
making abracadabra of mortal speech
poems and the music of the ear
hymning praises to blue-throat Vishnu
denying once and for all the Resurrection
leaving everything to the fate of Sound
echoes ricocheting through concrete
or the vast silences of the Deccan
how would you feel tossed out
of the speeding vehicle of Love ?
it isn't that I want you forever more
nor that even the pleasure of your eyes
looking back to see the drowned world
is what I crave—nonsense of passion
everyday money laundering pure theft
just to steal you and wait for the papers
to announce vast rewards for your return
to the simple innocence of married life
no I don't want the punctuations
that illustrate your hidden body
nor the exclamations and expletives
that inform the *selva oscura* of your mind
the spine grows erect in anticipation
of what can never be // love me
once and destroy for certain what
we can never have
goddess ! become inside out !
so I can wear your remains illegally
stolen all your parts one by one
intensities of the diameters
that separate circle from circle
in the never ending instant of illusion
steal you just once more Shadow !
for a week of minutes in isolation
one two three ! Bang

01-13-18

HIATUS

there is no hiatus greater than death
no death greater than the poem
that has yet to be written for You
always in regard to the body parts
to the sutures and spinal taps and
inlays before the tombstone and what'
s more listening for breath the in
and out the sky high mile measured
for you as movement and silence
and the impossibilities of thought
bridge their way between you and
oceans churning in the unconscious
islands you must have stopped in their
wake the surf and bubble and spume
riding into the cerulean absence you
call home-coming the longing episode
to be held furtively by the illegal
alien you name *lover* gunning his motor
loading you up with friction a pause
between mouths a wonder wet and
what language do they use speaking
lonely to you in troubled sleep a
sigh between vowels and for sure
prayers by the rote to the smoking
goddess with her lingerie and cutlery
wood deep in myth shadow and game
crossing where small deer dappled
or white pause to drink your reflection
in the dark pool beside the large
black stone the statue perhaps coming
to consciousness palms up head almost
to be within that sculpted marble
imagine you are and worlds of infinity
what can they say between leaf and margin
consonants anchored to invisible ink
composing as air moves eddying the poem
about what is greater than death You
instilled green like sap running where
the tree's wound seems to cry out a
voice yours demanding light again
even as day drains its star of sky
ear to the turf hearing in reverse
footsteps inevitable that bear away
unwary shadows tumbling hapless souls
into that small hole what seems to moan

taking with it your outline shape of
winds just born in the eastern hill
these are dawn verses you think an
attitude that requires a shoreline long
and absent waves becoming more
than their presence giving birth to
illusion and darkness on the very rim
where time scallops its siesta wide
as the oriental flame surging quietly
asleep take care of your back don't
whatever you do drown in mind
life won't come back as easily this
time the poem its origins in dance
rising you too will take the music
in your sleeping arms embrace death
like that it won't last as long as
love

01-13-18

ADONIS

I am the ruin of an alphabet
that has never been written
the omega without a zero
the omicron desperate for sigma
I am the past tense of a verb
that cannot be employed
in the first person plural
the significance of so many words
that lack meaning find in me
the symptomatic zoography
of a planet ruddy and blank
circling the noosphere noontimes
to be destroyed by a casual
phoneme known only to rishis
of the holy Vedas AUM
moon-dots riding a circumflex
of oceans boundless and white
triggered associations of alpha
yearning to enter beta
how many houses does it take ?
essence is non-existent !
little One take my hands
remove them one by one
toss them to the sun-flares
as they appear on the horizon
where sleep mounts its great horse

bringing night to endless time
I am exhausted by writing
the same book over and over
the first page never gets past
the last page and there
are paragraphs so empty
that only the letter Delta fits
and the rushing waters of
the tingling tributaries of
the enormous winds of
that give birth to mountains
little One take my head
and burn it precisely
where tau intersects with
gamma the holy Egyptian !
the rest is residue of sounds
echoes from the Hour
when Adonis was gored
and the ivory tusk high
in the air seemed to sing
my Venus little One
Thou art and Forever !

01-14-18

SWEETS OF SIN

"Why should those lovers that no lovers miss
Dream, until God burn Nature with a kiss?"
W.B. Yeats

the darkness the indwelling part of the soul
where men waste lives leaving senseless white
their absences leaning against cold autumn winds
yet within and without you the culminations
of light upon light like wings folded over you
bear you up through untenanted rooms of thought
to me you appear like a wave in the night bright
surf a once and only time a laving upon the rocks
that abut here and there in the soul's journey
making difficult the passage upwards and out
toward greater fires your small feet hidden as
if stepping on invisible sands your mind and hands
the best parts of your body the entirety of otherness
you assume if I could but hold the intensity of
that shadowy mass your hair and the swift
carriage of something else from within breaking
daylight into uneven hemispheres where you go

lost I don't know in which the mountain side
where wood and slope evolve into a labyrinth
or the concavity where myth takes shape in
the form of nymph dedicated to the deep water
wherein stooping to drink souls metamorphose
into planets or shaking comets in the noon glare
irises and lotuses brilliant white and red athirst
like your mouth the sudden time it offered itself
and the cleavage of air was loud ! and cliffs swart
and plangent fell sharply off the firmament falling
hard into the ocean of dreams the tremendous
echo of a sound followed by softer tracks a
goddess wrapped in diaphanous skins shining
making way through a city of leaves and hives
how did the bees make their alphabet about her ?
or was it you trembling in the instant of mystic
reunion eye intent upon the quivering spear-tip
that precedes twilight the ancient musk and
finally the depths where nothing can be spelled
a moon sigh a friction between space and silence
asleep at once in the distances the smoking wilds
of the world that lies behind the mirror's face
and then gone a faint vowel a fade indistinct
a hush kissing forever the oncoming absence

01-14-18

MYTH OF ETERNAL RETURN

how is it comes to me such passion
out of bitter fruit in my waning years
a soul arises from the Indistinct house
and steps that carry rivers and lands
from afar come toppling at my feet
to look and espy no common cause
nor nature nor a god has this wrought
I stand in mists no morning bears
yet hold in my arms a body sweet
that has never been before nor after
this hour will be not again a thing
to embrace and promise in the ear
undying thoughts of love the unending
such tumult in the sky without sound
thunders of the archaic ! what's to see ?
between eye and eye the lightning white
the immensity of a single mind lost
to the energies that govern the universe
among rock and dale I wend a missing

shadow a brain and hands remembering
what was that dream that seemed like
matter a substance perfumed and glorious
a halo of stars in rapture for a minute only
to disappear in the Heraclitean stream
images waver like water held in the air
small trance the infinite indissoluble
in which murmur the bees of intransigence
great eras have come and gone in the dew
heroes with shields large as the sun
felled by a single blade of grass AOI !
without memory cities have transgressed
their walls and turned to dust in a flue
histories the length of twenty Chinas
written on the back of a thumbnail
become black & without notice disappear
yet I stood here and here as well beside
the archaic Oak sensing in my embrace
the every second of eternal presence
my heart beating within the *other* heart
blood stirring in the moon's hidden wake
repeatedly sands shape the echo of *the* name
ancient wild and swiftly like a comet
passing through the stillness of Hearing
what a resonance the eternal syllables make
labyrinthine poetries meandering ideas
the image of a totality in sundered reds
a face emerges ! multiple blank visages
archaic as the quarries of the gods floating
on islands of the uncharted western sea
statue anvil lip and bliss ! marvels of
the untold Myth subterranean fleeting
which is the paragraph of encounters ?
which the hexameters of longing ?
come back ! this is no daily portent
but the Muse on rotation from the Library
simultaneous and non-existent unfinished
why do I keep returning to this Nothing
if not to redress the Kiss and its mouth
smoking unendurable restless and gone !

01-15-18

THE SOUL CUT FROM ITS MOORINGS
CIRCLES WITHOUT NORTH THE SEAS

and the boats how many of them lost
in the caverns of sea   agape the
mists swirling and caught me in his eye
the Master but recognized me not
swift circling above the curlew's
mourning mew adrift as if wingless
in darkening clouds the sky
never to meet earth but distances
hovering in the shattered wake
from afar espy curling blue smoke rings
never to be reached a
    fixed in prayer like a stone
heaven's swart denial not offer hope
a longing and lay the head down
waiting for the tide to carry the body's
shadow unto   broken stairs leading
netherward to where grasping shades
of men and forgetful of name
and rank   piteous is where I
stopped straining to see to know which
the dense mire   in between forms
    hallowed and numinous nouns
pronounced bitter accent a thread
following a thin mercurial line into a
cerulean   tipped the basin to drain
of impurities   we will not be there
again nor of day the sun's glare to
    entranced by a beguiling voice
a song as if emerging from rock
where were we after all ?
sound of water lapping near the ear
an echo in the dry brush a flint a
flame to   perhaps and within
from some depth of soul carried a word
bright in formation and holy
somehow the size of unknown
proportions and came full circle
nightfall treading stars without number
as if by some enchantment to draw in
the nets the sea-wracked boats
green death   waiting hours
for the Plow and the Wain and whatever
other luminous projections but naught
trading whispers like memories

        doomed to never return to
the place as foretold
but to remain shades among shades
in some imaginary world of dust-storms
of kindling and small urns
        had the Master but
explained what it was he *saw*
that we did not and left us to riot
all night in the tavern 'til witless
and one by one separately we fell
from the lip
        into this dank and
foul tenement that has no fundament
but error and lamentation
loosed from the old body
sound of water lapping near the ear
and dim sea-birds aloft
        the stars going out

01-15-18

NUMEROLOGY

we will begin with the numeral ten
and from there ascend the secret path
never knowing what we left behind
nor what lies ahead in furious light

when eleven is reached uneven raw
when counting does no more good
when clouds on their blind axle
roar turning purplish with dim flares

why move on to mystic number twelve ?
when multiples of three *Pythagoras*
declared can summon hundred-foliate
the Secret Rose that blooms within

in this mortal sphere why enumerate
cause and deficiency spirit and sight ?
not enough to have known for just
a fraction of time your Billowing ?

when we have ceased to commune
consciously and the welkin darkens
for all eternity why fix the suns as finite
wheeling flaming celestial orbs ?

infinity resides in the numeral One

above and below the separate quadrants
that divide known and unknown the cosmos
shatter infinitely in the maker's Ear

no more Zeus no more Hera the gods
rutilating like spent comets beautify
alone the ashen residue of the universe
as it plummets like a pail into chaos

in all thus numerological confusion
in this labyrinth of Ionian speculation
what is it you cling to so desperately
is it love's infirm and pallid genesis ?

the first is always the last time to *see*
what it is we are only meant to dream
centrifuge and sonata flickering wildly
in a poetry of sleeping ocean waste

come then Little one let us to the stair
that climbs midway between the elements
earth air fire and water sparkling nothings
that radiate rotating around the empty Sound

have enough of this burning planet
its frenzied ambulances and broken streets
the *other* side is but a vain promise
heaven is the vacuum Echo leaves behind

what of thirteen number death the Real ?
fictions of brain entities of subterfuge
you and I dancers in a lunar reel
front to front masks of one another

do then release the skin and sing its
unremembered song the flight to infinity
bees take your hair and ants your feet
what remains is the forever of your waist !

beyond the last possible number high
on the imaginary scale of time and space
your longing presence your enduring absence
uncountable and imperishable anti-matter

dot dot dot a resonating code in number Red
vast and ineffable never reaching fate
destinies like powders flung to the winds
your face the fade of total Oblivion

01-16-18

ΦΙΛΟΣΟΦΙΑ

three halves of the circle !
and all around the Ideal the rhombus
of ideas swirling to find place
in the whole if such a whole exists
hair and net and trident
sea rushes to meet its beauty Land !
under everything lies a single Word
when was the question ever asked
that never should require an answer ?
we leaf through pages of air
seeking the lost continent of Mu
shadows come and go passing on the wall
within the somewhere of music a soul
the very Soul that lives outside of mind
roves seeking entry into the *animate*
and clouds that dwell within the Eye
like sky that surrounds the ether of time
become that *animate* and learn
like statues to speak as mortals
inquiring of the Cave and its republic
wherein devotees of poesy and spheres
bank hand in hand musing aloud
Oh when was ever and then why
such and such the temple and the fly
are we bitten in order to think ?
the streets of Athens paved far and wide
the shops and leather-crafters
the isolated gymnosophist the drunk
the lewd and brave hero of Salamis
all gather like a knot around the dust
from above and *Crash !* the bolts of Zeus
the movie theater fills with din
who was the dissident in the agora ?
who the silent rhetor filing papers of voice ?
archaic the great and unhewn rock
the Acropolis rearing like a feathery horse
into now the distance of history
colors have Number ! red is twenty five
and black the opposite of every hundred
yellow is the score of fifties
all are mad who have looked into the Book
but especially mad are you and I
driven by Aphrodite's secret storm
we look deep into the marble
and read what was never written

remote the rumors of strife and war
Egyptian theories of sand and after-life
corpses that ruminate on the stars
and lovers forever bound by the Invisible
immortal as only gods can be !

01-16-18

ADDICTED

after all this time more than ever
to you addicted as only a poet can be
to lyricism where it least occurs
the street that puzzles its passage
east toward the darkest funnel
or at once the surprise of a door
slamming shut on fingers of grass
addiction to the exhalation of cars
because they send warnings to you
approach to heaven is for now denied
if only I could have half the dose
I got yesterday and multiply it
in a thousand smoke rings zooming
out of my mind repetition of your name
obsessed with the two syllables
that comprise an endless Trojan epic
you fundamentally exposed to laws
of irreversibility and lunacy
on days when noons are impossible
and the only hour that exists
is the one when I line up at the clinic
to get my prescription of you filled
blank scraps of paper tossed to sea
illegitimate signatures on the dotted red
long fusions of subatomic particles
in pre-Mycenean script ALOUD
is it wonder there is no room for my head
that sky is only a ring of vertigo
ensconced in dangerous moons
that sun no longer rises where it should
but in a cracked window in bedlam
where you can hear the passionate
reciting multiple verses of Nothing
addicts like me come a dime a dozen
looking for what they have only dreamed
days spent in the abattoir of mirrors
a rosary slipping between hands
that should be shaping cones of water

Help ! the ambulance careens
around invisible mountains sharp
with cliffs and the distances of Harmony
alone in a padded cell with *reefer*
and a needle and thread and Eyes !
to see what ? desperate to have another
of you the craving of paradise
sewing with my brain the synapses
that go in and out of echoes
telephone calls to the Marvelous !
air is only so far and the rest
is endless waiting for the gate
to open letting You out of jail

01-17-18

ON THE DEATH OF JOHN OLIVER SIMON
STILL ANOTHER POET GONE

this is not eternity we still eat
and fall deep asleep in our beds
and waking count the number of skies
in passing before night falls again
not eternity but close to it the dim
and pallid sunsets the winter
of our life they say and in the glass
reflections long altered fade
a distant din a small small noise
the ear seems to catch hesitating
sounds resembling words and
thoughts like bees in a lost vortex
every day brings news of another
gone the wrong path into the wood
the lake there cold and blue
spends little time to take that shade
comes back no more that missing
name the one turned to smoke
remote as the eastern hill beyond
the shadows of the leafless trees
this is not eternity we still eat
and fall deep asleep in our beds

01-17-18

TO THE UNNAMED GODDESS

what's a goddess like her
doing in the middle of the sea ?
thunderbolt and lightning arches
ocean swells mountain high
no land in sight just endless
water and the vacuum of sky
portents of the apocalypse
voices loud and swarming
oracles and debates rushing
which is the direction home ?
is there a submarine earth
replete with memories of Her ?
all books are but shadows
there is nothing fixed in sound
legends of watery origin
stars flooded with light
racing to complete the dark
what's a goddess like her
doing in the middle of nowhere ?
ampersands and asterisks
protocols of the welkin
minuscule versions of Red
tomes of empty letters
how can there be a way home ?
when was consciousness ?
if she moves her feet
the small lotuses of mind
turn blue and white and off
traffic of the Phlegethon !
flames and more flames
spelling and swirling bright
clouds and nemesis and Fate
itself declared null and void
there is only absence
punctuation of the dead
so what's a goddess like her
doing dancing on the waves ?
she shines she shines evermore
a fortune in rain and glass
recording devices turned up
to catch the parenthesis
of her eternal breath
do I stand amazed
if she turns to look just once
at the mortal world behind ?

a hand she has and two
that move like wings
white with spray and dew
come to me ! I pray
dreams the size of salt
or inky blossoms that
spread from all she sees
and me she takes uprooted
from the trance of life
and offers this brief
immortality of night

01-18-18

BIG BANG

so big the thunder sound must be Zeus
playing at the top of the stairs his powerful
games echoes boomerang and deafen
the all whole cosmic Bangs in flux asterisms
swept away in a single fist kiss the immense
drenched in the light of after-time nine
years in the task the irreducible walls
of Ilion piled high x and y and heroes
Argives and the horde of Priam's sons
how swiftly battle destroys Sleep the anchor
between lives this chain sways gives way
breaks the galactic link something begins
dream spent just after the end and wild
chaos of origination and the thrum thrum
of archaic drums rock and stone and cliff
heights of insuperable beauty split crashing
repeatedly into the numbed human ear to
sing to speak alone to chant go into trance
envision the everything at once before it starts
the ignition the neutral gear the mud guard
the cinema of atavistic reflection splinter
mirrors come and go taking with them
ghosts of the Immortals ! here are planets
the size of thumbnails and there are moons
like bottomless swills of ink and night
the ineffable with its hundredtrillionbillion
stars knocking this way and that trying all
to make an escape through a peninsula of gas
big Eyes looks through his rear view scope and
POW the infinitesimal inch of his powdered thumb
like a keg of dynamite smokes the ether blaze
for the fraction of a second it takes a nebula

to die what comes next in the tavern and all the
busy souls quaffing 'til dawn the elixir of Death
the joy of it all the terrific green smear of Dawn
aurora heeling her violent black steeds before sun-up
and the cities ! in one tremendous sunburst KABOOM
don't come back, *Little One* don't shake my hand
it isn't here that everything gets explained it's
not in the anteroom where they manufacture thought
nor the circle and the crypt and the all-consuming
pyre of Love roaring with its fluorescent flares
deep into the Hour when dot dot dot the enemy
RED trussed up as Mars comes in sequences
of alpha and omega mowing down the replicas
of man the indigenous statuary of earth the worm
and the trilobite the tortoise and the elephant
Gone ! nuclear waste to smithereens awash
in tides of lunacy and phantom intelligence
sand-clocks triggered to go off at midnight
at the reading of the Book of Books
page after page blank musings of Chacmool
watery feathers mysterious volcanic activity
just behind the medulla oblongata and then
Little One, Don't ! the dial and the button
the cipher that can't be read the metric unit
the false the fade the pale the unending dance
shanti OM shanti Om shanti OM

01-18-18

PERSEPHONE THE NEXT TIME

from anti-inferno comes news of your survival
legendary dark clouded in myths of regeneration
fountains hills tombstones depths of unknown
your face emerging from mists of the Hiatus
between this life and the countless others
light fixed or wavering between two systems
of metaphor and the great conjunction of sky
and the illusory fictions of archaic statuary
interposed as if love were a matter of sculpting
a shape and ready to fly from the Mind into what
secondary galaxy where you have never stepped
yet where memory of your body in trance passing
is engraved in tufa and sand like necrologies
of all the other goddesses like unto you in hair
and nerve and color bearing message of salvation
grass that discolors your cheeks enormous fade
of the thing your eyes see when first ascending

from that subterranean throne into a summer
distant with echoes and splashes and cries
distilled in the ear's complex recording device
how will you greet the flowers in their waking ?
what cycles of heat will crown your shadow
elegantly moving between issues of stone and rock
alert to the skies in their anachronism of ether ?
unrecognized you will shift from bright red
to blue the cool azures of infinite breath
mountains and lairs the abode of the absent
and of the silent who have arisen from the dead
to partake of flower and hive once again salute
you magically informing themselves with bees
and you will be known ! what dense and white
atmosphere raveling its cloud lattice about you
will burst into x-rays of the other world
announcing your footstep and golden rustle
clad in nothing but hues of celestial ruby
what will you be ? what will you do ?
this is the month of Eternity ! the solar week
when everything is forgotten and nothing stains
the swirling air but the nacre of your distance
whom have you embraced that you tremble so ?
a car is running its motor outside your ruins
what sense does it make to remember anything ?
tumulus of haruspex lightning bolts and egrets
radios barely catch your voice singing what ?
television sets blur with electric snow storms
whatever of you remains is an abstract painting
a photograph from pharaonic times of dew
is there a metamorphosis worthy of you ?
crocodiles floating lotuses horses and hummingbirds
lichen that covers the estuaries of the Nile
seven times seven thirteen plus zero !
all of the archaic shivers in your phantom wake
as you pass and pass over that small lawn
where first you succumbed to the Fruit !
whose is the voice that cries out woefully
You belong to me !

01-19-18

PARIS & HELEN

you I plan to steal and hide away
in my private hills and feed and keep
until dawn loses its swart steeds
why should anyone else have you ?
it's I who recognize in the dim set
of your eyes roses blooming perpetually
though you cry and plead poverty
the wealth of your hair alone will
sustain us both in dusky afterlife
entwined as ivy darkening afternoons
come away then become illegal
break all these customs of light
and transfer the night of your soul
to me listen no more to the sirens
that careen down avenues like squad
cars or ambulances of misfortune
for once give it up that holy home
that staircase those screens & beds
with me there'll be no loss of seas
no lack of storms and starless winds
come sink with me in the eastern shore
let those who claim warriors to be
scour the landscape for trace of you
what is that man to you who gambles
whores and struts in shining bronze ?
it's I who see heaven in your mouth
blank absences of yesterday cease
starting today on my small skiff
spindrift and salty surf and mists
you'll cling to me as shadow to rock
listening to the nocturnal rave
as moon embraces its lost other

01-19-18

THE MYSTERIES

winding and unwinding the thread
in and out through stone and light
it is not sleeping nor waking either
the nebulous cataract of mind self-
dissolved in the effort to recall the
what the whenever the various and
green passages the flares symbolisms
lamps and asterisks that dot the sky
to be read by mythographers nights
when moon's delicate shell vanishes
in the eye when the eye itself disappears
deep within love's deep recess a
multiple mask a persona marked
in shades of red a shadow walking
looking for its other the soul writing
with a lost finger in the grass verses
to be read in a mirror when the Hour
reverses and summoned the dead
from an afterworld of spilling sand
dredged the parts from the fundament
pyramid sphinx and tripod
called from afar the oracle and *Lo !*
after so many lives spent in limbo
the resurrection of the heart's
great memory the circular idea
that goes re-creating seasons and years
summers in the small pool to the left
and on the right the statues that talk
the cities and the living mountains
gods tripartite and ethereal swarming
in the brief inch of breath and who
will tell of such visions who will
remove the seal from the golden mouth
who will say : it is *She* once again
come from the curtains of absence !
house of countless rooms darkness
immersed in the ineffable beyond
yet shining the bright *Once*
no one can enumerate the splendor
the immediacy and the brevity
eternity's thimble the infinite spool
round which she revolves her being
come back to me ! corridors fill
with musk and amber a pale
distance an indistinct mile a forge

whole afternoons spent in idylls
beside her though she is not *there*
what is there ever to *know* ?
the greater signs cannot be read
there is no salvation but omega
the girl next door is missing
hills that capture sunset gone !
ebb and flow of time desists
legend of the western islands
wrapped in redundant fogs
nowhere to be found the footstep
nowhere to be heard the footfall
the lesser signs fixed in dew
symbols without interpretation
ciphers so great they explode
no number more significant
than Zero and its multiples
finite space time destroyed
magnificent replicas of air
astonishment of the empty
as it fills with poetry absurd
inkstained illegible totally
things dropping out of the sky
unnamable and holy
as is the body in its lack
mysteriously wending over
the inevitable fictions
for two minutes we wait
for each other to become One
what I am is your shadow
sacred moment of the Beloved
everything is ancient and
beyond recall primordial
there never was a first time
just this only time with You

01-20-18

TRINACRIA

out of rock bees pour swarming
sunlight bathes their intense sound
zzzing throughout high meridian
flowers offer all they have to the noise
air becomes dense sweet & heady
some muse must have inspired you
to move flashing swiftly through
the dense and hush afternoon
yellows beckon to cerulean skies
from here to zero and back again
without a shadow you brave speed
soon night and with it eternity
will envelope your heat wave
blazing otherness of memory
seized by grace and desire to *be*
poised on the lip of time *enough*
you have never really been except
as the mask worn in the dance
when you come to me unawares
in sleep's three perfect halves
darkening in the lunar mystery
it's time for the honeymoon !
bees rock flowers yellow highs
noon repeated a thousand times
in a single instant and cerulean
temples of the heavens bright
wherever we go whoever we are
what doesn't really matter nor
why like persons of the drama
reciting colors instead of words
Hybla with its mythical apiaries
greater than the Cyclops' eye
where hues of the spectrum *Loud*
accompany us from room to room
shores come running insane
with epic prescience of sands
phantom bards & doomed kings
fall full faint before the Door
where we pause for the oracle
are you the bride of last August ?
garlanded in marigold and rust
your hands tremble like rain
your face behind thirty veils
secret that cannot be revealed
daylight scours volcanic ash

scattered grasses like code
for sumptuous remote heavens
rustle in vagrant southern winds
but you ? transpiring in the fane
Diana's inflected arc aims straight
for the animal that transforms
what is it legend keeps from view ?
the *Island's* fierce cliffs and crags
resounding surfs billowing waves
to spend just one night there
isolated from insect topographies
nymph ! ransom your wet skin
involved in the labyrinth of Salt
become One with the splashing
that fills the ear with light
it's time for the honeymoon !

01-21-18

CONSULTING THE DELPHIC ORACLE

where is the hand that feeds the stars ?
and the bright eye that watches the sheep ?
where is the god of commotion and ecstasy ?
is there a name for the thing we know the least ?
who is the man who rows the oar of death ?
how many times did we hear the noise
              without comprehending ?
is there a place the light goes when we die ?
how much shadow does it take to remember ?
and on and on the waters sound lapping against
the Stygian bark and no wind to fill the sail
darkness that completes darkness night
that informs ear and eye of the unending
and by the bedside or in the opened book
or by the small lamp in the window or
what keeps happening is the incessant verse
repetition and circularity and madness
here take these syllables and translate them
where is the dry well that hides the face ?
I met a woman in the morning who walked
the mists and her hair and her mouth and
the invitation in her glance and I fell
as from a horse galloping to the *Finish*
what did she see that she looked so intently
into the small water where I lay unconscious
where is the poem you promised me yesterday ?
where's the money ? where's the breadfruit ?

over and over she put the key in the ignition
she gunned the motor and dawn surprised us both
a great and immense arm reached out of the clouds
a terrific roaring thunderous and echoing
knocked us out of bed—it's our wedding day !
where are the fingers that inscribe the skies ?
much as we like to imagine nothing really happens
there are doors that cannot open and a glass
that contains in its few drops a parallel universe
the woman who keeps coming out to greet me
though the hour is not even up who is she ?
the next time I wake and the house is in order
and the guests in the parlor talking and
exchanging tales of the demolition will look
as I descend the stairs a strange woman on my arm
who will say this is not the last day of time ?
that was a goddess and no mortal woman
didn't you see how her feet stayed above the ground ?
she is not of this earth nor of this space
she is the shining that has no form
we entered the theater to watch the spectacle
lions leopards and panthers
I am faint and a-tremble
where is the hand that feeds the stars ?

01-21-18

RITUAL MADNESS

I invented you out of Chaos
no intervention of earth or water
no skies above just sheer imagination
and up you rose like Venus
out of surf-foam bathed wet
shining darkly in your pink shell
arms out-stretched to gather light
and then *Poof* gone in a second
to what other atmospheres fled
to wash your hair to wash your hair
and let it shine and let it shine
so early in the morning ?
when next I met you by the sacred oak
you were not the same unrecognizable
a sylph a waif a nymph in name only
washing your hair in the flowing stream
rinsing your hair in the purling stream
so early in the morning
for what goddess do you wash your hair

for what goddess do you shine
so early in the morning?
you're mad she said downright crazy
I'm not me and you're not you
I wash my hair for no one
there are goddesses no more
from Chaos blessed dark I come
not from earth or water
from imagination fully formed
I rose one dawn shaking my hair
in the dense and violent atmospheres
I am not bright I know no light
ringed with nacre and roseate
I emerge from the hell zones
from where wild dogs get their fill
of carcasses and carrion
from swirling spills of liquid death
I rise daily to wash my hair
you are not you nor am I me
you're crazy downright mad
to follow what you only imagine to be
a shadow ritually plunged in darkness
from Chaos sprung to Chaos
nightly I return to wash my hair again
and disappeared she did into the foam
the ancient eddies before time
and still a third time we met
in a city without name on a street
a hundred times repeated in its length
wandering dazed her hair just washed
I stopped to look and gaze
in a trance she was and shining wet
her massive inky hair seemed to blaze
through me she walked
as through a vapor cold
and disappeared forever
to wash hair in eternity
to shine forever in eternity

01-22-18

BACON FAT

hey Joe it's our birthday again tomorrow
what do you mean *again* ? it's been 8 years
    since I celebrated them I even
have a hard time recollecting what snow
hardened on the terraced hills behind
Saint Mary's hospital felt like you know
where we were born and it was dusky
dark evening the carillon bells from
the Plummer building were hushed and
wasn't that one of the first times I lost
consciousness seeing the marvels of
the Mayan night sky as never before
and you trying to pick me up off the
cold ground and the tree stump and
on the radio they were playing Handel's
Water Music going to Granny's house on
First Street you dragged me do you
remember what year that was 1947 ?
and the ice skating rink at Lincoln School
and lonely the way we meandered over
to frozen Bear Creek the sky all grey
menacing it was like dying all over
but again , No , Man , no such word
as *again* or maybe it was the Hora
Staccato on the radio the cars moving
slowly down the street dim lights
plowing the inky ocean trying to sleep
upstairs between frozen sheets unable
to recall how we got here the train haul
all the way from Culver City by the
MGM studios it was always winter in
the mountains invisible to dreamers like
you and me and the way the Old Man
hiding his tear-filled eyes would console
us promising Mom would get out of the
san and we moved into the place on Seventh
Avenue how many more winters before we
got drunk and made ourselves look like
thugs outcasts poets painters in a movie
version of Toulouse-Lautrec's life
our lives too in wild situational colors
moving faster through great icy Chicago
winter blasts and the train hugging Lake
Michigan or the blues on the afternoon
radio *My Love will never die*

but *again* ? so hazy this mind gets
drugs maybe or the supreme vision
of all the after lives possible rolled up
into one little 45 RPM record with the
big hole in the middle going round and
round playing songs like *Bacon Fat*
remember—there's a new kind of dance
sweeping the south—*diddly diddly whump*
I forget so much after that we separated
on a street corner in San Francisco
kept looking back to see if you were
looking back to see if
but *again* ?

01-23-18

LOVE : A DEFINITION

perfectly a dream it has all been you
I mean rushing at me with your mouth
on mine high inspiration it says on the screen
would this ever happen in real life ?
sleepwalking doing somersaults recalling
other lives other loves just this once upon
a time driving through neighborhoods
much like Greek ruins shattered temples
and automobiles ditched on side streets
lacking all four tires a section of sky
ready to collapse on the morning hour when
the milkman used to deliver his bottles
placing them on the steps glass containers
of white distances reminiscent of goddesses
waking out of an epoch-long siesta eyes
troubled with something seen unnamable
your entrance to a world that does not exist
increments of red stealing on night a moon
adjusted to fit your eyes and what's more
at the end of a long garden path littered
with rose petals hyacinth narcissus and
shadows invented by your absence the
why can't I get it straight absolution
cloud stains bitters mineral waters &
the thing the phrase that comes to mind
utter me ! shooting for a trip to Jupiter
now that's a honeymoon circling and
recycling and making adjustments for
the loss of time in space travel a dawn
like no other spreading its feathery flares

across a juxtaposed universe a dream
it must have been as you breathlessly
down the stairs in a blur of pinks and
eyes the shape of almonds a radio
somewhere deep inside to announce
an end to all Punctuation worlds collide
trying to say something through glass
a vision tripled by reflecting mercury
wound me ! archaic and immense Rock
between here and the following infinity
suggestions that poetry can no longer
sustain colors named for characters
of an unknown alphabet residing only
in your mind *You Beautiful Thought* !
subsiding in the last part of the dream
you are both ascending and descending
and the stairs are multiple divided by
the fourteen hemispheres of Heat
isn't it exhausting to imagine so much
to be so out of control just breathing
as if life could ever come to an end
staring down that animal emerging
from the pre-history of sand *Love* !

01-24-18

ON OUR 79TH

in the second it takes for eternity
to complete its first round I heard
the music on the radio exactly as it
was played lives ago in some other
world where you were still walking
gracing the air as leaves grace light
on opposite sides of the same space
we both occupied mirrors were set
to reflect what in each of us was
the *other* parallels like snowflakes
or blades of grass inseparably identical
why do we collect these maps of night ?
that music put me in trance hundreds
of universes came and went in a single
note the horns wailed mournfully
and a drum relentlessly kept rhythm
restraining wild horses moving as
they pulled the vast coffin of history
down the street right in front of
the house that came to accept us

in the winter of lost memory
which of us is still sleeping hard
making a labyrinth of the sky
and which of us is sitting up
talking to the multiple dead
who inhabit the dream of mind
even as the sun drains the sky
and day buries its head in ivy
who will know which is which ?

01-24-18

THE DEPTHS

shining and arrogant Duke Agamemnon
what did he know about his palatial end
just as shadows bleeding on the walls
or submerged in stygian deeps lost souls
clamor for light // come back !
at this point in life when all eternity
pivots on a single second perceived suddenly
will be you there ? will the heavens
cancel a thousand resurrections ?
we are and we are not let's face it
weaving in and out of factories of breath
leaves that rustle in the ear grass underfoot
and then *Wham !* the descent into chaos
desperately reaching for the promised hand
whole landscapes glimpsed in the fall
nature and air and planets without name
the moon itself glows red and fractures
insensibly into a thousand destinies
yours and mine in the mix plummeting
into the inexorable Ocean-of-Being
it's all been a confused and aimless dream
living and living again for the Hour
big empires of cloud and memory rise
and decline the minute we try to understand
what it is that is happening in the depths
where we stir from sleep aggravated
by the pointillism of light that briefly
enters through the window of childhood
only to be deflected turned into dusts
powders assuming shapes of distance
and longing // of distance and longing
++++++++++++++++++++++++++++++
this morning will be different we say
bright the sun will host multiple

appearances of phantom others
will they all be in colors and fade ?
what can be the outcome of trust ?
getting dressed communing with a god
who is responsible for the stairs
and joining finger to finger
buttons and shirts and coming out
through doors that weren't there before
Oh day of possibilities !
or is it a cruel hoax a splendid lie ?
the deity of misapprehension shines !
kisses can't be owned !
a hundred dollars buys a one-way ticket
to Hades and nothing more
one can never come back from anywhere
the dice are cast the fates sorted out
depths and more depths without asterisks
lovers mutilated by passion
the darker it gets the deeper the thrust
inextricable miasma of Love !
why should there be a way out ?
today will be no different
repetitions of scars the holy
today will be no different than
all the previous days and wounds
light will never penetrate this far down
voices proceeding from torn leaves
will plead for an end to twilight
depths deeper than imagination
more remote than mind
what else can there be ?
an inch one way or the other
what does it matter to the dead ?
+++++++++++++++++++++++++
the minute I saw you it was darkness
depths in your eyes depths in your mouth
there were no heights no skies
only the rushing tide of the deep
taking me away with you

01-25-18

ULTIMA !

chromeplate illusion I told you so
warning shots fired through verse
shouldn't have touched that dial
the button connects to the wrong side
and soon the whole thing will blow
how can we keep this escapade up ?
the language led to its own loss
a description of you before the war
a singular anatomical detail was it ?
sensation that this is for real and
not a literary juxtaposition between
two frames of converging light
spectra wildly out of proportion
to the space they seem to occupy
or suddenly it's the moon a hive
of eerie sequences in slow motion
high above our delusional heads
so kiss me one more time beside
this artifice of nightly ampersands
quoting from the Book of Books
does no good when the accident
is already in the past tense and
staring out the window three gods
plotting harmonies too beautiful
to endure the human mind a case
study in fractions and longings
thinking cannot make it better
so you are what it seems to be a
delicate wing a petal a softening
of the vowels it takes to resound
darkly the name they gave you
ULTIMA ! shifting obliquely
into the red zone time lapse
a sound that cannot be rightly heard
a phrase unique to statues on the
verge of acquiring human speech
syllables stammered in dream talk
one and one you and the mask
that personifies you in the dance
so many tens and a single twenty !
who can ever count the ways
you appear and disappear great
as the eye that conceived sand
asleep and adrift on inky waves
weaving the song between fingers

of grass dense green bending low
to the Apollo of broken distances
ULTIMA ! drink deep the dark
night the unending fade beyond
nothing else can be pronounced
how can we keep this escapade up ?
annihilating angel your face
fractured marble from the Island
where the sun lies buried

01-26-18

THE SPACE WHERE DARK IS BORN

black mercury ! black mercury !
heart numbingly tender the cruel sun
whose apparatus is glass of the baleful reflection
who can name a lesser day than his light
sliding like a knife into the oviparous wound
come to rest on skyscrapers of dust

vertigo is short for rust
you fall and all the red of the universe
becomes the dark centered in your eye
nothing you see has shape
hands are a way of losing contact

look into the sky of blue ! fists
thunder of hidden fishes and a concrete eye
testosterone and flaming antibodies
swarming in the broken ventricle
Olympus of obsidian corpses crying out
for the leaf from which they were torn
neither silence nor the hell-hound
remain to savage their invisible entrails

great geysered the gushing Mother
of all beneath pellicules of filmy algae
to see beneath the warp of air into
that nemesis crawling with queen of hearts
foam and adrenalin and hopping
she prances into the vagabond of Myth
nacre jade ambrosia the toothless mouth !

who has brought night forth from his wallet
and counted out time in twenty dollar bills ?
I cannot nor do I ken which is which
the unbearable inch of the sutured stairway
or the witless gathering of evenings

in the suppository of archaic delirium
wild decisions to void the path
when no one knows why the death
at one end differs from the death
at the other flowering and sulfurous

black mercury ! black mercury !
she who turns on and off the switch
running like a water of unending sand
the eye catches an instant of that exploding ink
extrapolations from a poetry of lost fingers
grass and depths tunneled through night
she moves one hip on either side of space
it is death asleep at last in its skull
of all reverberating silences
whatever else shifts from red to blank
whoever else has decided to be the *other*
if not Dante Alighieri emerging from the dross
and miasma of his unwritten *Poem*
taciturn as an Etruscan haruspex
eyes inverted gaze fixed on the polar star
everything is to burn in his idiom
chapel and oil dump and whistling snows
wherever his girlfriend has gone
whoever she has been in memory
is nothing more sheen of gorgeous disaster
stellar rotations beyond the spectrum
Zoom of invisible wings of intelligence
to remember in order to forget

black mercury ! black mercury !

02-06-18

AFTERLIFE

the first thought is no longer possession
but absence from particles and profusion
alpha seems to be the norm and omega
the least accessible and least desirable
beta is the waiting for eternity to end
gamma is the plus below the surface
where matter yields to space and zero
water emerges from rock rock dissolves
in the conversation between spirits
who contend for the soul of Achilles
suddenly delta lifts its spear and hurls
its venomous tip into the core of Being

sand is illustrative of the intricacies
that occur between moonrise and dawn
stars like a vast woof of question marks
spackling the back brain with urges
to thought when no thought can exist
vacuum and reorientation and zoom
why else does lamba lap the distances
and kappa fiercely adorned with myrtle
recite to all the unknown dead a hymn
to a Demeter of worlds long gone by
of wheat and oak and spar and nettles
memories of fingers on the loom plying
great tales of homecoming and heartbreak
places where no one has really ever been
caves grottos libraries filled with asterisks
an Egypt no map can describe and basalt
mu stands erect on the rim of time a breath
like ice in vertigo a collapse of all space
diminished omicron a vacant mouth
declares philosophy to be a rent veil
masks that have entered a relentless dance
pyramids and cities jungles of mankind
languages that have no recall of sound
does it matter that sigma lacks shadow ?
you and I have been here before standing
on the ridge where the sun lies buried
recounting as if to no one the myth of sleep
days numberless passing on a screen
argent crimson by turns and the song
of eventualities tau and upsilon eyes
that migrate heavenwards taking paradise
with them into the unforeseen and gone
which of us can withstand the *other*
which of us can lying still end the game ?

02-17-18

NEFERTITI

like a sleep of twenties you reoccur
dream slipper argent feather wing
clouds of imitation distance and pearl
nacre of the substitute for the goddess
gilded tombs paraphernalia of sand
insubstantial as the predictions of air
nothing assumes shape least of all you
divorced from the context of space
other than your voice like a wire
unraveling across the universe of mind
what a double physics of entropy
and ivy what a proof of anti-matter
the syllables that devour the poem
nothing means ! nothing matters !
fictions of five mirages of fifty
lessons about the trebled moon
red haunting at midnight of zero
perplex of you woven through beta
between depths alone you happen
both invisible and pataphysical
in the sleep that follows sleep a wave
waters so steep no cliff can feel
and submerged in the middle of it
radiant as the Nile-born lotus
your image asleep never to waken
recurs immense and yet smaller
than the planet X adrift in Cairo
how is it we have yet to meet though
I know you as I know the palm
of my intricately sewn left hand ?
is the world only the suggestion
of a place where you walked pale
as the fade of a week of Thursdays ?
the damp masses of your hair
phantom of sleep nerveless winds
the eye but not what the eye sees !

02-07-18

MYRMIDONS

repetitions of ink and sand
armies of myrmidons unseen
republic of transgression and pleasure !
indictments of paradise ! screw the gods !
rituals of flypaper and anathema
no more plurals of water but
the neuter gender of every living breath
round and round the sarcophagus
worm skins and bleeding lichen
grasses that grow downwards
Proserpina in her army pinafore
gathering heads of the recent victors
when were we ever so drunk
as to forego one last embrace
nettles and briars and nail-heads
down to the lethal mulberry grove
to where Agamemnon and Croesus
in their gilded attire perspire to death
shadows of the future in slow motion
Greeks in their tragic circumflex
futile stairways into the unknown
section by section of sky bled
until only the universal white of oblivion
glows in its all enticing fade
clouds that smother antiquity with arsenic
vestals beheaded and dancing wildly
round the priapic lore of stone
naked shame of history
subterfuge treason denials of reason
politics of the insane and incoherent
peace treaties ad nauseam
Westphalia and Vienna and Actium
you know them as emblems of glory
blind spearheaded thrusts into the dark
entrails of the universal basement
held at the waist by anvils Venus
tortured into confessing lust after lust
who doesn't envy her ?
let me tell you about the Neapolitan
who stared down the effigy of Stalin
or the native of Ancona who dared Socrates
into one more game of dice
to both the hemlock maze !
judgment by shattered antennae
dozen and one fragments of the number Zero

numinous and idiotic shreds of justice !
heaven is in all the burning hay
the troops of red ants are here at last
Brazil upside down in its umbilical carnival
charge ! is there anything more indecent
than the military parade ?
black suns black mercury black fish
all flashing through the startled eye
porphyry columns felled in an instant
by termite hordes and the emperor
of Byzantium drowned in ice cream
flush out the ancient seers !
heaven is in the mown grass of eventide
in the tender thread of saliva
that links nipple to lip *pink !*
while outside the raging glass
black ants weaving drunkenly
capture the Ionian sea !
the tales about the tale of *Ending*
are winding up their insane prologue
inches and meters and light years
fogs of desire mists of longing
hellmouth fission and counter fugue
multiple and incommensurate the entrances
to Hades where angry shades
desperately contend for memory
with insect depravity of the brain
the notorious et cetera
contraband fugitive erroneous conscience
Nemesis swarming hives
the countless the unnumbered
deathless and inconclusive
                      the

02-08-18

THE DEATH OF HERODOTUS

forgetting to kneel and pray
startled by the sound of a lark
and a tremendous shaking of earth
and sky commenced and as of angels
a sound of wings whirring loud
resonant as the hives of mount Hybla
turned to look and amazed at the Light
flares of incandescent speech !
vowels of clouds orgasms of thunder
syllables of all the unknown tongues

what rapture of mind-loss witless
consultation of the unconscious map
and the lark and a thousand like it
flown into a transept of fire just above
the pinnacle that used to be his head
imagine ! of course this was death
death itself the charged white lightning
the byways of burning gravel
and the great Sicilian landscape
of sun-drenched fields ablaze forever
where was it to turn and look
who was it to encounter with palsied hands
a flickering instant of life recalled
of seas navigated in less than an hour
and the oracle and the sun beam
and the many rushing naiads fleet
with mountains of water and grass
what was it ? a pulse beating somewhere
an arm reaching down from Olympus
the aching the dolorous longing
to be just once and then the words
backwards jumbled unrecognizable
fragments of an archaic brain
come and gone in the breath of a minute
death gloriously informed with zinc
flashes of interminable mercury
days collapsed into a light year
gravid with all the futures before time
death the lapse of consciousness
lying in a ditch waiting for the messenger
the dog-faced one and the Bride
risen from a single spear of mint
gorgeously resplendent in skin of music
tympana and sistra and gongs wild
processions of unidentifiable insects
proceeding through the nostrils
and the secret of the Pyramid
revealed in a single grain of sand
death parade of nilotic irises
lapping of endless waters whispers
rock and what generates rock
vast and empty the final O

02-08-18

SHAKTI

what is the mind between us ?
stellar distances or a millimeter
floral sensation of the overcoming
beyond what space can contain
lipstick intrigue cosmic hairdo
moonrise undulation of the hips
dead as the cadaver of the sea
mountain-born daughter asleep
in the dynamo of ash and dust
painted and repainted to apply
skin all over the lost hemisphere
tongue sticking out the tease
intercontinental belly dancing
each foot planted on the marital
corpse halves of bliss and anger
one-armed kings on blind elephants
tortoise and serpent and roebuck
princes born from nowhere
bearing messages of salvation
and true death to the uninitiated
how can red ribbons fasten thought ?
thighs calves ankles and toes
swart polished glistening with sweat
the dance of tongues and knives
the event which has never happened
the story that can never be told
everything is mystery and hair !
a book fifteen thousand volumes
in length with no beginning and end
to be read to the paralytic and deaf
to be tossed into the universal dump
even as she swells growing like ink
into massive and sumptuous prayers
her body the spirit of the unborn
who has never been will see her !
who walks puny catalyst on earth
how can he ever know what it is ?
in her eyes total crazy wildness
narcotics and stupor of genuine love
idiocy and vagrancy on the loose
follow her into the madhouse
where one by one she devours
anyone who thinks ! PARVATI !
snakeskin riddle undone girdle
fires seven years long and more

smoke married to the ruddy moon
that fills her navel and planets
never to be named and floating
off kilter causing full collapse
of the empyrean *gorgeous lust*
she can be everywhere and nowhere
mantras chanted a million times
even a Buddha like a cigarette
in her wanton luscious mouth
or Krishna who is all women
that cannot be possessed is hers
pendant dangling from the left ear
and the milk cows at the end of day
the setting sun wasted in its water
futile aggregates of the unfinished
what is anything at all to her ?
jugs of enormous nights spill
and the universal lamp goes out
still but vibrating like a rock
the shapeless and unformed *thing*
Power sleeping in her ingle
jungles ! vast stony ridges !
distance alone can approach her
what is the sum of zero times zero ?
eternal orgasm of the diamond !

02-09-18

PHANTOM HELEN

rejoicing in the landscape the rain
from afar and worshipping trees
stone and cliff the heights adore
so many the deities hidden there
between single blades of grass
or in the ochre stripes of twilight
or blossoming in nettle and furze
crocus and delight the eye amaze
but where oh where are you gone
in this plenty and riot of green
all colors of the spectra adorned
secrets of tufa flint and marble
shapes that come and go asleep
illusory meadows yellow sleeved
things that fly in bright air wings
and sprites the atmosphere dense
making echoes a folly to the ear
but oh where have you gone so

leaving here and here the void
a glassy distance the world seen
diminished in its inky sphere
no more clouded passing sky
nor thunder intones its threat
as if dismissing natural gifts
mourn your absence gods
who once seemed real in flight
or in groves of rock sparred
with shadow men for destiny
Troy ten times built to fall !
hush is the all around of dust
ghosts phantom outlines heroes
once they were in gleaming
but now like you alone gone
to other woods inextricable
by day the hoopoe cries by night
screech owls do Hecate's bid
have fled you have leaving
behind a torn cloth a print
in the restless sand a scent
of musk and oriental balm
does Mycenae rear its head ?
vast and ominous the silence
spreading its quilt like a sea
over the western world's camp
moon its ruddy splendor sheds
revealing destroyed walls
turrets gone to mould and
gates gaping open rusted pins
scattered architectural illusions
some say to have seen you
flitting like a desecrated angel
over Egypt's deathless tombs
others claim you are *Selene*
the lunar double the archaic
forever and repeatedly dead
yet like a memory of sheets
and trebled mourning choirs
your own self weaves through
dreams and dreams alone
never more to see daylight
nor to traverse these meadows
this arcadia of never was
to no one you now belong
but to me your shepherd
your errant prideful fool

lying on this raving step
communing with an alphabet
drawn up by cranes on high
and dissolved in a single gust
time and space all nothing
                spent

02-10-18

THE RUDIMENTS OF POETRY

speeches oriental and otherwise
soft air brings us and poetry
colossal hewn from rock unformed
endlessly unknown the within
what man most ignores and rising
verses mantic and disheveled voice
breezes too winding round branches
that talk and singing loud unsound
oracles unbind to the ear unheard
longing as green in unfurled grass
visceral components of meter
strung out or shattered in mid-air
the swift and cunning mechanics
of the god schoolboys most adore
a region somewhere else that poetry
breeds fading pale as statuary
in an infinite noontime sun or
the intellect of bees raveling honey
spun in weightless ingots for mind
to contemplate if this is a poem
if a poem is this bracken weir
to the left of the great sonant vowel
if sometime a resounding theogony
bursts in the seamless sky a thunder
clap a vertebrate emotion to blaze
making beautiful what cannot
be kenned the unmeaning drone
chanted in the brain's cave
a fiercely wild string of syllables
never to be read or catalogued
what other than this poem is a poem
to be and salient thrusts of light
and bonfires in the shape of dusk
sundered from the ink of understanding
apply nothing to the blank sections
quadrants of the firmament afire
it is here once we plied the oars

and rowed unskilled to Circe's isle
so we dreamed in eddying waters
mid afternoons in childhood's abscess
when light and dark the hell of time
the underwood and grasping tufts
we strayed immense with pleasure
to the Source where poesy's stark rose
blooms underground with the Dog
quizzical the leaves displayed their
opaque design pages uncut of the Book
no poem but what lies underneath
behind the mountain and the wing
we will never get there no matter
how much we tread earth's history
unhewn masses shimmering distance
so much poetry so little sense
rings of shorn hair fingers missing
dactyls at last a nostalgia for

02-11-18

CORPUS

the body what is it but a field
fictitious yet pain laden love
's labor across it strays some
times shoulder and neck
aching back out thrown when
leaning into other spheres
really it is spirit a rock
inhabited by idea of motion
moving through grazing
star meadows to believe it
is matter with a name born
from somewhere come a
mystery that cannot be
recalled unless it is water
the rolling tides darkening
twin of night its death always
a threat in day's light maze
filling anticipation fuels
muscles drives legs spins
brain into thinking feet
can actually obtain length
distance of time it takes
to breathe deep hold it and
see inward where a deity
supine and puzzled thinks

for it is a legend of pasts
unwritten grottos lairs
where lay its ancestor in
wait for love's soul depart
then with me Little One
to where such things have
no weight nor height even
as hair grows and nails
paint and lips smoking rouge
concede lay the shadow out
sheets around illusion
mourn what the sinews
nerve wrack bone smitten
fall head over heels for that ?
coming to be and thinking
it is even as the frontiers
fade and sleeping makes
it worse to wake was it
a dream the after all
feeling for limbs to course
blood through vital sums
call this a life ? looking
out through a lens enlarged
skies clouds opus number one
music in the left ear but
what happens in the shell
resounding oceans longing
in the right hemisphere
and speech too tongues
rattling on about love'
s corpse the delight

02-12-18

NOCTURN

when least expected a volley of shafts
from the left flank near the sand mounds
all night an eerie whistling a wind of sorts
the sea whipped up around the listing barks
it was Apollo at his deadly keenest ready
to wipe out the entire argive team in no
time flat fuck the hawsers and nets and oars
what good's a prayer to the gods anyway
Venus got 'em into this ruckus and what
does she give a damn hosiery and pinks
torn garter what else is new disheveled
lurking behind some ancestral stone and

prepared to give Hera a brick's length
of trouble the raw oyster-eyed bitch they
eftsoons are at each other as anything
under the rotting moon the world is carrion
dogs and birds of prey bad omens lice
ant hordes peeling the skin off dreams
and night the color of the river Styx
enveloping the fuming camps in their
stews and Achilles pissed and brooding
behind his battered gear won't talk to
anyone but his darling sweet Patroclus
and on the other side haughty stuck up
Agamemnon king of men taking up
his brother's cause and stealing girls
hard won booty of his prize warriors
so what hand of cards is Zeus dealing
tonight strip poker or is it Russian roulette
loves to watch 'em die dumb mortals
cast about on their pine-wood skiffs
across the back of the unruly waters
what's it all about these walls and gates
raving bards mantic words shoveled out
into the impending death-watch on the
steps slivers of moonlight ruddy oasis
of thought the whole lot of 'em cursed
unable to turn fate around on its wheel
feverish talk about afterlife underground
shadowy fades of memory is it true ?
who has been there and back who has
spoken with the long-gone ones amiss
heavy heads wine sloughs despond hoar
the ground dampens chill with awesome
reading of the planets high circling lost
can one measure time by their motions ?
drop the laden body down for another
bout with Morpheus softening brains
whorls of yellow distances the mind !
someone something howling in the murk
is it Menelaus dreaming in his arms
Helen almost immortal with her beauty
white armed pillow bosomed deathless
writhing beside her shepherd Alexander
puce colored dandy in his leather strips
a hog's head of venom on 'em all shivering
in the multilayered chambers of Palace
Hector in their midst the big one best
of the fifty sons and how many wives

Priam doddering old thing sceptered and
one eye already dead in the beyond of it
how many of 'em would survive the day
to come dusty moiling ruts of horse dung
thongs unpaired sandals rusting greaves
what does it all come to ? a messy pile up
of corpses unidentifiable from either side
sleep on heroes ! images wavering come
and go in the museum of illusions what !
turn aside the longing visions of home
islands bedecked in fogs and thyme
come away the end has been foretold
delicate arms beckoning from other lives
eyes inviting you all to lasting pleasure
disoriented the great bodies in rags
sublime wasting fragments lost
echoes only echoes
gone

02-13-18

THE ENVELOPE WITH YOU INSIDE IT

a valentine poem

not huge sums of money wadded tightly
nor secrets buried in coded script
nor contraband photographs of Venus
how could she compare to you anyway ?
locks of hair smiles perfumes lip gloss
the intent to convey loss of identity
borne on the wings of egrets on high
you never were anything but thin air
light enough to elude life's contours
fitting as only distance can in the envelope
and sealed and stamped to be carried
around in the vellum lining of a god
one who controls each step of the way
up the spiral stairway to the clouds
to the invisible mansions of long dead
deities now passed from mortal memory
unlike you impassioned with new wings
and a face radiant as t'ang dynasty brass
bright fulminating and yet absent as
the verses of the great unwritten poem
the one about you and only you unformed
elemental sourceless beaming darkly
underground sun radiating the depths

will you ever conform to the light ?
how did you happen to invent this space
small dense breathless like the moon
as it rises over the poetry of lost hills
your poetry your unencumbered words
that can never be pronounced right
how did you ever ? and is there nothing
afterwards but the enormous silences
that occur between alpha and tau ?
should I ever receive this envelope
should I dare to carry it with me to
the House of the Dead where daily
I levitate and practice the drone of time ?
are you really within this folded paper
sleeping and sleeping as if night
would never end and dreaming myths
and speaking too yes talking to blanks
subterfuge of heaven recondite vowel
the shape of your mouth in trance
longing and aching and a cigarette
the careful decision to smoke inside
when no one can be looking and signs
that the flame is your heart alive
beating like a sparrow's pulse
somewhere in the recess of that thing
to open it just once to spirit away
the essence of the poem's abracadabra
green violet and especially red !
the rest is a parenthetical conclusion
haunted asterisks fading commas
a wind the shape of your hair blowing
far and far away into stardust

02-14-18

THRENODY

Juno unable to hold back her wrath
and so it goes cloud troubling menaces
from the peaks of Mount Ida daily it seems
purplish thunderheads the wreck of summer
wasted fields of once yellow bright
withered on the vine the coming harvest
and from afar unseen mourning voices
whose corpse washed ashore this time ?
air spackled with torn winding sheets
winds from the underground whoosh
bringing chill to even the hottest sands

how many times to hear this dirge ?
only the dead know the precursor of
the alphabet the mortal zetas & mus
intransigence of anything that follows
zero anything that precedes alpha
numinous hieroglyphs carved from air
bespeak the human condition aloud
yet in silence other bodies wash ashore
faint vowels and dissipating consonants
language was ever the dangerous line
beyond which heroes ran precipitous
into the abyss they said was glory
howling and rabid cries ululations
manifestations of truth and lies weeping
diphthongs and circumflex accents
humming and droning recitations
of an unheard poetry across skies
yet to be invented heavens and paradise
itself the gorgeous untruth and walls
dividing tongue from tongue madness
what is ever the supreme noise ?
tides keep rising like blood swells
mothers on balconies blanched
blind with crying oblivious of rains
and tempests and thunderstrikes
how many worlds have come and gone
in an instant between what has been
and what can never be a speaking
among statues and tombstones
between quarries and cliff sides
tons of water dense as a Cyclops' eye
herds of phantom cattle slaughtered
by the sun in dawn's single radiance
over and over again hexameters
meant to praise the emperor fail
their marmoreal verses resounding
in a cacophony of ink and ampersands
detritus of clouds homophones of light
destiny in a clump of grass tossed
into the ditch where a hundred sons
of men lie moldering and unwept
why go on ? mothers ! mothers !
silence swings its rusty scythe over
the landscape and Juno pompous
in her unjustified ire sways on her chair
golden sandals bracelets ringing wildly
ear pendants like jewels of blood

how much more the poet can descry
nothing allays the deep threnody
overdue conclusion to world history
rock and strife grief and stone
lingering hues of the last sunset
lamp sunk forever in Tartary's depths
Persephone herself whitened to the
point of no return an echo of color
a fade wringing her heart
mother ! she tries to cry
but lacks voice no sound
not even a whisper

02-15-18

THE END OF THE WORLD

Shostakovich's 5th symphony

do words matter anymore ?
snatches of sound rags of air
tripartite vowels bleeding sense
leaves torn from their own voices
a music of kettle drums and harp
underlying harmonies of menace
gone the arcadian flute & pan's pipe
here on the edge the circumference
of hell episode and cracked metaphor
laying the ear to the floor board
to listen to water rotting in its shell
mythiform clouds on the wrack
carbon copies of Troy ten times over
seashores eaten by atomic rust
verses of inextricable density waft
like swarms of stunned fireflies
shattered idioms of dead atmospheres
does language in all its violence
have meaning for the drugged mind ?
porches where evening gathers in knots
and girls in summer wear learn dying
by hearing for the first and last time
Shostakovich's 5th symphony *Loud*
grasses crash and unbearable ivy
like violins hitting an impossible high
bittersweet aftermath of the pyramids
everything sotto voce in the rains
that descend in unending decibels
what is the construct of syntax

when the orchestra of mind is gone !
etched in soot over the left eye
paradigm of the holy suture of Apollo
the bow and the lyre and the tortoise
beckoning with a distant melody
the fevered thought of the undone self
what is ego in this panoply of asterisks ?
note by shivered note the music
by turns brass and reed and pounding
nothing can be spoken unless by statues
in a parody of the human condition
vision punctuated by quarries
where rock is mined for wings
to take aloft the remains of sound
beyond the tongue's dumb prattle
into a surfeit of Olympian silence
seraphic as the final unheard note

02-16-18

EROTIC

rush of cellophane and camellias
what sounds like rains in the stoned ear
fluids and detritus of the last visible planet
anxieties about the grass growing
in unkempt patches near the lost well
supreme addiction to wind and ether
what cannot breathe rock and sand
moss intense as an unmoving thought
gathering nights in the dissembled noon
of statues that are learning to speak
blind sight homophones of fire and ice
and tongues restless and uprooted
seeking mouths twin fictions of depth
wherever you turn there are houses
darker than the base of mount Everest
or windows that fly and rooms vacant
of floor and ceiling and whatever else
is impossible to relate in attic Greek
resemblances of hair to shapes of ink
you in the midst of typhoons of perfume
offering only your shadow to the god
of intellect and debasement hungry
as he is for mortal inches for honey
for whole hives of incontinent poetry
yours is the last verse alive ! *Lyrica* !
pictures of Aphrodite passed around

from palm to palm unseeing witless
great movie theaters of antiquity
screening the abyss of love and time
star fucked ruins circling outer space
incredible to say that you are Nowhere
you have never been and have ceased
to exist but in rumors spread by stone
to the remnants of water lapping
the gorgeous shores of Cyprus long
ago when telephones made of ivy
related monotonous descriptions
of you performing speech acts while
smoking cigarette after cigarette
in an effort to eradicate the afternoon
will the flight of bees from the porch
finally reduce this minute to its eternity !
evenings come and go in the quarry
sensation of leaves rustling in the camera
taking your photograph in negative
outlines of philosophical miscomprehension
it has never been white nor black
it has always been red only *Red !*
when you wake you are on the moon's
back side oblique faint panting
for light to consume years of flame
you turn and disappear thin as air
mountains argue over your essence
suns rise and fall in perfect harmony
with the incontestable death of the Hour
come away My Friend to where jazz
archaic as Osiris shattered resounds
leaving us deaf and wildly unshaped
one and the other absolutely Undone !

02-17-18

BROWARD COUNTY

the thing at the top
where does it come from
where is it going
it's not noon yet and
what's in the middle
I'm tired of this talking
vegetating between stone
and stone the world too
is a hiatus between
what is more abrupt
than this dying in music
a fane to the side fading
temple ware statuary
broken off at mid point
just when speech begins
to alter what is perceived
I'm thinking a radical
light is becoming sleep
or sky following a line
straight to the source
of red and its homophone
a brilliant luster at the
tip or the end of time
easily a conjecture aren't
you as well in your store
bought shoes and hose
a listening close to the
ear where the hair falls
over a section of cloud
really destined to meet
somewhere off the map
a junction of asterisk and
ampersand syntax devolved
cannot make it a sense
when meaning is else wise
correct me if the thing at
the left beginning to sound
its noise a fix of words
making a poetry seems
if one could get over
the tragedy the loud awful
a god bawling his eyes out
in the corridor and kids
running over the maze
epic quotes big in the air

smoking blue and grey
the one in the pinpoint skin
the other one I mean falling
off the cliff of reason
madness aiming its dereliction
like a gun at the portrait
of a former president or
his insane wife azure hair
ink blot brain a flame
can become great a line
from a radio lyric
come back to haunt
as always the ones left
behind in the detritus
who mourn them the
sea comes up to its knees
a long sad siren you
can hear it forever

02-17-18

INEFFABLE

an exercise in red falling down
all about the intricacies of light
fascination with darkness with night
the all encompassing in its many
shapes and forms and the voices
deep within resounding like seas
in the ear's small shell speaking
about nothing yet great with mind
pursuing love's longing distance
never can be obtained never be
felt unless sleeping in stone inside
porous rock inside the libraries
of unknown alphabets where sand
designates its ciphers of zed and
beta symbols for houses emptied
of history how many times must
it be and begin to write and sign
on pages of air the multiple thought
that has no beginning and numinous
clouds deities mansions of ether
so many myths tangled in ink
and the legend of hair and smoke
witnesses of a beauty taking on
a statuary of the remote body
whose is it why does it emerge

from a water the size of memory
what can never be understood
ineffable moments in an afternoon
punctuated by nostalgia's mountains
is there a who we are is there a
mask and a persona recited
to an audience of rock and moss
echo is the color of its fading
weaving in and out of woods
and dales there where for a brief
whoever it is has looked in a well
to discover the moon's face
which is the face of the other
resembling white and the pallor
of a goddess gone underground in
search of the poem about the poem
various the hues and ringing
enormously distant contained
in a single vowel unpronounceable
unless in dreams stringing sounds
sublime and haunting of a return
but it remains sleeping alone
yearning for its double in a glass
set up to refract the passing stream
the subterranean rush to nothing
the poem itself an eddying vanish
the fade of impossibilities
you could never have been *there*
you were never anything but love's
illusion the unwritten poem
fragment and ruin
loss and

02-18-18

ELEGY : HENRY THOMAS r.i.p.

paranoia dishonesty and suicide
such as the world is and more
how tender then childhood memories
when explosions of atmosphere and
cruel metaphor conjoin to annihilate
do you recall how he got out of the car
moving slowly to the schoolhouse door ?
that was before mythology took over
reading the sky like a book
opening cloud after cloud to discover
a Pandora's box replete with evils

smoking subterfuges alien dispositions
a life ahead without foreseeable stakes
who was the rosy cheeked cherub
climbing the stairs toward a future
as much tragedy as comedy ?
can never gain back those lost years
episodes that took a whole summer
grasses of longing totem beasts
lurking in the eaves a distance
of immense and indecipherable poetry
how many times does it take a minute
to resolve its own eternity ?
a fabric worn away to nothing
life's poorly punctuated syntax !
no one can really understand it
to make sense of an illusory topography
sailing over suburban lakes
smoking one endless cigarette
taking a chance with alcohol
or pretending that July is forever
when winter dominates the hills
and a music at once pounding thrill
and a threnody of sobbing violins
come on ! make it last !

02-19-18

THE GIRL I LEFT BEHIND

tumbling out of a toy-filled attic
unkempt wistful dressed in pinks
eyes brimming with what can never last
how did she come to age so swiftly
what does it take to keep her
forever young boundlessly joyful ?
forget her ! illusion and deceit
money laundering tickets to hell
desperately anchored to a dream
sudden encounters with spirit world
in which jade transfers ego to zero
literary subjects quarrel with stone
goddess in transparent oriental skin
makes music to the deaf of heart
little by little the shoreline recedes
cliffs respond with defiant echolalia
skies burst open their favorite month
clouds of ink thunder rattling sulfur
yellow ochre indigo violet Red !

she cancels green she favors crimson
valentine gifts dangerously unseen
comes and goes she does in a waft
of nicotine and opiates a vision
to be embraced like treachery
does the soul really know itself ?
listening to a small year-long radio
a song about skin and adultery
combs and purulent lip gloss
hunger for forbidden meats
fruit kept on ice for weeks on end
she makes circles of heat and radiance
underground sun bronze planet
itching to have a go at her shadow
at the outline she makes passing
through miles of glass and Lo !
when the street finally decides
the houses on either side collapse
in heaps of cardboard and rubbish
dust gathers its encomia and flies !
in the midst of centennial ruin
she stands tottering like Cassandra
raving on her ant-consumed steps
cannibal fictions of the girl
I left behind of the girl I bought
and sold and put up for auction
wild as she was in her moment of flame
a distance a longing a rage to know
what can never be revealed !

02-19-18

IUDICIUM PARIDIS

the judgment of Paris

old story the same as ever was
mountaintop culmination flowering
bees and ivy sun florid
dense the tropical beauties thigh
and curve essentially shining
what a measure to wrap around
waist and hip the limelight
in their eyes goddesses in name
stepping around coral and jade
small feet smaller minds yearning
what is it you want ?
basis of addiction the first hit

of the day wanting still more by noon
shepherds of the court flute and lyre
arrows laid aside hearts stoned
with adjectives of love
scenic drives zigzagging hills
what with ancient sun fixed
in the meridian of time far from
the sea where it will die tonight
for now the contest is on and she
who will gain the most in her skin
of sea-blue mist steps carefully
crowned with iridescent something
Paris away from home dazed
not knowing whether asleep and dreaming
or in an otherworldly trance
adjusts his gait mailing a secret kiss
to the purloined bride just waking
in her palace of oriental hours
how many the attributes of passion
grasses and weeds and small birds
alive with the joy of youth
a stone comes undone from its dark
someone on the other side
of the color red recites a poem
long and distant with the unheard
why won't you come forth
Bright One ? such is the tale
as it unravels its parti-colored threads
each for the unit of sky it takes
to compose the music that accompanies
the various acts of the tragicomedy
and mountains with their rills
chorus the pageant unfolding
stepping over pebbles and moss
each of the three divinities
but only one—*You !*
will receive in italics
and without further punctuation
the prized apple the fruit
myth and symbol of death
mouthed and garlanded and signed
by devotees of Mystery
with her hair undone and still wet
from her morning sea
takes the *thing* to her breast
and fleet as dawn's moist zephyr
disappears in a cloud of sand

aloft wondrous of love
labyrinth of light
enigma !

02-20-18

PERSEPHONE : THE DIFFICULTIES

the next time will be one of difficulties
to believe that it was you waiting on the steps
it must have been someone else one of the dead
one of the many who have come and gone
denying the light of day and breath
but certainly it was not you impatient
your face a lunar engraving tinted copper
not you but an imposter a moving statue
a color of remote hills and a wind
as if grazing on naked treetops in winter
shaping the chasm of your hair blowing
in the damp afternoon air a difficulty
to compare this resemblance to that of
an angel broken in sudden flight down
to earth only to meet an invisible barrier
yet there was no sound no crashing nothing
but the eerie sense of an archaic ruin
were you waiting for someone else
for a smoking wraith a spirit from hell
come back to inveigle you to accompany
it underground where intricacies of white
wrap around dim and shattered distances
a symbol only your presence almost shaking
did you lift a hand to the difficulty
that was approaching you as in a dream
did you reach out to hold an expectation
a less than familiar being voiceless and
where was I going then if not to the still
point where the cosmos pauses before
annihilating itself in a burst of sleep
immensely yellow then fading the bloom
of difficulties alternately azure and crimson
petals failing falling fading dizzy hues
was there a deep pool where your feet edged
difficult to say or even to imagine
a motor purring then the silence of otherness
a step forward without shadow you
more difficult than ever trying to talk
to transmit something of what you had seen

descending effortlessly below the grass
have you really returned then ?

02-21-18

FOOTNOTE TO HISTORY

what of the dictionaries incunabula
palimpsests hermeneutic tools lacunae
lexica disordered grammars *what !*
syntactic derangement textual hiatuses
illegible indecipherable fragments missing
pages unnumbered exordia postscripts
no known authors anonymous chronicles
undigested formulae black magic unreason
insanity poetry that has no origin no end
massive sections in untranslatable languages
madness to adhere to logic to assume
when it is chaos a nilotic palm leaf torn
to shreds what was there in the fading ink
to read misinterpret and misunderstand ?
wedged between the lines notes inscribed
centuries later small red dots squiggles
ampersands broken in half loud almost
in their insane need to divide the heavens
into what can be and what can never be !
almanacs astrological charts celestial maps
rendered useless by the light principia
ultimatums apparent forgeries lyrical
passages so sublime they cannot be finished
who is there to understand the ineffable ?
come away from the dark room with
negatives still wet microscopic thoughts
insect shapes caught between parchments
illusory conjectures about the script
itself a sequence of faint hieroglyphs
on rotting linen wrapped around mummies
death threats personifications of the goddess
rumors of intellect and pomp musical
digraphs in the corners pieces rubble
dust heaps really nothing more than
absences of mind stylistic deviations
exhausted sand remnants the descent
down crumbling stairwells into libraries
plundered a dozen times over histories
forever lost beneath vast grassy plots
where the river used to wind a finger-thin
trail leading nowhere enigmatic clues

chemical abstracts acid stains speech ruins
statuary mangled by religious fanatics
the City ! labyrinth of unplanned streets
buried under centuries of darkness
where there is nothing left to conjecture
night swelling its damp corpus over lands
that have ceased to exist nameless wilds
is there anything for us to inherit ?
silences dim shifting movements oblivion
the lamp and the wheel and the pyramid
gone forever from use and category
numbers that can never be counted aright
only the sky revolving on its eternal axis
unsighted now remains a distant memory
fading pale small useless incoherent
such was

02-21-18

THE ARCHAIC

out of the stubble emerging white
like a wraith bound invisibly to air
crying out for an archaic presence
to come forth a shaking of things
stone rooted to darkness yet aching
speech acts in rock sundered by rain
sand and melancholy together in
sleep where melded to a bright shape
come together daughter and light
wrapped and woven in a lamp
begin here the tale of loss weeping
above ground searching the grasses
for the finger and its ring unscripted
how many years and water rising
to the sculpted knee of a goddess
rushing like a dark wind over hills
that have never known the sun's rays
or eyes suddenly opened to night
haunted by voices proceeding from
leaf and ivy and whirring wings
a bead of dew an ear of wheat
three times around the mill pond
taught to pray backwards to trees
letters mysteriously engraved
on a marble slab fire springing
from ancient bone-texts in the west
what is to wake the violent mind ?

who is to endeavor the plow ?
cattle heard talking at midnight
sheaves learn to walk the fields
a river is born flowing from the ear
of the deity who governs storms
not in moderation language dreams
speaking and being silent in amber
whose hand reaches out to touch
the adjacent linen clad shoulder
arousing from a profound slumber
the genius of time a radiant *female*
combustible from the waist up
who treads the serpent kingdom
her enormous and plangent face
sheds tears for all sentient beings
heat circles her passing shadow
gravity fails to act in her aura
who can the mountain-born be ?
a verse gnomic and preterit issuing
from a crevice in the Sybil's mind
listen carefully to the vowels
rounding out of the unformed mouth
legend separating space and matter
small reeds playing breezes softly
a melancholy sets upon the world
ancient consonants caught in branches
work to summon thundering sky gods
and summers brilliant and lost
with their thousand children manifest
only to wane into the pale beyond
nothing but unfinished fables
tales of bees and remote fastnesses
where nymphs are born to beguile
unto the death unsuspecting men
the afterwards is a silent flood
a drowning of the senses a fade
tiny eddies faces swirling in myth
no sooner seen than forgotten

02-22-18

ISIS MY ISIS !

balsamic fragrances wafting Lord of the West
is come sleeping gifts of sand and myrrh
in his hands and tripartite skies open up
and clouds with mysterious inscriptions
and blue and green skin and ostrich feathers
decorating the crown and everywhere shadows
follow issuing from the great Underground
where men go to be relieved of their flesh
sacrosanct testimonies oracles inscrutable
who will accompany him ? chosen among
girls of the Secret Palace *you* linen draped
solemn pausing to drink of the immortal
stream that runs under and through stone
and affixed to your brow the sun Sign
tilting always to the vast unknown occident
you proceed like a wraith through radios
announcing the morning of the ritual bath
the multitude of unseen listening for a voice
paradise ! someone offers the self to you
for indigo and sashes of crimson-dyed silks
clothe your being inky insubstantial thing
yet to be lauded hummed sung chanted
ever in the rooms where no one enters
allow yourself then ! shake the sistra
signal to the ones on high the Hour is nigh
loved and loving in a ceremony of powders
red and thrice red the air blossoms wild
adore you ! no one has ever come so close
to the Text no one has never been so far
from the Text and everywhere there is Loud
boom and banging of the seed of Creation
dustless your feet graze earth's slight skin
your hair amazed with its voluptuous waves
takes the atmosphere and strangles it !
color yourself azure hyacinth and jade
swim downstream to the Nether world
and there become one with the lotus eaters
those who make holy all detritus
with them you partake of the bits of heaven
the 26 pieces of Osiris ! luxuriate
in the densities of after-time the deeps
unfolding before your awesome motions
one and one are three and you see *it* !
many-named a hundred goddesses You
are the unnamable One the errant star

celestial embodiment of the unthinkable
numinous ! what does it take to see you
repeated asterisk in the hemline of space ?

02-22-18

A SMALL LOVE POEM

dreaming about it doesn't make it so
daylight and the question of ownership
the sun's enormous contribution fails
to illumine the mysteries at the root
every time you come into view scathed
from another of life's untoward buffs
your radiance hidden by a wounded
partnership with light the edges frayed
why don't you admit the impossibilities
of ever being mine however much you
multiply your colors your eye shadow
the sense of danger in your mouth *the
the the* and all the other articles of
faith and understanding floral sprays
celestial hints at nothingness depths
the alternate to climbing the stairs
flight ! does the door slam shut ?
where does the window end and air begin ?
oracular phrases that occupy the mind
without being translated and the famous
disregard of the cigarette to elucidate
what it is the smoke is gathering around
its disappearance other than your lips
the once and only time is forever kissing
departures and arrivals on the clock
when no one is looking start the motor !
I can't remember where I left my hands
nor what it is I was doing when I left you
the last time we met at the crossroads
it was midnight in your pupils inky
distances stretching out into the galaxy
echoes of echoes star glitter moon drop
ancient as all things really are !

02-23-18

JOE ! INTIMATIONS OF ETERNITY

running the hand over the surface of sleep
a bas-relief with figures half hewn from myth
craving for the ever absent light the shapeless
effort of a landscape totally dark night-swept
beings partially human apparently agile moving
over frozen waters carved from impossibilities
and the drowned voices visible as luminous
fish or darting algae-like things in a rush
to find fusion with a distance not perceived
marble and jade and basalt structures hazy
lingering in the bottom land of dream image
configurations of thought becoming speech
yet unutterable unheard emissions of sound
vowels freed from stone and silences of rock
sand shifting in great storms like clouds
over the moon's erratic eye and sky *deaf!*
posing as a mountain of bluish air propelled
slowly across the enormous red shift of time
where in this turbulent fixity of things are
you ? yearning to wake within the tree's
ineffable soul blind root white streaming
nerveless juncture of fingers groping dazed
in a ferment of new grass dew and tufts
seeking atmospheres and ether and heights
a legend of unwritten roles transforming
the strange riddle of mind into potentials
of consciousness and otherness illusory
visions like paintings on a passing screen
depicting the lives of others never yours
never the stasis of the dormant idea of you
but fluid antinomies like fogs of blue acid
flaring across the back brain reaching out
to fasten a childhood with the skin of memory
to grow ! flowers come running back to you
embrace them ! eternal moment when green
alters the cosmos with its budding rapture
stars erupt out of an intransigent breath
universes glittering like pinwheels high
in the bright second when all things come
to be then pass from the evidence of time
back into the circular origins of space
somewhere out there where you are running
pacing your shadow with an unseen dog
racing to the stream of endless summer a

moment a single instant of bursting light
Joe ! intimations of eternity

02-23-18

HIATUS ii

glyphs of improbable beauty to be read
only in sleep dreaming faceless dark
punctuations that isolate your name
obscured by fantastic cloud passages
you will never be more than a hiatus
between lives an ampersand at best
interpolated among the various moons
that dot the transient western horizon
evenings gone by in the history of hills
mountains cliffs endless sand the ruddy
fading at the margins of being
alone at last you drifting misty beyond
any syntax a momentary illusion
as you appeared in the text of myths
waterfalls grottos dark recesses wild
entanglements of thought and hair
Nymph of the radiant distance !
sometimes there are inches of heaven
or avenues blind exits to paradise
where in a car driven by dusky horses
you pass by waving at the signposts
of language green and circular and
meaningless ultimately pale vanishing
soundless echoes ! what were you trying
to say to the mute legendary beings
whose lives like so many parentheses
shone for a brief haunting instant ?
myself among them dazzled and
striving to recognize in the glass
dense as an ink flowing through time
You ! what is it to wake in the Beyond?
multiple the mystical brides ! but only
One who survives longing and silent
out there nocturnal among planets
of unnamed dust oracular events
whispers opaque vowels dying shifts
when red is finally put to rest
what is it we are forever seeking
              but never find ?
what is it the hiatus separates ?
the inhabited world is lost !

02-24-18

ENIGMA

what does dead poet dream if not
the cancelled erased forgotten line
the one about the mountain's
dusky hue the distance between
water and air the fine distinction
between heaven and paradise
the infernal final sense of ending
before starting the following line
dead poet's qualms about illusion
the everywhere following love's
inky trail into madness and oblivion
what was her name where was her
house how did she come to be so far
which was the way out of the mess
why and why again did the line not
possess the right meter or syllables
which was the vowel and which the
consonant cluster to be avoided
and all the time was red the answer
were there really gods on the stairs
who was the vacant one down below
could one begin writing the same
thing all over again repeating always
the same errors and misgivings
choice of words not of subject but
how could the poem ever justify
itself sleeping in context of night
darkness taking over infirmity
of purpose a second thought a fuse
ready to go off an accident of love
yes virtual longing and myth
landscapes of emotion and trouble
dangerous syntax of the unavoidable
the once and for all ineffable that
should have been spelled out high
and loud as the recurring echo
bees swarming in the grassy ear
lying down pretending it wasn't so
gazing at the passing clouds above
where the *Name* dissolved pale
then reassembled itself unrecognized
how could the lyric be other than
a bell resounding in the archaic
a calling forth of the Muses !
one by one weaving through mists

clad in a skin of song and bright
only to fade before being perceived
by the poet already dead in mind
lost in the seemingly endless maze
of her hair and earth's fragments
enigma and grief the forlorn

02-25-18

WHAT ARE THE GODS UP TO ?

Salve ! birds bells feathers ringing
earth an inky rumor in the fuming
disregard of space loss of consciousness
by the dry well in the eastern field
small animals pause for divine light
disguised as a hag Gaia passes by
not daring to cross the lintel of mortality
what has been lost ? do grasses throng
underfoot ? thunder ! hail stones the size
of moons bang ! bang ! bang !
glass shatters omens split wide open
each of us has a mind to shift
moving from city to city in the dark
longing and subterfuge like derricks
why does one die while the other
survives wrapped in cool dewy sheets
intense activity in the ant heap
marauders with fading Greek faces
emerge sawing hemispheres of air
night like pinpricks in the eyes
of doctors who move ice blocks
back and forth on the southern border
altars half built temples insect hoards
skies menacing but decreased in area
where is the Cloud-Gatherer ? where is
the dancing Deity ? where is the goddess
serpent-haired and violent in her
triple-form ? where are any of the thirty
thousand three hundred and thirty three
gods ? marble sand and limestone
libraries drug stores football fields
artists dragged from their brains
involved in the instant of divine madness
chaos ! lumberyards ready to blaze
where is the memory to return ?
who doesn't ache in groin and heart ?
who doesn't pray for deliverance ?

who doesn't suffer pornographic syntax ?
language embedded in the arterial
design to implode all of humankind
I am with you Shiva ! cannibalism
headhunters microscopic murderers
cosmic intimations to annihilate purely !
skulls of Rudra ! blood-thirsty Kali !
can we add to the number of the Unknown ?
jungles swamps unassailable cliffs
mountains and more mountains !
Ahura Mazda invisible eternally aflame
take us from this transept of lies !
where is the spirit world ? where ?
unformed others hands lacking thought
poppies incarnadine and countless
on the Anatolian heights forever
what are the gods up to today ?
fever insanity and nostalgia
fever insanity and nostalgia

02-26-18

Iván Argüelles is an innovative and widely published Mexican-American poet. He was raised in México DF, Los Angeles, and ultimately Rochester, Minnesota. He received a BA in Classics from University of Chicago, and a degree in Library Science from Vanderbilt. A professional librarian, he was employed by the New York Public Library and the Library at UC Berkeley. A prolific writer, he has published numerous poetry collections, foremost among them: *"That" Goddess*; *Madonna Septet*; *Comedy , Divine , The*; *FIAT LUX*; *Orphic Cantos*; *Fragments from a Gone World*; and most recently *HOIL*, and *Twilight Cantos*. He received the 1989 William Carlos Williams Award for *Looking for Mary Lou*. In 2010 he received an American Book Award for his collection *The Death of Stalin*. In 2013 he was given a Lifetime Achievement Award from the Before Columbus Foundation.

www.ingramcontent.com/pod-product-compliance
Lightning Source LLC
Chambersburg PA
CBHW032125160426
43197CB00008B/515